THE REALLY PRACTICAL
TO
PRIMARY ENGLISH

Diana Bentley • Christine Burman
Rosemary Chamberlin • Suzi Clipson-Boyles
Denise Gray • Jackie Holderness
Margaret Lynch • Dee Reid

Text © Diana Bentley, Christine Burman, Rosemary Chamberlin, Suzi Clipson-Boyles, Denise Gray, Jackie Holderness, Margaret Lynch, Dee Reid 1999
Original line illustrations © Nelson Thornes Ltd

First published 1999 by:
Stanley Thornes (Publishers) Ltd

Reprinted in 2001 by:
Nelson Thornes Ltd
Delta Place
27 Bath Road
CHELTENHAM
GL53 7TH
United Kingdom

ISBN 0 7487 2937 2

01 02 03 / 10 9 8 7 6 5 4 3 2

Illustrations by Oxford Illustrators and Kathy Baxendale
Typeset by Northern Phototypesetting Co Ltd, Bolton
Printed and bound in Great Britain by Martins The Printers Ltd., Berwick upon Tweed

Contents

Acknowledgements

The authors and publishers would like to acknowledge the following people and organisations for permission to reproduce tables, diagrams and other material: Ann Davis, Christine Firman, Claire Robinson, Christine Salter, Badgemoor School, Henley-on-Thames, Oxfordshire, Bass Publications, Birmingham, David Fulton Publishers, Hodder and Stoughton Limited and The Qualifications and Curriculum Authority. This publication contains material which was produced by the Department for Education and Employment. © Crown copyright 1988. Reproduced with the permission of the controller of Her Majesty's Stationery Office.

Every effort has be made to contact copyright holders and we apologise if any have been overlooked.

1 Introduction

OBJECTIVES

By the end of this chapter, you should understand:

- the historical context in which the English language has evolved

- the central place of English in the whole curriculum

- the controversial nature of English and recurrent debates about literacy standards and teaching methods.

This is a really practical guide to teaching English. That means it:

- takes account of the fact that there are about thirty individuals in a class, with different abilities, interests and problems
- recognises that teachers are busy
- is mainly about *what* to teach, and *how* to teach it.

However, intelligent reflective teachers need to know something of the why as well as the what and the how. If they know something of the background and underlying principles they are less likely to fall prey to passing fads, and more able to adapt what they do when necessary. For that reason, this chapter looks at English – the language and the subject – and answers some questions about its history and place in the primary curriculum.

What is English?

English is a language, and languages are composed of sounds and symbols which convey meanings. Every language has a vocabulary, which includes all the words given to objects, concepts, actions and states. All languages have a structure, a system of word order and rules known as grammar. The users of a language need to learn and then use the agreed structures in order to make sense of one another.

Varieties of English

Regional variations and standard English

English is now the most widely spoken language in the world, though each continent has evolved its own variety of English and there are now several acknowledged Englishes. Any language is liable to vary from region to region, and as anyone who travels around Britain (or just watches television) will know, English also varies in different parts of the country. Speakers may use the standardised form but have a local accent, but if they also use vocabulary and grammar peculiar to their region they are said to speak a dialect (see Glossary).

Most societies give greater status to one particular language or dialect. This language becomes the language of control and, in literate societies, it is standardised in a written form. English has a standardised form, called standard English. This is the English we associate with written English and with English as it is taught in schools. It is the English taught to speakers of other languages, and a common language that should be comprehensible to everyone in all parts of Britain and the English-speaking world.

Teachers who know something of the development of the English language, however, will not make the mistake of thinking that standard English is in some way better than other dialects. It is descended from the dialect spoken in the region which included the Court and the University of Oxford and so gained a higher status, and after printing was invented it became known to an even wider audience.

Teachers have a difficult balancing act. On the one

1

hand children must be taught to speak and write standard English. To neglect to do this would be to leave them at severe disadvantage. On the other hand teachers need to respond sensitively to children's dialects and home languages. Even as adults we can find criticism or ridicule of the way we speak painful and extremely personal. For young children, to be told the way they speak is 'wrong' is also criticism of their parents. In Chapters 7 and 8, Suzi Clipson-Boyles talks about the central place of oral language and explains the importance of avoiding negative responses to a child's home language. She describes how teachers help children to develop an increasingly wide repertoire of oral language to a point at which they can choose whichever way of speaking and writing is most appropriate for the occasion.

Change over time

All languages change over time and will reflect other languages which have been significant in their history. English contains words brought in by invaders such as Vikings, Romans and American film makers and words brought home by empire builders, soldiers and holiday makers. It is changing all the time, and not only from the introduction of words from abroad. Investigating the origins of words can be interesting and is a way of developing children's awareness of the language they speak.

Perhaps the most visible examples of language changing over time are the new words that are introduced or adapted to describe inventions and discoveries. Obviously, before there were telephones, televisions or the Internet, the words to describe them did not exist, but these inventions have brought about changes in our language in other ways as well. It is interesting to realise, for example, that a debate went on about what to call the people who listened to the radio (or wireless) or watched television, before the words 'listeners' and 'viewers' became commonplace; and that, before the telephone, 'hello' was an expression of surprise or a way to attract attention rather than a greeting. Somewhere, soon, a child may be surprised to discover that a mouse is 'also' a small live animal and that surfing can be done on a board in the sea.

Sometimes the meaning of a word changes because of mistakes and misuse, and this often causes fierce debate. For example, for a while some people tried to stick to the strict meaning of 'decimate', arguing that it meant destroying a tenth of something (originally Roman soldiers), but so many people used it to mean 'bringing about widespread destruction' that eventually this has been accepted by almost everyone as its meaning. Other changes involve using nouns as verbs or vice versa, and, again, such changes are topics of discussion and disagreement. Older readers may not be comfortable with the use of 'access' as a verb, or 'quote' as a noun. (e.g. 'I'll access that information'; 'Shall I include this quote?'). Younger readers may be surprised to learn that the words were not always used in this way.

Knowing that language varies from place to place and changes over time does not mean that anything goes. It does mean that some of the 'rules' are not hard and fast, and that teachers need to teach children how to use appropriate language in a variety of situations. As the National Curriculum General Requirements for English state: 'In order to participate confidently in public, cultural and working life, pupils need to be able to speak, write and read standard English fluently and accurately' (DfE 1995, para. 2).

All primary teachers need to have a good knowledge and understanding of the English language in order to teach children about the power of language. They also need to understand language change and variation as well as its rules, and in Chapter 21 Christine Burman explains more about how teachers can develop children's knowledge of the language they speak, read and write.

Where does English fit into the curriculum?

English is one of the three core subjects in the National Curriculum, but it is often regarded as the most important subject of all. Language is crucial in the learning of other subjects in the curriculum. It is the medium through which children learn, whether in their maths, science or humanities lessons. For this reason, many schools have policies for language across the curriculum (LAC) and they emphasise that all teachers, whatever their specialism, even at secondary level, are also teachers of speaking and listening, reading and writing.

Language across the curriculum
Because English is the chief language of instruction in our schools and because of an emphasis in

many schools on the importance of language across the curriculum, some teachers have believed that children's language learning needs could be addressed completely through cross-curricular work. English can be integrated successfully into topic work, as Christine Burman shows in Chapter 15, but if English is never taught as a subject in its own right, there is a danger that language study and analysis may be neglected.

The principles of planning English are investigated in Chapter 5, where Jackie Holderness explains how, when planning English work, teachers have to operate at several levels. One level is planning which English work should be part of the class topic and which should be taught separately from other areas of the curriculum. Another level involves the three planning time scales – long, medium and short term. Teachers also need to plan to introduce specific concepts at word, sentence and text level and plan for children to practise their skills and consolidate their knowledge.

The introduction of the National Curriculum in 1989 had contrasting consequences for the teaching of English across the curriculum. On the one hand its written demands encouraged teachers to plan discrete English work as well as cross-curricular English. On the other hand, the extremely heavy content of other subjects meant that teachers often felt the only way they could cover everything was to plan 'two for the price of one' lessons. This sometimes meant that, even if English was not squeezed out, it was hard to ensure that all aspects of the subject were covered and that continuity and progression were ensured. The easing of the demands of the National Curriculum in 1992 made it possible for teachers to teach English separately as well as across the curriculum. The guidance of the National Literacy Strategy *Framework for Teaching* (DfEE 1998) makes it clear that this is what should happen.

The Framework for Teaching is a file intended to help all primary teachers to teach literacy successfully. It is part of the National Literacy Strategy – a major government initiative planned to raise standards of literacy. In 1996, under the last Conservative Government, the DfEE set up a five-year National Literacy Project coordinated from Reading with regional centres in a selection of LEAs. At the same time, while still in opposition, the Labour Party formed a Literacy Task Force chaired by Professor Michael Barber and asked it to design a

strategy to raise standards over a five to ten-year period. The aim is that by the year 2002, 80 per cent of 11-year-olds will reach Level 4 of the National Curriculum for English – the standard previously set as the level expected of 'average' 11-year-olds – and by 2007 the percentage of children reaching that level would be near 100 per cent. Since the General Election of 1997, the Government has combined these two initiatives and extended the National Literacy Project to cover all LEAs. The National Literacy Strategy Framework for Teaching has been published, giving specific guidance to teachers on what to teach and how to teach it. This does not override the National Curriculum but complements it, and both make it clear that English should be taught as a separate subject as well as across the curriculum.

As Dee Reid describes in Chapter 3, the National Curriculum divides English into three strands or attainment targets: 1) Speaking and Listening, 2) Reading and 3) Writing. Despite having separate areas within the English curriculum, however, it is important to remember the interrelatedness of these language skills. Teachers who consciously try to synthesise the various areas of English have a holistic view of language learning and can be said to subscribe to a whole-language or language-experience approach. Well-paced, stimulating literacy teaching will provide many opportunities for children to develop their speaking and listening skills, as well as making connections between their reading and writing.

What is the place of literature in the curriculum?

There is much greater understanding these days about the importance of teaching children how to understand a variety of non-fiction texts. Gone are the days when stories formed the whole diet of primary school children and extracting information from tables, reading instructions, finding information in encyclopaedias, etc., was left to the secondary school.

Nevertheless, fiction is still important and many effective teachers use literature as a starting point for children's written English work. Good books help children to understand other people's lives and ways of thinking, to explore feelings, understand motivation and come to terms with their own problems. The National Curriculum for English provoked considerable controversy when it included booklists of recommended texts, proposed as our 'literary heritage'. It neglected important sections of modern British and world literature, but did mark an attempt to ensure that people who share a common language also share knowledge of a common literary heritage.

As teachers consider the various strands and elements of the English curriculum, it is useful to remember the underlying purpose of English teaching. Margaret Meek (1991) reminds us that:

> the tendency to see literacy as useful has often kept the attention of teachers on the need to emphasise its controlling aspects, spelling, grammar and getting the words right, rather than on its liberating feature, the exercise of the imagination.

The National Curriculum Order (DfE 1995) says that children should be 'telling stories both real and imagined …' (Speaking and Listening, KS1, para. 1a). They should read 'poems and stories with familiar settings and those based on imaginary or fantasy worlds … traditional folk and fairy stories … stories and poems from a range of cultures … books and poems by significant children's authors' (Reading, KS1, para. 1d) and 'myths, legends and traditional stories' (Reading, KS2, para. 1d). Primary teachers need to become knowledgeable and enthusiastic about children's literature if they are to encourage the children in their care to become lifelong readers who see books as a source of information and pleasure.

Language study in the curriculum

Through a wide range of language experiences (stories, discussions, rhymes and songs, chants and raps) young children come to appreciate the richness of language, long before they come to school. They learn to recognise language patterns in speech, in stories and in songs. In their English lessons in school they will gradually be helped to make explicit their knowledge of the language they speak and read.

The National Literacy Strategy Framework for Teaching emphasises the importance of language study. In it, English is divided into three strands:

- word level: phonics, spelling and vocabulary
- sentence level: grammar and punctuation
- text level: comprehension and composition.

At first glance it might seem that language study belongs at sentence level with punctuation and grammar, but in fact it has a place in all three lev-

els. For example, at word level, children have to learn correct terms such as 'synonym' (Year 3) so that they can discuss language, and to investigate words such as 'spaghetti' and 'bungalow' which come from other languages (Year 5). At text level, children are required to identify the features of different types of writing, investigate word play or analyse poetic style (Year 5).

Language study is an important element in the National Curriculum. It should underpin all English work, heightening children's awareness of the richness of the language they use. With effective and enthusiastic teaching, children can discover that English is an exciting and powerful medium of expression and communication. Through other areas of the curriculum, children can be encouraged to explore local dialects, geographical variation in vocabulary or the history of words and phrases. Through literature, children can appreciate the power of language to persuade, move or inspire. Learning about English and how to use it effectively and with pleasure needs to be purposeful. It should not be reduced to isolated grammatical exercises, and the reasons for studying it at school should be made clear to the children.

Are standards in English really falling?

Throughout the centuries, older people have tended to claim that standards (of manners, morals or scholarship) have deteriorated since they were young. Writers in Ancient Greece and Rome complained about the younger generation in terms very similar to those we read in newspapers today. Concern about falling standards of literacy is not new either, and not confined to Britain. Reaching conclusions about whether standards of literacy really have fallen, however, is extremely complex.

Firstly, there are problems about comparison. Bearing in mind the changes in language that have taken place, we are not comparing like with like if we give 1940s reading tests to 1990s children. There is one test which contains the phrase 'the milkman's horse' – a common enough sight in the 1940s, but today's children may never see a milkman, let alone one with a horse. Secondly, there is the matter of whose standards go up or down. Standards achieved by the most able children could rise while those of the less able were falling (or vice versa). Thirdly, there are issues to do with what we require pupils and students to do. As has been mentioned, the literacy demands of today and the next century are different from those of the postwar years.

There is some evidence that reading standards fell in the years after the introduction of the National Curriculum. The curriculum was seriously over-crowded and teachers did not have the time to concentrate on English as they once had. The National Curriculum was streamlined in 1992, however, and in 1998 schools were given even more flexibility in terms of curriculum content for the non-core subjects, so that they could concentrate on English, maths and science.

Generally, however, research suggests that standards have not fallen overall, though there is no shortage of employers and college lecturers who believe they have. There are possible explanations for this belief. Higher education now recruits many students who would not have gone to university in the past, while other young people who might once have found a manual job which did not require literacy skills no longer have this option, and their poor literacy becomes more obvious. It is also possible that industry requires different literacy skills from its workers than those which are (or were) taught and tested in school. Until recently, English lessons were mainly fiction-based, while most employers do not require workers who can write stories and read novels. As the debate continues, therefore, about what skills young people have and what they need, the question of what literacy is needs to be addressed.

What is literacy?

There are different opinions about literacy, as the following definitions show.

> The ability to read and write. The ability to use language proficiently.
> (*Collins Concise Dictionary*)

> The ability to read and write a simple message.
> (UN 1942)

> The essential knowledge and skills … to engage in all those activities in which literacy is required for effective functioning in [the] group and community.
> (UNESCO 1962)

> Literacy saves lives. It enables you to express yourself, to be yourself, to find yourself, to free yourself.
> (M. Morgan, prison literacy tutor, 1996)

> I want to read and write so I can stop being the shadow of other people.
> (Paulo Freire 1978)

According to the definition given by the UN in 1942, almost everyone in Britain today would count as literate. Morgan's and Freire's definitions, on the other hand, emphasise the liberating power that literacy has for individuals, while according to UNESCO, what would count as literate for a peasant farmer in the last century would not be literate for an 11-year-old today. This shows us that literacy is neither a clear nor a static concept.

The National Literacy Strategy Framework for Teaching (1998) asks 'What is literacy?' and concludes:

> Literate primary pupils should:
> - read and write with confidence, fluency and understanding
> - be able to orchestrate a full range of reading cues (phonic, graphic, syntactic, contextual) to monitor their reading and correct their own mistakes
> - understand the sound and spelling system and use this to read and spell accurately
> - have fluent and legible handwriting
> - have an interest in words and their meanings and a growing vocabulary
> - know, understand and be able to write in a range of genres in fiction and poetry, and understand and be familiar with some of the ways in which narratives are structured through basic literary ideas of setting, character and plot
> - understand, use and be able to write a range of non-fiction texts
> - plan, draft, revise and edit their own writing
> - have a suitable technical vocabulary through which to understand and discuss their reading and writing
> - be interested in books, read with enjoyment and evaluate and justify their preferences
> - through reading and writing, develop their powers of imagination, inventiveness and critical awareness.
> (p. 3)

5

Children today need to be literate in a variety of ways: TV literate, computer literate, advertising literate and book literate – topics that are dealt with in the chapters on information technology, media education and reading. Children need to be taught about persuasive writing, and helped to detect bias – an important skill for consumers and members of a democratic society. This is a broader and deeper view of literacy than the dictionary definition of 'able to read and write', and schools need to address all these forms of literacy if they are to prepare children for the future.

How do we raise standards?

Perhaps we should not quibble about whether standards have fallen or not: what matters is that they must rise. As the needs of society and the opportunities for individuals have developed, the literacy requirements have grown also. As manual jobs decline, it is more important than ever that children become fluent and confident speakers, readers and writers, but literacy is not valued simply for its usefulness in the world of work. As Wragg *et al.* (1998) say:

> **Anyone unable to read a work of literature or peruse the vast amounts of written information in our society, compose a letter, prepare and present a report or understand and follow written instruction, may find that opportunities for further study, prospects for promotion, or even satisfying personal and social relationships are diminished. In a fast moving society poor levels of literacy can have dire consequences.**

Over the years there have been many successful initiatives aimed at improving children's reading and writing: some introduced in individual schools, some in clusters of schools or LEAs as well as nationwide schemes such as the National Writing Project. Even the nationwide schemes, however, were voluntary programmes for teachers who identified a need for improvement in their own individual schools. The National Literacy Project, on the other hand, is designed to affect the work done in every class in every primary school. The methods it suggests follow many years of argument about the best way to teach reading.

What is the best way to teach reading?

Throughout the twentieth century there has been controversy about the best way to teach reading. Until recently the major debate was seen as a competition between two contrasting models of reading:

- the bottom-up model which starts with letter and word recognition and progresses towards understanding the meaning of text
- the top-down model, which emphasises the way readers use their existing knowledge to make predictions about what they expect to read.

The majority of teachers have continued to use a combination of methods, but some people seemed to believe that there was one perfect method, if only it could be found.

The search for the perfect method

Teachers and psychologists are always searching for new teaching methods and approaches and ways to help children overcome particular problems. For example, the Look and Say method of teaching reading, which became popular in the 1960s and 1970s, was thought to be an improvement on the phonics method. With phonics children were taught to sound out letters and blend the sounds together, but Look and Say was based on the idea that:

- breaking down words into their component sounds was difficult because English spelling is irregular
- children often recognise whole words by their shape, and can read 'difficult' words like 'aeroplane' or 'elephant' more easily than 'this' or 'that'.

English is irregular and the second point is valid for some words, but any child taught exclusively by this method had no way of tackling unknown words, and had, in effect, to learn every word from scratch as if learning a logographic script like Chinese.

The debate between phonics and Look and Say (both 'bottom-up' methods) was followed by that between decoding and meaning-based approaches. In the 1960s, Kenneth Goodman (1967) claimed that reading was a 'psycholinguistic guessing game' in which readers guessed at words according to what would make sense. Again, there is some truth in this, but it cannot explain how we read everything. Readers cannot guess every word! This method emphasised the importance of context, and of readers' prior knowledge, but it was a very partial account of the reading process.

Some methods were pioneered by teachers dissatisfied with traditional teaching because they were worried about children who could read but did not want to. This was the case with Liz Waterland (1985), a practising infant teacher, who believed that written language could be learned as easily and in the same way as spoken language, by an apprentice working alongside skilled practitioners. The Apprenticeship Approach placed emphasis on meaning and enjoyment, and was associated with the so-called 'real books' movement.

Some teachers, unhappy with the stilted, contrived language of commercial reading schemes, advocated replacing these with good commercially produced books. 'Real books' versus reading schemes became the next reading battle zone, and elements of the media and some politicians combined to blame 'real books' for alleged falling literacy standards. A few experienced teachers with a detailed knowledge of children's literature succeeded in steering their children along a progressively more challenging course of carefully chosen, excellent non-scheme books. A few others presided over classes in which children continually re-read the same easy books and made little progress. Most teachers did neither of those things, however, as a survey by HMI (1991) found that only 5 per cent of teachers were using 'real books' as their sole approach.

For most teachers with a normal-sized class, total commitment to 'real books' was impractical. The debate drew attention to the need for children to read more widely and beyond their graded readers, however, and an unlooked-for benefit has been the great improvement in reading schemes. The disadvantages of reading schemes were that they could be boring and repetitive, used contrived language of the 'Jack lacks the hack's tack' variety, and encouraged unhealthy competition at the expense of intrinsic pleasure and interest in the content. ('*I'm* on Green 3. *She's* only on Blue 5.'). Some children would not venture beyond the scheme.

Many published schemes are now designed to minimise the competitive element. Books are different shapes and sizes with a variety of layouts, and, unlike many of the old schemes, they say who the author and illustrator are. Schemes include non-fiction, plays and poems. In other words, today's reading-scheme books are 'real books'

with the benefit of structure, progression and continuity built in.

The growth of consensus

After years of argument a consensus now appears to have been reached that, to become literate, children need:

- pre-reading stories and rhymes
- early intervention for those who make a slow start
- interesting, meaningful texts
- phonic instruction
- enthusiastic teachers
- interested and involved parents who read with their children regularly
- personal involvement
- lots of practice.

There is also consensus on the importance of teaching children to use a multi-faceted approach to reading combining contextual understanding with phonic, graphic and grammatical knowledge in order to make sense of what they are reading. This is described in the National Literacy Strategy Framework for Teaching as a series of searchlights, each shedding light on the text.

Much practical advice about the best way to teach reading is given by Diana Bentley in Chapters 9 and 10, and there are comprehensive modules on reading provided by the Framework for Teaching. When the National Literacy Project was piloted in a selection of LEAs and schools, teachers introduced a literacy hour in which attention was fully focused on language activities. This is now recommended as an excellent way of teaching literacy

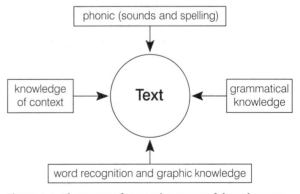

Figure 1.1 **The range of strategies successful readers use to make sense of text**

What is the literacy hour?

Before the National Literacy Project went nationwide in September 1998, arrangements were made for all schools to devote two days in-service training to the teaching of literacy, and they were provided with materials including copies of the *Framework for Teaching*. This sets clear expectations of what should be covered each term, in an unprecedented level of detail. The project emphasises the importance of extending reading skills at Key Stage 2. It stresses careful classroom management, direct instruction and a systematic approach to phonics, spelling and vocabulary at both key stages. The teaching objectives are set out under the three interrelated strands of word, sentence and text level, and it is important to remember that the 'levels' do not relate to levels of difficulty or ability but to the content of what is taught. Nor do they replace the National Curriculum attainment targets or the programmes of study.

The literacy hour is made up of four phases – three of whole-class teaching and one of independent and group work.

Although one of the key elements of the literacy hour is that the teacher is actually teaching the whole time, with a significant proportion of whole-class teaching, it is important to note that this does not signal a return to 'chalk and talk' aimed vaguely at the middle of the ability range. The Framework says that:

> **The most successful teaching is:**
> * **discursive** – characterised by high quality oral work;
> * **interactive** – pupils' contributions are encouraged, expected and extended;
> * **well-paced** – there is a sense of urgency, driven by the need to make progress and succeed;
> * **confident** – teachers have a clear understanding of the objectives;
> * **ambitious** – there is optimism about and high expectations of success.
>
> (p. 8)

The *Framework for Teaching* and the pack of support materials (nicknamed the 'Lunch Box') provide a great deal of support and information for teachers. There is help with planning as well as a detailed breakdown of what needs to be taught. For the literacy hour to be a success, however, teachers will need to plan a variety of stimulating language activities suitable for their own classes. Practical suggestions on how to do this will be found in the following chapters of this book.

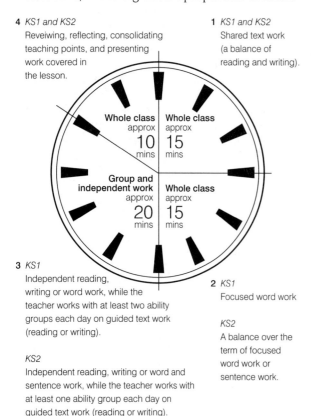

4 *KS1 and KS2*
Reveiwing, reflecting, consolidating teaching points, and presenting work covered in the lesson.

1 *KS1 and KS2*
Shared text work (a balance of reading and writing).

Whole class approx **10** mins | Whole class approx **15** mins

Group and independent work approx **20** mins | Whole class approx **15** mins

3 *KS1*
Independent reading, writing or word work, while the teacher works with at least two ability groups each day on guided text work (reading or writing).

KS2
Independent reading, writing or word and sentence work, while the teacher works with at least one ability group each day on guided text work (reading or writing).

2 *KS1*
Focused word work

KS2
A balance over the term of focused word work or sentence work.

Figure 1.2 The structure of the literacy hour
Source: DfEE 1998

SUMMARY

This chapter has introduced some of the controversial issues surrounding the teaching of English. It has looked at:

* the evolution and status of standard English, language diversity and the need for language study

* the important place of English in the curriculum, as the medium of instruction for other subjects and as a subject in its own right

* the debate about standards of literacy, including an overview of different methods of teaching reading and an introduction to the National Literacy Project and the literacy hour.

It has attempted to provide teachers with a background to the teaching of English so that they can respond positively and professionally to research-based initiatives while avoiding commercial fashion fads.

References

DfE (1995) *English in the National Curriculum*, HMSO
DfEE (1998) *The National Literacy Strategy: Framework for Teaching*, DfEE
Freire, Paulo (1978) *Pedagogy in Process*, Seabury Press
Goodman, K. S. (1967) 'Reading: A Psycholinguistic Guessing Game', *Journal of the Reading Specialist* 4: 126–35
HMI (1991) *The Teaching and Learning of Reading in Primary Schools*, DES
Meek, M. (1991) *On Being Literate*, Bodley Head
Morgan, M. (1996) 'Literacy Saves Lives', in Bobbie Neate (ed.) *Literacy Saves Lives*, UKRA
Waterland, L. (1985) *Read with Me*, Thimble Press
Wragg, E. C., Wragg, C. M., Haynes, G. S. and Chamberlin, R. P. (1998) *Improving Literacy in the Primary School*, Routledge

Further reading

Bourne, J. (ed.) (1994) *Thinking through Primary Practice*, Open University Press
A thoughtful collection of papers on the primary curriculum with useful chapters on Reading, Grammar, Bilingualism, and Reading and Language.
Clay, M. (1992) *Becoming Literate*, Heinemann
Well known for her work on Reading Recovery around the world, Clay provides teachers with a thorough knowledge about literacy teaching and provides practical guidance about supporting children's development.
Meek, M. (1991) *On Being Literate*, Bodley Head
This very readable book offers us a perceptive and experienced perspective on the issues which relate to being literate. Based on research into how children become literate, it encourages teachers to think for themselves about English in education.
Sealey, A. (1996) *Learning about Language*, Oxford University Press
This book provides a clear overview of issues which underpin teaching about language in the National Curriculum. It also provides practical suggestions for teaching children about spoken and written texts.
Wray, D. and Medwell, J. (1997) *English for Primary Teachers: An Audit and Self-Study Guide*, Letts Educational
This is a very helpful check and guide for students and teachers who are concerned about their own knowledge of English. It sets out what teachers need to know and how they can go about filling in any gaps.

2 Language, literacy and the under-fives

OBJECTIVES

By the end of this chapter you should:

- be aware of the principles which underpin a high-quality language and literacy curriculum for the under-fives

- have sound knowledge of the *Desirable Outcomes for Children's Learning* for language and literacy and how under-fives can be supported towards achieving them

- have a framework for planning, assessing and recording an appropriate language and literacy curriculum for the under-fives.

Introduction

This chapter begins with an explanation of the current national framework for those working with the under-fives. It then discusses how teachers can plan an appropriate language and literacy curriculum which recognises the centrality of play. Examples of good practice in discrete and cross-curricular contexts are suggested in order to promote progress towards the set goals for five-year-olds. The final section discusses how teachers can work with other supporting adults to build a full picture of children's overall achievement in language.

Language and literacy and the under-fives: the Desirable Outcomes

The term 'under-fives' is now used to refer to the non-statutory stage of education at nursery or in a reception class. The *Desirable Outcomes for Children's Learning on Entering Compulsory Education* (DfE and SCAA 1996, currently under review) is a very useful document for all those who work with under-fives across the full range of provision. Generally the outcomes are goals for learning for children by the time they enter compulsory education. Presented as six areas of learning, they aim 'to provide a foundation for later achievement'.

These six areas of learning are:

- Personal and Social Development
- Language and Literacy
- Mathematics
- Knowledge and Understanding of the World
- Physical Development
- Creative Development.

If we look at Figure 2.1 we can see how the goals can be separated into the three strands of Speaking and Listening, Reading and Writing, and how these relate to the Level 1 and Level 2 descriptions at Key Stage 1. SCAA's model of key features of progression in language and literacy is apparent here, together with how the Desirable Outcomes provide a foundation for Key Stage 1 of the National Curriculum.

In addition to specifying goals for children's learning on entering compulsory education, the outcomes restate some long-established principles of good practice in language and literacy with the under-fives. The curriculum should be essentially child centred so that children feel secure, valued and confident and develop a sense of achievement through learning which is pleasurable and rewarding. The activities we provide should take account of their interests and promote their self-control and independence. The importance of assessment recording and reporting is stressed in order to ensure continuity. High status is also given to the role of parents and other agencies.

AREA OF LEARNING	DESIRABLE OUTCOMES ON ENTRY TO COMPULSORY SCHOOLING	NATIONAL CURRICULUM LEVEL 1 DESCRIPTION	NATIONAL CURRICULUM LEVEL 2 / END OF KEY STAGE DESCRIPTION
Language and Literacy	In small and large groups, children listen attentively and talk about their experiences. They use a growing vocabulary with increasing fluency to express thoughts and convey meaning to the listener. They listen and respond to stories, songs, nursery rhymes and poems. They make up their own stories and take part in role play with confidence.	Pupils talk about matters of immediate interest. They listen to others and usually respond appropriately. They convey simple meanings to a range of listeners, speaking audibly, and begin to extend their ideas or accounts by providing some detail. *(English: Speaking and Listening)*	Pupils begin to show some confidence in talking and listening, particularly where the topics interest them. On occasions, they show awareness of the needs of the listener by including relevant detail. In developing and explaining their ideas they speak clearly and use a growing vocabulary. They usually listen carefully and respond with increasing appropriateness to what others say. They are beginning to be aware that in some situations a more formal vocabulary and tone of voice are used. *(English: Speaking and Listening)*
	Children enjoy books and handle them carefully, understanding how they are organised. They know that words and pictures carry meaning and that, in English, print is read from left to right and from top to bottom. They begin to associate sounds with patterns in rhymes, with syllables, and with words and letters. They recognise their own names and some familiar words. They recognise letters of the alphabet by shape and sound.	Pupils recognise familiar words in simple texts. They use their knowledge of letters and sound-symbol relationships in order to read words and to establish meaning when reading aloud. In these activities they sometimes require support. They express their response to poems, stories and non-fiction by identifying aspects they like. *(English: Reading)*	Pupils' reading of simple texts shows understanding and is generally accurate. They express opinions about major events or ideas in stories, poems and non-fiction. They use more than one strategy, such as phonic, graphic, syntactic and contextual, in reading unfamiliar words and establishing meaning. *(English: Reading)*
	In their writing they use pictures, symbols, familiar words and letters to communicate meaning, showing awareness of some of the different purposes of writing. They write their names with appropriate use of upper and lower case letters.	Pupils' writing communicates meaning through simple words and phrases. In their reading or writing, pupils begin to show awareness of how full stops are used. Letters are usually clearly shaped and correctly orientated. *(English: Writing)*	Pupils' writing communicates meaning in both narrative and non-narrative forms, using appropriate and interesting vocabulary, and showing some awareness of the reader. Ideas are developed in a sequence of sentences, sometimes demarcated by capital letters and full stops. Simple, monosyllabic words are usually spelt correctly, and where there are inaccuracies the alternative is phonetically plausible. In handwriting, letters are accurately formed and consistent in size. *(English: Writing)*

Figure 2.1 The strands of the Desirable Outcomes and relationship with Key Stage 1 programme of study
Source: DfEE and SCAA 1996

Planning an appropriate language and literacy curriculum for the under-fives

Looking at Children's Learning (DfE/SCAA 1997), a booklet produced to complement the Desirable Outcomes, emphasises the need for planning to take account of the principles described above. It also stresses that planning should be at different levels: long term (across a year) medium term (across a term) and short term (day to day).

Within this framework planning should:

1 Build on children's prior experiences, skills and knowledge
2 Promote individual children's progress towards the Desirable Outcomes
3 Show major links across aspects of the areas of learning.

In this next section we will explore how these headings can guide us in planning an appropriate curriculum for language and literacy.

1 Building on children's prior experiences, skills and knowledge

All children in today's society experience a wide variety of print in their environment. In their local area, print is all around them in the form of street and shop signs, notices, instructions, advertisements, supermarket packaging, and so on. Given the support and guidance of a well-attuned parent or carer, this contextualised print can help young children to understand that writing comes in many different forms and is used for many different purposes, such as to instruct, entertain, inform, persuade and organise.

At home, young children also interact with many forms of print on toys, TVs, computers and games and in books. They often see adults reading recipes, hobby books and manuals, newspapers, magazines and catalogues. Sometimes they watch and join in the writing of messages, shopping lists, greeting cards, invitations and letters, expecting others to read and respond to their own attempts. In such literacy events children are learning that print communicates, that it is used to sustain rela-

tionships and meet a wide range of personal needs.

When working with young children we can build on this prior experience by ensuring that print of different types is all around the classroom and that it is used to meet a range of purposes. The role-play area can include print in the form of signs, labels, packages, lists and notices. For instance, signs might read: 'Please leave the shop very tidy.' Or: 'Only five children can work in the shop.' Not only does this help keep the role-play in some order, it serves to highlight the functional and communicative nature of written language.

On displays and in other areas of the classroom, we can include print that is used to instruct, inform and carry on the classroom business of the day. For instance, we might write and encourage children to read simple signs like: 'Take the register'; 'Collect the milk'. In certain areas such as the sand and water areas, rules and instructions can be particularly important, as in 'Only three children play in the sand please'. Or we might have a sign reading: 'Quiet please!' in the reading area, although children will still need frequent reminders!

Such a print-rich environment encourages children to explore literacy, to experiment, investigate and generate print for themselves, but we need to remember that under-fives should not be left to learn all about written language on their own.

The vital role of adults

Before school, children are often drawn into joint social activities and conversations where print is created, shared and used in a wide range of social contexts. Parents and other adults frequently engage children in conversation around print in the home and community. In so doing they intuitively act as models, providing powerful demonstrations of the role of spoken and written language in everyday life (Vygotsky 1962). In the nursery or reception class, we too can continue to model and demonstrate the forms and functions of written language and what reading and writing can do by:

- labelling with and in front of children
- scribing stories, accounts or reports for individuals or small groups
- reading different texts like newspapers, magazines, telephone directories to demonstrate how they are used in the everyday world
- talking about texts, illustrating their different types

and purposes, e.g. lists, notices, messages, signs, invitations, etc.

- writing in front of groups or the class using a white board or paper clipped to an easel
- reading back children's writing to consolidate their understanding of print and punctuation in a real context.

Of course the literacy hour framework, with its emphasis upon whole-class shared reading and shared writing, provides regular opportunity for this kind of explicit, focused language work.

Linking play and literacy

In pre-school learning there has always been a strong link between different kinds of play, first-hand experiences and literacy. During play we have all seen children pretending to be mothers, fathers, doctors, shopkeepers, and using reading and writing as appropriate to the particular role. Given the opportunity they will often have a go at writing their own shopping lists, notices, messages, greetings cards, or they might play at reading and 'behave like a reader' as they read maybe to a favourite toy.

At school we can keep play central and reinforce its high status by organising the room into clearly defined play areas where effective bridges are built between play and literacy. These play areas normally include:

- a quiet, carpeted reading or book area
- a listening table containing a listening unit, taped stories and accompanying books for children to listen to, read and discuss
- display tables with books and other media linked to a topic
- a role-play area – matching the current topic or interest, e.g. café, hairdresser's
- a writing area
- a computer area
- an art/craft area
- a construction area
- a sand and water play area.

Even where space is very limited and areas cannot be retained for specific learning purposes, we can work with our colleagues to develop resource boxes on the theme of an office or a café, moving the boxes to different classrooms as and when appropriate. With the introduction of materials like paper, pencils, pens, coloured crayons, white boards, clip boards, books and book-making resources these areas can be transformed into highly literate areas which offer children a contin-uous daily diet of play-based language and literacy opportunities which meet their different needs.

This approach is in direct line with the Ofsted Handbook, *Guidance on the Inspection of Nursery and Primary Schools* (1995), which recognises that much of the work with under-fives is practical and built around ongoing continuous activities from which children choose; as it says: 'The teaching of younger children should be linked to the organisation of the classroom where planned activities are set up and resources for teachers and children to select and use over longer periods of time' (p. 68).

Figure 2.2 shows how one reception-class teacher has developed a plan for her reception classroom in order to provide a range of practical continuous activities that make natural links between areas and build bridges between children's play and literacy.

Such an environment encourages children to explore literacy, but again the role of adult intervention and talk is vital. We should:

- give children the opportunity to build real conversations around what they are doing, while they are doing it
- recognise their interests and build upon them
- encourage them to reflect on their own experiences and to order their thinking
- use talk to consolidate early learning, develop more complex ideas, extend understanding and set off new lines of thought and enquiry.

2 Promoting individual children's progress towards the Desirable Outcomes

Planning continuous work for the under-fives

In this section we explore three major language and literacy activities set in key areas of the nursery and reception classroom: the reading area, the writing area and the role-play area. The intention is to highlight the kinds of activities which both build on children's prior experiences and learning and promote individual children's progress towards the Desirable Outcomes (references to the Desirable Outcomes appear in italics). Although the focus is upon the outcomes, many of these activities reach into the word, sentence and text-

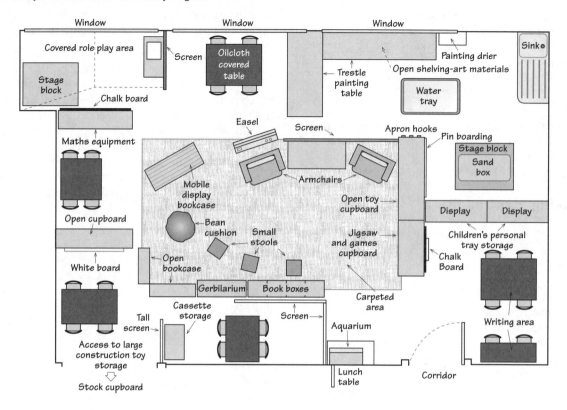

Figure 2.2 Plan of a reception classroom
Source: Christine Firman

level work set out for the reception year in the National Literacy Strategy's Framework for Teaching (see Chapter 1); there are numerous opportunities for children to understand print, to develop their phonological awareness, to recognise words and to extend their vocabulary through the all-important contexts of story and play.

The reading area: sharing big books with the whole class

The outcomes for language and literacy expect that children should listen and respond to stories, songs, nursery rhymes and poems, make up their own stories and take part in role play with confidence. An emphasis on story-based activities can help children visit most of the language and literacy outcomes. For example, stories always seem to engage children's interests and emotions, so they want to *listen attentively*. The book talk around the themes and characters in the stories provides an ideal context for them to *express thoughts and convey meaning to the listener*; it seems that young children have a natural, almost overwhelming

urgency to relate their own life experiences to the story and back again.

If we can use enlarged stories and 'modelling' with the class we can develop important concepts of print which constitute most of the reading competencies. For example, by pointing to text and discussing the story, we are modelling that words carry meaning and that (in English) print is read from left to right and from top to bottom. Certain big book stories are also particularly effective in helping children associate sounds with patterns in rhymes, with syllables, and with words and letters. Here are just a few examples from Story Chest's *Hairy Bear* (Thomas Nelson 1990):

> **Hairy Bear, Hairy Bear, You're just a scaredy bear**

And

> **I'll crim, cram, crash em, I'll bim, bam, bash em, I'll fim, fam, fight em**

After frequent class and group shared reading sessions with such texts children will often spot some familiar words like 'I' and 'the'. They also get to learn from this and other activities the relationship between the shape and sound of letters of the alphabet, so that children reading a text like *Hairy Bear* can clearly learn a great deal about the letters (onset) *cr* in 'crim, cram, crash' and the onsets *f* and *b*.

Sharing stories also provides ideal starting points for a whole range of writing activities linked to the story theme. Children can write and read a simple story for a class book on 'What frightens us at night', or they can make up similar nonsense rhymes to be displayed on the wall for others to read, or write captions for their pictures on animals at night, thus showing *awareness of some of the different purposes of writing*. Finally, adding their names to these self-created, meaningful texts provides them with a real purpose and audience for *writing their names with appropriate use of upper and lower case letters*.

The writing area: making books
Collaborative book-making is a particularly effective means of developing the under-fives' concepts of books and print and their general understanding of what reading is all about. Here our role is crucial in that we explicitly use book-making to demonstrate many of the fundamental processes of reading and writing.

What happens is that the teacher or supporting adult works with the children to compose and construct a book, which is then 'published' and added to the existing classroom reading resources. First of all we would read and celebrate a published big book so that children could listen and respond to stories. We might focus attention on the cover (picture, author, publisher, illustrator), the title page or any end papers, and maybe scribe a list of these features on a flip chart for use as a working framework to help children to enjoy books and understand how they are organised.

The class might consider a whole range of different starting points for their own book: classroom or school activities and events (e.g. an outing or a visiting speaker); personal experiences; songs (e.g. 'There was a princess long ago'); plays; rhymes (e.g. 'Five little speckled frogs'); instructions (e.g. How to make fairy cakes). Here children can make up their own stories and take part in role play with confidence.

Of course, we should help the group make decisions about the form of the book. Will it be shaped, have pop-ups, flaps, or photographs? Is it to be scribed by the teacher/typed into a word processor/printed out and pasted/written by children? How will it be illustrated – by drawings, paintings, moving parts or real items?

In all of this, small and large groups of children are likely to listen attentively and talk about their experiences using a growing vocabulary with increasing fluency to express thoughts and convey meaning to the listener.

If we can act as scribe we will be able to model the behaviours of real writers by:

- re-reading as we progress
- crossing out
- inserting omissions
- discussing how words might be spelt
- highlighting features of print: word, initial sounds, onsets and rime, punctuation, sentence.

Similarly as we write and re-read the children's story we will be modelling how pictures, symbols, familiar words, and letters communicate meaning whilst demonstrating some of the different purposes of writing, how reading works and how readers use many different clues to make sense of texts. In particular we will be:

- developing concepts of print by discussing directionality, e.g. left to right, top to bottom, page, etc.
- discussing how to use pictures as cues
- helping children to recognise letters of the alphabet by shape and sound (e.g. How many b's can you count on our page?)
- reinforcing sight vocabulary (e.g. How many I's can you spot?)
- encouraging anticipation and prediction of what is to come next.

In all of this, children are *developing knowledge that words and pictures carry meaning and that, in English, print is read from left to right and from top to bottom*. They are also beginning *to associate words with patterns in rhymes, with syllables, and with words and letters*.

The role-play area: planning, constructing and resourcing an area incorporating different texts
The Desirable Outcomes expect that by the age of five children should take part in role play with confidence. Role-play areas offer a variety of rich non-threatening literacy learning opportunities for the

under-fives, who can interact with a range of written material for different purposes in real-life situations like an office, café, library or shop. Through role play children experience a wide variety of texts and learn the importance of being resourceful in using and developing a range of strategies for making meaning.

Many adults working with the under-fives base their role-play areas on themes like travel agencies, shops and restaurants. This encourages children to write and read a wide range of texts *across the curriculum*, so for example in a shoe shop children can read labels on shoe boxes, read when measuring and estimating for shoe-fitting, etc.

Whenever possible the children should be involved in the planning, constructing and resourcing of the area as this not only increases engagement and ownership but it also offers extra language opportunities. In small and large groups they can listen attentively and talk about their experiences. They can use a growing vocabulary with increasing fluency to express thoughts and convey meaning to the listener. Remember that even the very youngest children have the most creative ideas and a most careful attention to detail.

A flip chart or an easel can be used to record results of discussions/brainstorms/lists of resources. In sharing these texts we can encourage children to know that words and pictures carry meaning and that, in English, print is read from left to right. We can also encourage the group to decide upon ground rules for how to use the area, for example how many children at a time, where to hang costumes, etc.

Children and their parents can all help with the resources needed. Real-life objects should be collected to give an authentic feel. For an optician's the class might visit and acquire posters, magazines leaflets adverts, etc. A shop can have labels, receipts, cash register, stock book, order forms, lists, catalogues, special offers, signs, advertisements.

A collection of story and information books that tie in with and extend the theme should be displayed attractively and be readily available for children to handle. In terms of the Desirable Outcomes children are learning to enjoy books and handle them carefully, understanding how they are organised. They are listening and responding to stories, songs, nursery rhymes and poems.

We can, in addition, make and display labels which inform, instruct, guide or decorate. Some might suggest possible activities or the general use of the area, but what is important is that children are learning to use pictures, symbols, familiar words, and letters, to communicate meaning, developing awareness of some of the different purposes of writing.

When everything is in its place we might organise a Grand Opening ceremony. This can extend the possibilities for further planning, collaboration, reading and writing (invitations and letters for the guests!).

Note that SCAA's booklet *Looking at Children's Learning* describes in detail many activities similar to those described above.

3 Making links across areas of learning

It is obvious that very young children do not learn in separate subject areas, nor do they separate talking, reading and writing. Rather they learn about different aspects of language as they use language to communicate, make sense of the world and share meaning with those around them.

Many nursery and reception activities are integrated in that they relate to more than one subject. For example, most simple cooking activities using recipes will include scientific processes, number work, concepts of measurement, talking, reading and possibly writing.

Looking at Children's Learning stresses that planning should show major links across aspects of the areas of learning. The Desirable Outcomes for language and literacy also state that other areas of learning make a vital contribution to the successful development of literacy.

But first we need to be familiar with the key aspects of language and literacy in different areas of learning. Then we will be in a better position to offer activities which develop both language and literacy and the knowledge and skills specific to each area of learning.

For example, in Mathematics the outcomes stress the importance of children using and understanding language in the development of simple mathematical ideas, understanding and recording numbers through practical activities using the language involved.

In Knowledge and Understanding of the World the role of talk is given high status in that children should talk about where they live, their environment, their families, and past and present events in their own lives. They are encouraged to talk about their observations, sometimes recording them and asking questions to gain information about why things happen and how things work.

The Creative Development area of learning focuses upon the development of children's imagination and their ability to communicate and to express ideas and feelings in creative ways.

Figure 2.3, an example of medium-term planning (across a term), provides an outline of a term's topic on movement (7–8 hours) with a nursery class of 24 children. Each aspect of the topic interrelated different areas of learning and provided rich opportunities for language and literacy development.

Assessing and recording the language achievements of the under-fives

Careful assessment and record keeping underpin all good educational practice. They are essential elements in securing continuity and progression.

DES, *Starting with Quality* (1990)

Characteristics of the under-fives: implications for assessment

At this stage of development it can be very difficult to make accurate assessments. Many young children have far greater knowledge than they can express through language, and may fail to respond or carry out a task because they misunderstand the question. Under-fives can also have a very limited span of concentration and be very sensitive to variables like the time of day, hunger, fatigue, etc.

Medium-term planning:
Linking language and literacy, knowledge of the world and mathematics

Theme: Movement   **Starting point:** How do we come to school?

Learning aims in relation to areas of learning: Desirable Outcomes

Language and literacy
In small and large groups, children listen attentively and talk about their experiences. They use a growing vocabulary with increasing fluency to express thoughts and convey meaning to the listener. Children enjoy books … understanding how they are organised. They know that words carry meaning and that in English, print is read from left to right and top to bottom. They recognise their own names … In their writing they use pictures, symbols, familiar words and letters, to communicate meaning, showing awareness of some of the different purposes of writing.

Mathematics
Children use mathematical language … to describe … quantity … Through practical activities children understand and record numbers … and begin to use the language involved.

Knowledge and understanding of the world
Children talk about where they live, their environment … events in their own lives.
They talk about their observations, sometimes recording them and ask questions to gain information …

Activities/experiences
The children to talk about how they travel to school. In pairs to ask staff how they travelled to school. The children to listen and report back to a larger group.
Use of transport shapes and sorting to help pupils count how many come by car, bus, bike, etc.
The data to be presented in the form of a simple chart with labels produced by the word processor and printer.
The class to share stories, poems, rhymes and songs about how people and animals move.
Sharing of simple information books on movement to deepen understanding and develop knowledge about the subject.
In groups children to make books entitled 'How we come to school'. The teacher/helper to use a language-experience approach and scribe simple sentences such as 'Mrs Smith travels on the bus', 'Mr Kent travels on his bike' …
Pupils to draw pictures to illustrate their page and write their names as authors at the front of the book.

Figure 2.3 An example of medium-term planning for under-fives showing links across areas of learning

They are also particularly sensitive to social context; unknown adults can often increase the level of their anxiety.

It is vital therefore that we assess children's achievements in language and literacy over a period of time and across a range of learning and social contexts. It is also better if assessments are carried out by familiar adults who know the children best; clearly joint assessments involving nursery nurses and teachers are particularly valuable at this phase.

A framework for assessing and recording

Below is a possible framework for assessing and recording language and literacy achievement in the under-fives.

1 Teachers' comments/records

These can record positive aspects of children's developing knowledge, skills and concepts in language and literacy, including statements related to the Desirable Outcomes and, where relevant, Key Stage 1 attainments. We can use informal or structured observation procedures to assess children in play and in a range of spontaneous learning situations and social groupings. This information is invaluable in supplementing and complementing the data we may have collected in more formal literacy events. In particular it gives feedback on children's developing awareness of functional print in the environment; what it is for and how it works. Close observation can also reveal the use of specific reading strategies, some of which might not have been demonstrated in more open contexts.

In Figure 2.4 a teacher has made notes/jottings as children used a 'have a go' approach to writing labels for observational drawings of fruit and berries.

2 Parents'/carers' comments

To ensure continuity we also need information about the child's language use at home, as well as the contexts in which it takes place, so that we can build experiences into learning at school.

The parent–teacher conference is increasingly seen as an opportunity for the teacher to learn about each child from the adult who knows her or him best. They provide an excellent opportunity both for parents to discuss their own priorities for

When asked to write on own
Rebecca – wrote her name then wrote groups of letters. She's aware of lower case and capitals and makes the letters confidently.

Fay – very aware of print and began by writing familiar names. She then asked how do you write rose hip? She then wrote R O on her own and copied the rest from her friend. She is very interested in print. I'm sure she would write on her own. She said 'ROSE starts like ROSS'.

Figure 2.4 Teacher's notes/jottings on 'Have a go' writing as labels for observational drawings of autumn fruits and berries
Source: Ann Davis, Curriculum and Advisory Service, Birmingham

their child and for observations to be shared. The *Primary Language Record* (Barrs *et al.* 1988) provides a useful range of topics which can be used as a framework for such parent–teacher conversations; they include:

- the child's knowledge and enjoyment of story
- the kinds of reading the child enjoys at home
- whether or not there are community schools in the area which the child attends
- the writing opportunities at home
- the child's special interests at home, including toys, games, TV programmes
- what parents have observed in their child's language and literacy development and any concerns they may have.

3 Contributions from children

Children's self-assessment can be highly motivating. All children like to know how they are getting on. With support even the youngest can be encouraged to reflect on what they can do well and what they can do to improve. Gradually they can set their own targets to improve their work and develop a greater sense of responsibility for their own learning. In addition what children say can be used to plan for what they need next. These insights in turn contribute to any other diagnostic and formative procedures, like baseline assessments, we might use.

4 Samples of children's work

Samples can offer us more information about a child's progress and achievement than many other forms of assessment. They can take the form of final end products or drafts/notes, etc., and could be used by:

- present teachers and other nursery/reception staff
- receiving teachers
- the child
- parents/carers/guardians
- the headteacher
- governors
- outside agencies
- Ofsted inspectors.

They can be selected because they show:

- significant steps forward/progress over time
- particular growth points
- a child's strengths and weaknesses
- attainment related to the language and literacy outcomes in the Desirable Outcomes and where relevant the Key Stage 1 attainments.

They can take the form of writing, photographs, audio/video tapes, diagrams, charts, computer printouts.

Remember it is important to date and annotate samples. We need to describe the social context, that is whether the work was completed individually, in pairs or in different kinds of groupings like mixed ability, all girls or boys, or common language. Similarly we need to describe the learning context in terms of how and where the work originated – a play area perhaps, or a different curriculum area of learning.

Baseline assessment

As from September 1998 all children will be assessed when they first start school, which for most children will be when they start in a reception class at the age of four or five.
The two key aims of baseline assessment are:

- to find out about children's knowledge and abilities so that teachers can plan effectively for each child's learning needs
- to help schools measure and monitor progress from when they start school so that they can check whether children are achieving as well as they might be.

The assessments are to take place as part of everyday classroom activity (for example looking at a book with a child) within six weeks of the child starting school. Schools must now choose a baseline assessment scheme formally accredited by the Qualifications and Curriculum Authority, but may use the scales provided in Part 3 of their baseline assessment information pack (1998). These have been designed to cover aspects of the Desirable Outcomes for each area of learning. Item 3 on the scale relates to the Desirable Outcomes, which of course come into effect in the term following the child's fifth birthday. Item 4 is seen as representing Level 1 of the National Curriculum. The following list shows the major criteria for Reading, Writing, and Speaking and Listening (more details of what to look for under each heading can be found in Part 3 of the information pack, pages 3 and 4).

Reading A: Reading for meaning and enjoyment

1 Holds books appropriately whilst turning the pages and retelling the story from memory
2 Able to predict words and phrases
3 Uses memory of familiar text to match some spoken and written words
4 Reads simple texts

Reading B: Letter knowledge

1 Recognises his or her own name
2 Recognises five letters by shape and sound
3 Recognises fifteen letters by shape and sound
4 Recognises all letter shapes by names and sounds

Reading C: Phonological awareness

1 Recites familiar rhymes
2 Recognises initial sounds
3 Associates sounds with patterns in rhyme
4 Demonstrates knowledge of sound sequences in words

Writing

1 Distinguishes between print and pictures in his or her own work
2 Writes letter shapes
3 Independently writes own name spelt correctly
4 Writes words

Speaking and Listening

1 Recounts events or experiences
2 Asks questions to find out information and listens to the answers
3 Makes up own story and tells it

4   Makes up a story with detail and tells it to a small group, and listens to stories

There is still much developmental work to be done in this area, and scales will never give us a complete picture of what a child achieves in language and literacy; it will always be important to gather evidence of achievement over time and in different contexts as recommended above.

towards achieving the current set targets for five-year-olds.

You should by now:

- have a greater awareness of some of the commonly agreed principles which underpin a high-quality language and literacy curriculum for the under-fives

- have more knowledge of the Desirable Outcomes (SCAA) for language and literacy and of the kinds of early activities that can help children develop the required competencies

- have a framework for planning, assessing and recording an appropriate curriculum in language and literacy for the under-fives which recognises the crucial importance of stories, play and talk.

SUMMARY

This chapter has attempted to offer ways of planning and assessing a stimulating, high-quality language and literacy curriculum for the under-fives which will promote their progress

References

Barrs, M., Ellis, S., Hester, H. and Thomas, A. (1988) *The Primary Language Record*, Centre for Language in Primary Education

DES (1990) *Starting with Quality: Report of the Committee of Enquiry into the Educational Experiences Offered to Three and Four Year Olds* (The Rumbold Report), HMSO

DfEE and SCAA (1996) *Desirable Outcomes for Children's Learning on Entering Compulsory Education*, DfEE

DfEE and SCAA (1997) *Looking at Children's Learning: Desirable Outcomes for Children's Learning on Entering Compulsory Education*, DfEE

Ofsted (1995) *The Ofsted Handbook: Guidance on the Inspection of Nursery and Primary Schools*, HMSO

QCA (1998) *The Baseline Assessment Information Pack: Preparation for Statutory Baseline Assessment*, QCA

Story Chest Big Books (1990) *Hairy Bear*, Thomas Nelson

Vygotsky, L. S. (1962) *Thought and Language*, MIT Press

Further reading

Clipson-Boyles, S. (1995) *Language and Literacy in the Early Years*, David Fulton
An accessible and practical handbook to support teachers and assistants in nursery and primary classroom settings. The book contains useful activities, some of which are supported by photocopiable activity sheets.

Garton, A. and Pratt, C. (1989) *Learning to Be Literate: The Development of Spoken and Written Language*, Basil Blackwell
A comprehensive but readable review of the development of children's spoken and written language from birth to about eight years of age

Hall, N. (1987) *The Emergence of Literacy*, Hodder and Stoughton
A readable survey of the emergence of reading and writing in young children. It examines current research and provides a strong rationale for classroom practice in the early years.

James, F. (1996) *Phonological Awareness: Classroom Strategies*, UKRA
An excellent booklet which outlines the research background into phonological awareness. It also describes activities that have been drawn together by teachers and LEA support staff. All are part of a rich language curriculum which builds on children's knowledge and experience and which draws upon the literary tradition of rhyme and poetry.

3 The National Curriculum for English

OBJECTIVES

By the end of this chapter you should:

- have learnt key aspects of the history of the National Curriculum

- understand the structure of the National Curriculum

- be familiar with the terminology of English in the National Curriculum

- understand the nature of assessment in English in the National Curriculum.

The history of the National Curriculum

In 1988, after an extensive consultation process that invited feedback from all interested parties, the National Curriculum became law. It was embedded within an Education Reform Act which brought to schools in England and Wales a degree of control over the content of the curriculum that was hitherto unimaginable in primary education.

Prior to the introduction of the National Curriculum the headteacher or, more often, an individual class teacher, determined the curriculum in any primary school. They chose topics for study based on their particular interests or on the availability of books in the school which could support the study. The curriculum for English and maths was often determined by graded books produced by educational publishers which set out the areas to be covered and proposed an order in which to teach them.

In secondary schools the content of what was to be taught was dictated by the public examinations at GCSE and, as well as prescribing the curriculum

for Years 10 and 11, the GCSE tended to dominate the curriculum content for Years 7–9. However, in the primary sector, with no public examinations to set the curriculum, teachers were able to exercise considerable freedom to determine what was to be taught and how it was to be taught. A team of Her Majesty's Inspectors (HMIs) assessed schools and made suggestions about improving teaching techniques but, because there was no national framework of a curriculum against which to set this advice, it often had little impact other than on the individual school which had been inspected.

It was into this environment, which was essentially individualistic and broadly unaccountable, that the Conservative Government of the time introduced a curriculum which specified exactly *what* was to be taught and *when* (although it stopped short of specifying *how* the subjects were to be taught). It was understandable that it threw the teaching profession into turmoil.

Ten years on, the concept of a National Curriculum, its characteristic terminology and its comprehensive assessment procedures seem so familiar to practising teachers that it is hard to imagine the unbridled freedom of the days prior to 1988.

The structure of the National Curriculum

The National Curriculum covers nine subjects at primary level:

Core foundation subjects: English, maths, science

Foundation subjects: art, geography, history, music, PE, technology (design technology and information technology)

It is organised on the basis of two key stages:

	Age	Year groups
Key Stage 1	5–7	1–2
Key Stage 2	7–11	3–6

The curriculum content for each of the different subjects is described in the same way, i.e.:

- *programmes of study:* what pupils must be taught
- *attainment targets:* expected standards of pupils' performance
- *level descriptions:* at the end of Key Stages 1, 2 and 3 for all subjects except art, music and PE, standards of pupils' performance are set out in eight level descriptions of increasing difficulty.

In July 1998 the DfEE published the leaflet *Maintaining Breadth and Balance*. This provides guidance to teachers about restructuring the amount of time to be spent on the foundation subjects in order to free time for the core subjects and to prepare for the implementation of the National Literacy Strategy Framework for Teaching in both English and maths.

English in the National Curriculum

The programmes of study are organised into three subject areas, or attainment targets:

1 Speaking and Listening
2 Reading
3 Writing.

The division into three subject areas or attainment targets is intended to give equal status to each area (there was a fear that otherwise Speaking and Listening might be overshadowed by the other two programmes of study). However, despite this division, the National Curriculum Order is at pains to stress that 'Pupils' activities should be developed with an integrated programme of speaking and listening, reading and writing' (DfE 1995).

Integrating all aspects of English

Prior to the advent of the National Curriculum it was fairly typical for English to be seen as one subject without teasing out the linked skills of speaking and listening, reading and writing. The danger in this approach was that it was possible for teachers to concentrate upon one aspect, such as writing, at the expense of another, such as speaking and listening. The National Curriculum has tried to balance giving separate attention to each aspect of English whilst at the same time encouraging an integrated approach to the teaching of English.

Teachers will address this tension between the separate programmes of study and the importance of integrating the subject when they organise medium-term planning. Teachers may be very clear about their focus on skills to be acquired and range to be covered with particular emphasis upon one area, for example Speaking and Listening, but the context for this might be a task in the classroom which engages the children in talking, reading and writing.

The National Curriculum encourages this overlap but it does require teachers to ensure that all three programmes of study are addressed appropriately.

Teaching English skills separately from other curriculum subjects

Because of the nature of English as a subject there is a real danger that assumptions are made regarding the teaching of English as a by-product of other subjects. That is, it is assumed that as language skills are needed for all subjects then English is automatically being taught across the curriculum. For example, writing up a science experiment could double as English 'information writing'; talking about Victorian poverty might be considered to suffice for the Speaking and Listening programme of study – 'using talk to develop thinking'. Whilst there is obvious overlap it is also very important to ensure that these particular skills of communication are taught in their own right and are not just treated as aspects of other subjects.

General Requirements

Unlike other curriculum subjects the National Curriculum for English has General Requirements for teaching the subject across all the key stages. This broad overview of the English curriculum sets the tone and maps the area for the three programmes of study. It gives guidance about the requirements for children to develop as *effective* speakers, listeners, readers and writers. It also explains the relationship between 'standard' English and non-standard English. It describes how each form should be taught and how children should be made aware of when it is necessary to use standard English and when non-standard forms might be used to achieve a particular effect.

The programmes of study

The programme of study for each strand of English is organised under the same headings: Range, Key Skills, Standard English and Language Study, as shown in the following chart.

	Speaking and Listening	Reading	Writing
Range			
Key Skills			
Standard English and Language Study			

Range

Range in the English National Curriculum outlines the opportunities to which children are entitled. It describes the context within which the other sub-divisions of the English curriculum (i.e. Key Skills and Standard English and Language Study) are to be interpreted.

Speaking and Listening

This describes the broad sweep of speaking and listening opportunities with which children should be provided in order to develop as effective speakers and listeners across a range of experiences.

Reading

This describes the broad sweep of literature and information books in print and on screen that should be made available to children.

Writing

This describes the stimuli that may prompt writing; the purposes of writing and the audiences for whom the children may write.

Balancing fiction and non-fiction

An important consideration within the National Curriculum is the attention paid to children as readers and writers of texts which are not exclusively fiction. Prior to the National Curriculum it was generally thought that children of primary age should learn to read fiction and that their writing should primarily be imaginative stories. Reading for information and writing in a non-personal style in the form of a report or a set of instructions were thought to be skills taught in secondary school. The National Curriculum has placed great emphasis upon the importance of teaching children to be readers and writers of all kinds of non-fiction texts as well as fiction.

Fiction texts that are specifically mentioned at Key Stage 1 include rhymes, stories with predictable language, traditional stories and stories from other cultures. Non-fiction texts include signs, labels, simple information books and dictionaries.

At Key Stage 2 the range for both fiction and non-fiction is more extensive and includes legends, mystery stories, science fiction, classic poetry, reports, arguments, journalism and diaries.

Although the extent of the range increases from Key Stage 1 to Key Stage 2 it is, broadly speaking, addressing similar areas. This is because there is no clear hierarchical order of difficulty when describing ranges of writing experiences. Writing a formal letter to a policeman could be a suitable task for children working at Key Stage 2. However, one could easily imagine a situation in the Year 2 classroom where the teacher has arranged for a police officer to come and talk to the class and then the teacher might model for the children the writing of a thank you letter to the officer, thereby making it an entirely appropriate task for those younger children.

This typifies some of the problems that have faced teachers as they try to map the diverse skills of English on to the requirements of the National Curriculum. It is fair to say that the authors of the National Curriculum would undoubtedly agree that English has been a particularly problematic subject to fit into the National Curriculum framework because of the nature of the subject, which does not conform to neat linear lines of knowledge development. Whereas in other subjects experts and others can broadly agree upon an order in which to introduce skills, in English such an order cannot readily be found. For this reason there is considerable overlap between skills and experiences described under the heading Range at both Key Stages 1 and 2.

Key Skills

This section of the programmes of study describes the knowledge, skills and understanding to be taught in each attainment target. Unlike the content of Range it is, on the whole, easier to describe skills in a clear hierarchy and this is what the National Curriculum sets out to do.

Speaking and Listening: Key Stage 1
The knowledge, skills and understanding of *speaking* to be taught are:

- that effective communication is clear, fluent and interesting
- how to speak with confidence
- how to incorporate the relevant and omit the less important
- how to take turns in speaking.

The knowledge, skills and understanding of *listening* to be taught are:

- to listen with growing concentration
- to ask appropriate questions
- to use talk to develop thinking
- to build upon the utterances of others.

Speaking and Listening: Key Stage 2
The knowledge, skills and understanding of *speaking* to be taught are:

- to express themselves clearly
- to make careful word choices
- to engage in purposeful discussions
- to evaluate their own discussions.

The knowledge, skills and understanding of *listening* to be taught are:

- to recall salient features of, for example, a TV programme
- to identify the gist of a discussion
- to make relevant contributions
- to listen attentively and ask questions to clarify information
- to defend opinions courteously.

The difficulty in attempting to map out a hierarchy of skills in this subject area is reflected in the language of the requirements, which are unavoidably vague. For example: What is 'confident' speaking for a five-year-old? What is it reasonable to expect a six-year-old to be able to produce in terms of 'appropriate' questions? How can teachers assess whether a child has fully engaged in 'purposeful' discussions? However, all these difficulties in precisely defining a hierarchy in no way invalidate the importance of attempting to do so. Prior to the National Curriculum teachers were rarely required to assess children's speaking and listening skills at all other than to sum up a child as 'a chatterbox' or 'shy'. The National Curriculum has been invaluable in raising awareness about expectations and standards in speaking and listening skills, which are arguably the most important of all life skills taught in school.

However, for the programmes of study for Reading and Writing it is considerably easier to map a progression of skills.

Reading: Key Stage 1
The knowledge, skills and understanding to be taught are:

- phonic knowledge (the relationship between print symbols and sound patterns)
- graphic knowledge (how word meanings are embedded in consistent letter patterns, i.e. relationships between root words and derivatives, such as help, helpful)
- word recognition (developing a swift and effective sight vocabulary)
- grammatical knowledge (understanding sentence syntax)
- contextual understanding (supporting meaning from context)

These are the core building blocks of learning to read. The curriculum stresses that all these skills need to be introduced within a balanced and coherent programme. This clear guidance helps teachers to avoid the pitfalls of over-emphasis of one component skill at the expense of the others.

Reading: Key Stage 2
By Key Stage 2 the Key Skills section concentrates more upon children responding to texts and using their newly acquired skills of decoding to interpret and fully understand what they have read. They are to be taught the importance of reading with fluency and intonation. There is also emphasis upon using the skills of reading to find information from books and other sources; for example:

- skimming (reading to get an initial overview of the subject matter and main ideas of a passage) and scanning (reading to locate information by locating a key word)
- identifying the purpose of the enquiry
- using reference books effectively
- extending vocabulary beyond the everyday and familiar.

Writing: Key Stage 1
The knowledge, skills and understanding to be taught include:

- learning about the purposes of written language
- learning the alphabet
- experimental writing
- structuring writing on paper and screen
- the importance of word choices
- punctuation: capital letters, full stops, question marks and commas

- spelling: simple words and spelling patterns
- handwriting: developing a legible style.

Writing: Key Stage 2

The knowledge, skills and understanding to be taught include:

- appropriate writing styles for different purposes
- the importance of drafting writing
- punctuation: full stops, question and exclamation marks, commas, inverted commas and apostrophes to mark possession
- spelling: a bank of useful words and complex polysyllabic words
- handwriting: legible handwriting in joined-up and printed styles

Standard English and Language Study

The third section in each of the programmes of study for English is Standard English and Language Study. This is an area of the English curriculum that has generated some lively debate, and a full explanation of the requirements is provided in Chapter 21.

Speaking and Listening: Key Stages 1 and 2

The emphasis is upon children learning standard English to add to the repertoire of their own spoken language. The differences between standard English and other non-standard forms usually lie in differences in vocabulary and syntax. The National Curriculum does not set out to undermine the importance of any child's use of language but rather it invites children to see how language can be used differently in situations to achieve different effects. The emphasis is on appropriateness of language for different occasions.

Reading: Key Stages 1 and 2

This emphasises teaching children to be aware of textual characteristics, for example how different story genres employ different kinds of story openers. This develops into a vocabulary to discuss texts – for example author, setting, plot, format – and an increasing awareness of how authors use standard English or non-standard English for particular effects.

Writing: Key Stages 1 and 2

This covers drawing children's attention to the correct use of language within a context of understanding why variants of the correct form might be used in certain circumstances. It is really looking at how language works and encouraging children to have the terminology with which to dissect language in order to use it appropriately.

Testing in the National Curriculum

Children are assessed at the end of each key stage. The assessments have two separate components:

1 Standard national tasks and tests for all children in reading and writing. The tests show what children have achieved in selected parts of English at the end of the Key Stage.
2 Teachers complete their own assessments at the end of the Key Stage to give a level for each aspect of English.

Standard national tests

For Key Stage 1 the test involves:

- an assessment of oral reading
- a written reading comprehension test
- an assessment of writing
- a spelling test.

For Key Stage 2 the test involves:

- a written reading comprehension test
- an assessment of writing
- a spelling test.

These tests are written and set by outside agencies commissioned by the Qualifications and Curriculum Authority (QCA), but the teacher administers all the tests.

Teacher assessment

To accompany all the national tests teachers also make judgements about the level of work being achieved by a child. The benchmarks for progress are detailed in the attainment targets, which set out the expected standards of children's performance in each of the profile components for English. These standards are set out in eight level descriptions of increasing difficulty.

Teachers are expected to make judgements about a child's performance against the level descriptions. With guidance and practice teachers can become familiar with what the standards set out in the level descriptions mean in practice and how the level descriptions can be used to make accurate and consistent judgements on a child's performance. Deciding which level description best describes the overall performance of an individual child is a professional decision. There will not always be an exact fit. This is why it is very important for teachers to keep evidence of children's work and to discuss exemplars of standards with colleagues.

Assessing performance over time is somewhat easier when considering the development of writing ability or reading performance. It can be more of a challenge to the teacher to keep evidence of a child's progress in speaking and listening, but it is worth remembering that children are awarded a Speaking and Listening level on teacher assessment only; there are no tests for speaking and listening.

These teacher assessment levels are averaged to form an overall subject level. Teacher assessment takes into account strengths and weaknesses in performance across a range of contexts and over a period of time. In this way it provides a different but equally important assessment of a child's performance to run alongside the formal testing at the end of the key stage.

Note: More information about assessment procedures for the national tests can be found in Chapter 6 and in the relevant chapters on Speaking and Listening, Reading and Writing.

SUMMARY

This chapter has given a general overview of the content of the National Curriculum for English. More specifically it has:

- considered the balance between teaching speaking, listening, reading and writing as separate skills and as part of an integrated curriculum

- given a flavour of the content of the English curriculum with reference to range, key skills and language study

- introduced the two strands of assessment in English – standard national tests and teacher assessment.

Reference

DfE (1995) *English in the National Curriculum*, HMSO

4 Integrating the areas of language

OBJECTIVES

By the end of this chapter you should:

- understand what is meant by an integrated approach to language and appreciate its value

- understand the integrated framework adopted by the National Literacy Strategy

- know how to plan some integrated activities for the under-fives and for children at Key Stages 1 and 2.

Integrating language: what does it mean?

When we talk about integration in English teaching and learning we are talking about making links between each of the three areas or 'modes' of language: speaking and listening, reading and writing.

There is currently much emphasis upon the importance of integrating speaking and listening, reading and writing. When the National Curriculum was revised in 1995 a new preface was introduced to each English programme of study. This stressed that children's abilities should be developed within an integrated programme which 'interrelated' speaking and listening, reading and writing.

More recently, in a huge effort to achieve better literacy standards, the National Literacy Strategy has established a Framework for Teaching (DES 1998) which makes very close connections between the teaching of speaking and listening, reading, writing and knowledge about language. Before we look more closely at these two documents let us first consider what we mean by integration of language, first from an adult perspective and then through specific classroom examples.

In everyday life we all make links between speaking, listening, reading and writing. Imagine wanting to make travel arrangements to visit a friend. We might first jot down when we would prefer to travel. Then we might ring train enquiries using our notes to remind us what information we need about relevant departure times. We would listen to what was said and make notes again during the conversation. Later we would probably read our notes and reflect upon them before making a final decision.

In classrooms too, children can be found working on activities which make natural links between talk, reading and writing. Many teachers at Key Stage 1 use children's own talking and writing experiences as starting points for reading in what is described as 'a language experience approach'. What usually happens is that children tell the teacher what they want to say about a recent experience, picture or model and then the teacher writes the text and invites the child to read it back. Often children make such a strong emotional response to their self-created texts that they want to return to them time and time again. This builds their self-esteem as a reader but also develops sight vocabulary and many important reading skills. So a language experience approach is a clear example of integrating language in that speaking and listening, reading and writing are all reinforcing and extending each other.

Many teachers also use book talk as part of their continuous integrated language and literacy programme. Aidan Chambers (1993) writes:

> **Talking well about books is a high value activity in itself. But talking well about books is also the best rehearsal there is for talking about other things. So in helping children to talk about their reading, we help them to be articulate about the rest of their lives.**

At Key Stage 1, book talk often takes place as the

whole class are involved in shared reading of a story during the literacy hour, and at Key Stage 2 teachers now use book talk during shared and guided reading in order to develop children's comprehension of more challenging literary texts. After reading the text they might talk about the setting, characters, plot or use of language. This might lead on to different kinds of shared writing which enable children to get closer to the book and develop a deeper understanding of its meaning.

Why integrate language?

A functional approach

For both adults and children, many experiences of language and literacy are integrated in that talk, reading and writing are all used together to help fulfil particular needs. This model of language is often called a 'functional' model. (Halliday 1989). At the heart of a functional model of language and learning is an emphasis upon meaning. In addition a functional model:

- looks at how language enables us to do things
- emphasises that language activities should have real purposes
- avoids empty decontextualised exercises or simply teaching language for the sake of teaching language
- is concerned with real whole texts rather than individual words and sentences in isolation.

Integrating language: what are the advantages for children?

Continuity
In our first example we saw how adults integrate language in order to function in everyday life and in society as a whole. Very young children do not learn about talking, reading and writing as separate aspects of language either. In the real world they use them in interrelated ways to communicate and share meaning with those around them. So when we use integrated approaches in the classroom, in many important ways we are respecting and building upon the way very young children acquire and use language at home and in their communities.

Purpose and relevance
Integrating different language skills enables children to learn through language while learning more about language – the focus being on the meaning and the purpose. It can help children feel that what is taught is worth learning because it serves useful and real purposes, including their own. When language is kept integrated and purposeful, children are more likely to see it as relevant, which leads them to a greater sense of control and ownership over their own use of reading, speaking and listening and thinking. At school the learning of language and literacy skills can be exciting and stimulating if the emphasis stays upon meaning and if children are allowed to develop control over making sense.

It is important to mention at this point that bilingual children, in particular, require as many opportunities as possible to use their second language in real, meaningful contexts. They need to be able to practise English in a pleasurable and meaningful way as opposed to decontextualised and isolated drills. Similarly the struggling reader or writer can find learning particularly hard when it focuses upon specific isolated speaking and listening, reading and writing skills out of context. All too often this approach 'bears little relation to who they are, what they think and what they do' (Holdaway 1979). Sadly it can also remind them of the distance between their world and the world of school.

Planning for integration: the National Literacy Strategy Framework for Teaching

The National Curriculum Orders for English and Welsh are set out as three separate modes of language: Speaking and Listening, Reading and Writing. The National Literacy Strategy's Framework for Teaching is, however, a completely integrated model of language and literacy. Each term's work focuses upon a particular range of fiction, poetry and non-fiction. Reading and writing objectives are closely linked throughout as the texts children are reading provide a structure for their writing. In the framework, there are three strands to the work – word level, sentence level and text level – and all are closely interrelated. The overall structure of the framework is shown in Figure 4.1.

The objectives are subdivided for each term, as shown in Figure 4.2. Notice how the headings for word-level work change at Key Stage 2 to focus

YEAR TERM		
1 1		
Range: **Fiction and Poetry** **Non-Fiction**		
Word level work: Phonics, spelling and vocabulary Pupils should be taught:	**Sentence level work:** Grammar and punctuation Pupils should be taught:	**Text level work:** Comprehension and composition Pupils should be taught:

Figure 4.1 The overall structure of the Framework for Teaching
Source: DfEE 1998

Word level	Sentence level	Text level
Reception year • Phonological awareness, phonics and spelling • Word recognition, graphic knowledge and spelling • Vocabulary extension • Handwriting	• Grammatical awareness	• Understanding of print • Reading comprehension • Writing composition
Key Stage 1 • Phonological awareness, phonics and spelling • Word recognition, graphic knowledge and spelling • Vocabulary extension • Handwriting	• Grammatical awareness • Sentence construction and punctuation	*Fiction and poetry* • Reading comprehension • Writing composition *Non-fiction* • Reading comprehension • Writing composition
Key Stage 2 • Revision and consolidation from Key Stage 1 (to the end of Y3) • Spelling strategies • Spelling conventions and rules • Vocabulary extension • Handwriting (to the end of Y4)	• Grammatical awareness • Sentence construction and punctuation	*Fiction and poetry* • Reading comprehension • Writing composition *Non-fiction* • Reading comprehension • Writing composition

Figure 4.2 The Framework for Teaching: the objectives for each term
Source: DfEE 1998

less upon phonological awareness and word recognition and more on spelling strategies, conventions and rules.

The framework emphasises that shared reading and shared writing should be interlinked as follows:

- introduction of a text
- working on it through shared reading
- using the text as a frame for writing or as a stimulus to extend, alter or comment on it.

Strong links are constantly being made between spoken language, reading and spelling. Here the project relates to recent research evidence (Adams 1990 and Goswami and Bryant 1990). This has shown that an early understanding of sounds (phonemes) and their spellings has an important effect on children's reading and writing development.

The objectives in the basic work section emphasise the importance of identifying sounds in spoken language through exploration, and playing with patterned and predictable language, like poems, rhymes, games, tongue twisters, etc. Children must then make the connection between these sound patterns and the letters on the page in order that they will recognise and use phonic cues when they are reading. They are also encouraged to use analogy, by using their knowledge of known words to read and spell previously unseen words.

The importance of integrating grammar, reading and writing is emphasised. Members of the draft project held that grammar is not systematically taught in most primary schools and regarded sound knowledge of grammar as essential to an understanding of reading and writing.

The framework also makes strong links between reading and writing for information. Through Key Stage 2 the range of reading and writing increases and with it the need for children to understand the organisation and purpose of a wide variety of texts. More specifically it links, for example, the scanning of a text to the making of written notes which capture key words and ideas.

The importance of shared reading

Shared reading is a whole-class reading activity using a common text like a big book, a picture book or poem. It now plays a central role in the first 15 minutes of the literacy hour, but in reality shared reading has been an established part of many teachers' practice for some time. These teachers share texts with the whole class because it provides a purposeful, enjoyable context for integrated language and literacy work. They feel it promotes awareness that writing has a real purpose: to communicate and share meaning with others. It also provides them with an opportunity to model the reading and writing process and so develop children's understanding of the features and purposes of written language.

In early years classrooms the whole class usually share an enlarged text by reading aloud together with expression and intonation, the teacher possibly using a pointer to focus the children's attention on the words. At an appropriate time she might stop to discuss the themes and characters in the story. She might also encourage children to guess what is coming next or to discuss certain spelling patterns and phonic rules.

The Literacy Training Pack produced by the National Literacy Strategy (DfEE 1998) includes a number of video extracts of teachers engaged in shared reading with the whole class. The Ofsted video *Literacy Matters* (1997), produced to complement the work of the National Literacy project, also features a class engaged in this kind of shared language experience. The class are currently working on the rime of 'ush' and their attention is drawn to the fact that two words 'rush' and 'brush' have this same rime. The teacher then encourages children to make analogies with their family or word bank of words – displayed on the classroom wall. The children are invited to spell some of these words aloud, so making the connection with their sounds and appearance as letters on the page. They then receive a quick and simple grammar lesson on how common suffixes can change the tense and meaning of words as the teacher adds -ed and -ing to rush and brush. The session ends with all the class joining in once again with the reading of the story they all obviously enjoy. This is a clear example of an integrated activity in which the teacher has provided opportunities for learning by making links between the three modes of language.

This next section offers examples of the kinds of integrated language experiences which might be planned as group activities in the literacy hour. They could be planned either as independent group work or as guided text work with the teacher.

Reading and writing information

Teachers at Key Stage 2 frequently use integrated approaches as a way of helping children read and write information texts without resorting to decontextualised worksheets and comprehension cards. In one class, children were encouraged to make an information book and used talk, reading and writing at each stage in the process. The work covered a period of 2–3 weeks and involved a number of integrated and differentiated group activities. These included:

- sharing the differences between factual and literary texts
- discussing what made a good research question
- helping each other to locate, read and use the different structural devices like blurb, chapter headings; subtitles, diagrams and labels
- using different reading styles like skimming, scanning, intensive and reflective reading, writing notes
- discussing first drafts and reviewing each other's work for meaning – re-presenting the information, talking and agreeing upon the final text and format for the book.

Finally the children celebrated their achievements and presented their information book to another class. (See Cairney 1990, pp. 98–105: 'Getting it all together: integrating the reading and writing of factual texts'.)

Developing response to literature

We saw at the beginning of this chapter the importance of book talk. The following activities promote all kinds of interesting purposeful talk about books, their settings, characters, themes, plots and language. In their different ways, these creative approaches help children develop a love of literature as they discuss, assess, interpret and criticise texts using talk, reading and writing in interrelated ways. (See Cairney 1990 and Benton and Fox 1985.)

Character interviews

The children read and discuss a story, then decide upon one aspect for an interview, which is conducted as if it were part of real life. In pairs or groups they generate questions an interviewer might ask one of the characters . Then they discuss possible answers and role play the interview. This kind of integrated activity encourages children to develop a thorough understanding and appreciation of the text by 'getting inside the character'.

Character grids

After reading a story or play, children are asked to plot various characters' attributes and motives on a simple grid. For example, whether they are selfish or considerate, courageous or cowardly. Children become involved in quite intense discussion around the characters. Some children go on to develop their own systems for analysing the characters in books.

Written conversations

Children have a written dialogue with a character from a book they have been reading. They might assume the roles of characters from two different books, for example the BFG conversing with Jack from 'Jack and the Beanstalk'. The purpose here is to encourage them to become actively involved with the people and events in the text as they try to understand the way they think, act, talk and write.

Story-mapping

This works well where a journey is important, as is the case in many books for young readers. The children discuss and interpret extracts of the story. Then they create one or several large wall maps on which the movements of the characters are plotted and perhaps illustrated by groups in the class using art, painting, 3-D effects or other techniques.

Book-making

Book-making is another example of an integrated language activity and one which is a common feature of good practice at all phases. Here children make their own books about particular experiences, areas of interest or personal stories.

The starting point for the book can be a school or classroom experience, a story, a poem, a rhyme, a play, a class topic (see Figure 4.3). The formats might be pop-up, zigzag, enlarged or shaped, and include photographs, drawings, flaps or even real items (see Figure 4.4). The children can write independently or in groups. Less experienced writers might dictate their text to the teacher, or other adult, who can then act as scribe.

This enables them to write at greater length than they can manage to write for themselves. Audiences can be children themselves, parents, other classes, governors, etc.

WHERE TO START?

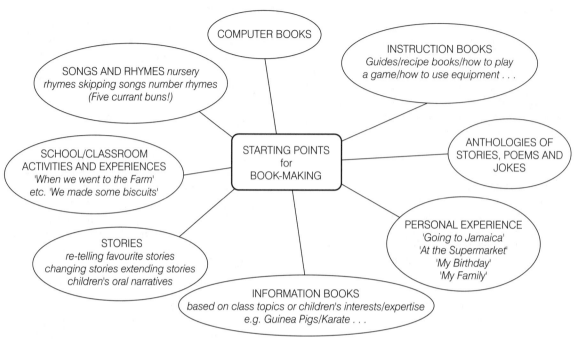

Figure 4.3 Examples of different starting points for book-making

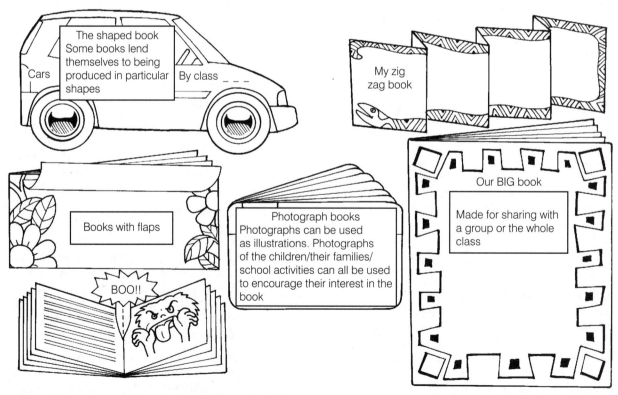

Figure 4.4 Examples of different formats for book-making

Teachers find that when they make books for and with groups of children they are highly motivated to read them. They also find that in the process of book-making the children develop a whole range of interrelated speaking and listening, reading and writing skills, such as:

- using different kinds of talk for different purposes, including deciding, narrating, problem-solving, negotiating, collaborating, justifying, explaining
- writing and reading a range of texts like brainstorm webs, notes, first drafts through to the neat and clear final copy
- seeing how different texts are ordered, shaped and sequenced, and how choice of words and correct punctuation can enhance meaning.

Planning an integrated programme for the under-fives

In Chapter 2 we established that pre-school children do not learn about reading and writing as separate aspects of language. In the real world their learning is integrated. They learn about language as they use it and they use language for a wide range of powerful, purposeful functions.

But where should we start with planning for the under-fives? The Desirable Outcomes for Children's Learning (DfEE and SCAA 1996) are essentially goals for children to achieve by the age of five. In no way, however, do they represent any kind of programme of study as that provided by the National Curriculum and the Framework for Teaching for Key Stages 1 and 2.

The challenge for those of us working in nurseries and reception classes is therefore to identify worthwhile activities which will promote children's development towards achieving these outcomes by the age of five.

In the following example of blocked planning for under-fives, Jill Murphy's 'Peace at Last' and her other stories provide rich contexts in which children can work in an integrated way towards achieving many of the language and literacy outcomes. Activities around the stories offer opportunities which build upon and develop children's likely pre-school experiences of functional literacy. They also emphasise play, an essential element in all planning for the under-fives. In addition, by dealing with the theme of caring and sharing and

in touching on issues of personal identity, uniqueness and diversity in family life patterns, they provide ample opportunities for embedding equal opportunities in terms of race, gender and special educational needs. All the ideas can be used quite successfully within the framework of the literacy hour.

Example of blocked planning for the under-fives

Time: 7–8 hours
Class/Group: Reception, 4–5-year-olds
Theme/Topic/Subject: Author study – Jill Murphy

Learning aims in relation to Desirable Outcomes

- To encourage children to listen and respond to stories expressing preferences and opinions about characters
- To understand how books are organised
- To communicate meaning in writing using familiar words, symbols or pictures
- To write their names

Teaching methods

First of all we can introduce Jill Murphy using an autobiography from a magazine article. Here we are trying to develop children's awareness of authorship. Children can then listen to 'Peace at Last' and other stories over four to five sessions, responding to the themes and characters. We can also highlight the sounds, letters, rhymes and patterns in the books and thus develop children's phonological awareness in a fun and exciting way.

The class can talk about favourite scenes and possibly act out different roles or maybe use dressing-up clothes in the role-play area. We can talk about their experiences of night time and make up stories about hearing noises in the night. We may wish to write a class story on an easel with and in front of the children to show the purpose of writing and that it communicates meaning. In this we are acting as scribe, modelling concepts of print such as left to right and how sounds relate to letters and patterns of letters as recommended in the Framework for Teaching.

One group could then read multiple copies of 'Peace at Last'. Another group could sequence aspects of the story using photocopies of key scenes from 'Peace at Last' and other stories.

Others might dictate simple labels for each one. For example, 'Mum and Dad Bear are asleep in bed'.

Individuals can draw or paint favourite scenes and write their names. They can also be encouraged to write on themes suggested by the story, such as what I like/dislike about the dark; bad or good dreams, etc.

Some groups could make books on the theme of bedtime routines, such as 'Getting ready for bed'. It is important here to build in repetitive sentence structures and introduce familiar words to support the development of sight vocabulary, for example 'I wear pyjamas', 'I wear slippers', etc.

When all is completed the children love to write their name as authors at the beginning of the book and then read it to as many people as possible!

Although the emphasis here is upon story, there are many opportunities for working with information books. For example:

- finding out more about how things work: cars/fridges/clocks/phones, etc.
- people who work at night
- daytime and night-time animals.

In this context we can show children how to handle information books; how they are organised and are different from stories; how their purpose is to inform and instruct.

Some of these activities can obviously be planned as differentiated group activities for the literacy hour, if appropriate. In guided reading we might act as a scribe for some less confident/experienced writers. More able/confident writers can use *Breakthrough to Literacy* materials or word banks during independent group work.

When assessing children's achievements, we might consider the following assessment criteria:

- Can they use terms like 'title', 'author', 'illustrator' page, front, back, cover, etc.?
- Can they express a preference for a particular book/scene/character?
- Can they retell a part they enjoyed? Can they express opinions about the characters?
- Can they work with other children – listen, participate and cooperate?
- Can they write their names?
- Can they attach meaning to their own writing and attempt to read it back?

(*Looking at Children's Learning*, the complementary booklet to *Desirable Outcomes*, is an excellent resource for short-term planning for the under-fives. It describes in detail the planning and implementation of over 30 integrated activities.)

SUMMARY

This chapter has emphasised the unity of the three areas or modes of language: speaking, listening, reading and writing. It has also suggested activities which trainees and new teachers might try with children aged from three to eleven.

You should now:

- have a better understanding of what is meant by an integrated approach to language and appreciate why it is important to interrelate the different language areas

- know that the programmes of study interrelate

- have an understanding of the integrated framework adopted by the National Literacy Strategy Framework for Teaching

- know how to plan some integrated activities which are appropriate for the under-fives and for children working at Key Stages 1 and 2.

References

Adams, M. J. (1990) *Beginning to Read: Thinking and Learning about Print*, MIT Press

Benton, M. and Fox, G. (1985) *Teaching Literature 9–14*, Oxford University Press

Cairney, T. (1990) *Teaching Reading Comprehension*, Open University Press

Chambers, A. (1993) *Tell Me: Children, Reading and Talk*, Thimble Press

DfEE (1998) *The National Literacy Strategy: Framework for Teaching*, DfEE. See also DfEE (1997) *Implementation of the National Literacy Strategy: A Summary for Primary Schools*, DfEE

DfEE and SCAA (1996) *Desirable Outcomes for Children's Learning on Entering Compulsory Education*, DfEE

DfEE and SCAA (1997) *Looking at Children's Learning: Desirable Outcomes for Children's Learning on Entering Compulsory Education*, DfEE

Goswami, U. and Bryant, P. E. (1990) *Phonological Skills and Learning to Read*, Lawrence Erlbaum Associates

Halliday, M. A. K. and Hasan, R. (1989) *Language, Context and Text: Aspects of Language in a Social Semiotic Perspective*, Oxford University Press

Holdaway, D. (1979) *The Foundations of Literacy*, Ashton Scholastic

Ofsted (1997) *Literacy Matters*, video pack including workbook, CLF Vision

Further reading

Cairney, T. (1990) *Teaching Reading Comprehension*, Open University Press
An excellent book which offers a variety of integrated activities teachers can use to develop children's comprehension of both literary and non-fiction texts.

Chambers, A. (1993) *Tell Me: Children, Reading and Talk*, Thimble Press
Now something of a classic. Chambers offers exciting ideas to stimulate all kinds of book talk for a range of purposes in the busy primary classroom.

DfEE (1998) *National Literacy Strategy: Literacy Training Pack*, DfEE
Each module contains a pack of photocopiable activity resource sheets. There are ideas for integrated work with the whole class during shared reading and writing, and group activities at word and sentence level. Many are highly creative ideas which aim to interrelate speaking and listening, reading and writing.

5 Planning for English

OBJECTIVES

By the end of this chapter, you should:

- understand the principles of effective planning for and differentiation in English

- be able to plan continuous work, schemes of work and blocked or linked work

- be able to plan for English and the literacy hour

- appreciate the planning implications of the National Literacy Strategy's literacy hour.

Principles of planning

Whether or not a school has an effective whole-school policy on English, messages about language are evident on the walls, in the children's books, in interactions between individuals and in the quality of the library.

Planning for English, whether long or short term, will need to take into account the following:

- the requirements of the National Curriculum and the guidance of the National Literacy Strategy (NLS)
- the resources available, including other adults or children and materials
- the time allocated, e.g. one hour's literacy, half an hour's silent reading, twice-weekly class assemblies, etc.
- other topics to be studied across the curriculum
- the children's previous language and literacy experiences
- individual and group learning needs.

A teacher's planning for each year will also be influenced by his or her personal and professional development. Inevitably, a teacher will be affected by initiatives in English teaching, such as reading intervention programmes (e.g. Catch Up or Reading Recovery); family literacy support programmes and community initiatives (e.g. Bookstart, Story-sacks, PEEP); or new approaches and materials such as *First Steps*, *Jolly Phonics*, *PAT* or *THRASS* (see Glossary).

Who benefits?

If planning is both informed and conscientious, the child, the teacher and the school will all benefit.

For the child, effective planning ensures:

- progression, along a developmental continuum, in each strand of the National Curriculum for English
- a wide range of language experiences at text, sentence and word levels (DfEE 1998)
- continuity, in that lessons and skills build upon each other
- coherence in terms of the interrelatedness of the four English skills (speaking, listening, reading and writing)
- coherence in terms of the integration of English skills in other areas of the curriculum.

For the teacher, effective planning offers:

- a clear and achievable timeframe within which to work
- a means of checking adequate coverage of the content of the curriculum
- an opportunity to consider classroom organisation, e.g. groupings
- advance warning of resources required
- an opportunity to think ahead about teaching strategies and prepare for children with special needs
- an opportunity to consider approaches to assessment.

For the school, effective planning ensures:

- effective management of time
- a greater chance of continuity for the class if the class teacher has to be absent for any reason
- an opportunity to adapt teaching in relation to assessment
- an opportunity to identify the resources needed to

implement the English curriculum effectively

- whole-school liaison so that staff share a consistent approach to English teaching and literacy learning
- making the most of links across the curriculum and staff expertise.

Since 1998, the NLS, with its focus on whole-school INSET about literacy, has promoted a common debate on the teaching of English. However, before considering long, medium and short-term planning in English, let us first consider what is meant by the terms progression, continuity, coherence and efficiency, for they are important objectives of planning.

Planning for progression, continuity, coherence and efficiency

There are two main dimensions in planning. The first identifies development through time and ensures *progression* and *continuity*. The second dimension relates to planned curriculum coverage at any one point in time and ensures *coherence* and *efficiency* (see box).

Dimension	Objective
Development through time	Progression (movement through attainment targets)
	Continuity (managing progression so that learning builds upon prior experience)
Coverage at any one point in time	Coherence (coverage of different strands in a holistic way that makes sense to the child)
	Efficiency (covering all programmes of study, by effectively using the time allocated and available resources)

By looking at each objective in more detail, we can more fully understand the planning implications of this model.

Planning for progression

Effective planning for progression will involve making sure that all the children in a class are making as much progress as possible, depending on their level of ability and prior experience. In order to ensure that appropriate progress is being made, a teacher needs to make accurate judgements about a child's development and achievements:

- in relation to his or her peers in the class
- in relation to his or her prior experience and level of ability
- in relation to the national norms.

By comparing the programmes of study for each key stage, we can begin to appreciate the National Curriculum's approach to progression and skills development.

Progression in Speaking and Listening

They should be taught to incorporate relevant detail in explanations, descriptions and narratives …

(KS1, Attainment Target 2a)

By Key Stage 2, children

should be taught to organise what they want to say, and to use vocabulary and syntax that enables the communication of more complex meanings.

(KS2, Attainment Target 2a)

Progression in Reading

Pupils should be taught to use reference materials for different purposes …

(KS1, Attainment Target 2d)

More detail is required at Key Stage 2:

They should be given opportunities to read for different purposes, adopting different strategies for the task, including skimming to gain an overall impression, scanning to locate information and detailed reading to obtain specific information.

(KS2, Attainment Target 2c)

Progression in Writing

Pupils should have opportunities to plan and review their writing, assembling and developing their ideas on paper and on screen.

(KS1, Attainment Target 2b)

More detailed demands are prescribed at Key Stage 2. Pupils should be taught to:

- plan (note and develop initial ideas)
- draft (develop ideas from the plan into structured written text)
- revise (alter and improve the draft)
- proofread (check the draft for spelling and punctuation errors, omissions or repetitions)

	Autumn	Spring	Summer
Year 1	Growth (Prehistory)	Rights, Wrongs (Vikings)	Places and Maps (Sailors)
Year 2	Pattern/Colour (Aztecs)	Mountains (Explorers)	Animals (American Indians)

Figure 5.1 A curriculum overview for topics for Years 1 and 2

- present (prepare a neat, correct and clear final copy)

(KS2, Attainment Target 2b)

Some materials for teachers, such as *First Steps* (Heinemann 1997), provide detailed guidance to help teachers chart a child's progress along a continuum of development.

Planning for continuity

Most schools have begun to plan a whole-school curriculum, for each subject, across both key stages. Many schools operate three two-year, topic-based cycles, for example for Years 1 and 2. (See Figure 5.1).

Continuity in learning suggests that new learning builds upon prior knowledge. To plan successfully for continuity, teachers need to use accurate assessments of children's previous experience and levels of understanding and competence.

Below is an example to illustrate one teacher's attempts to ensure continuity of planning in English over four lessons.

The children's understanding of speech conventions was steadily developed, while the cross-curricular links gave the children's learning a sense of coherence.

Planning for coherence

Planning for coherence means looking for and reinforcing links between different subjects. Coherence between strands of the English curriculum is especially important. The National Literacy Strategy focuses primarily on reading and writing, but teachers need to plan for speaking and listening across the curriculum. The emphasis on text-based work, which includes sharing big books or multiple copies of texts, echoes the way many teachers have planned their English work around a rich range of children's literature, thereby trying to ensure coherence for the children. (See the example in Figure 5.2.)

A teacher wanting to develop her Key Stage 2 children's awareness of written dialogue in text started by looking at speech-bubble picture books.

Lesson 1: The first task the children were given was to design a zigzag book for very young children with only speech bubbles as text.

Lesson 2: The following week, the children were asked to write their own comic-strip page. This task combined work in history because the dialogue featured had to tell the story of the Gunpowder Plot.

Lesson 3: Next, after discussion and direct teaching about conventions of speech in writing, the children had to present one of their dialogues in narrative form, using speech marks.

Lesson 4: Finally, the children were asked to write the conversation between a spider and a fly, using direct speech. Once again, this related to another area of the curriculum. In this case, it was science, where children were looking at minibeasts and discussing the concept of predators and prey.

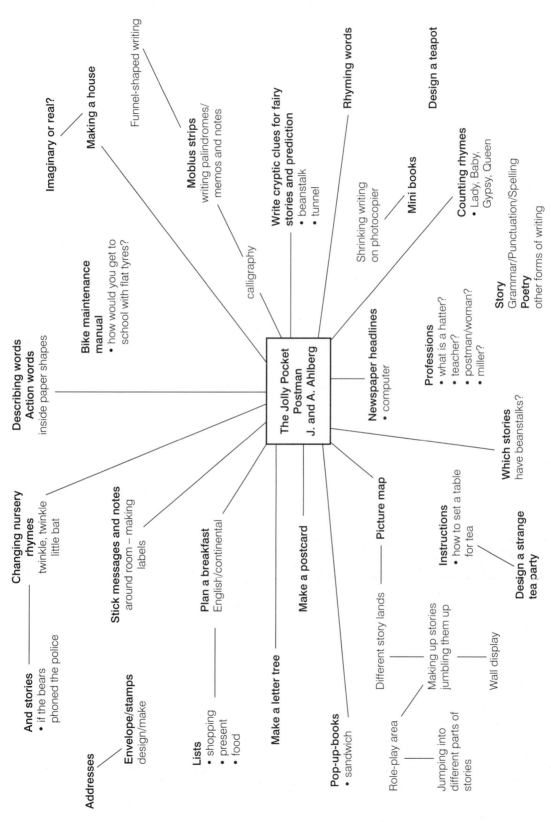

Figure 5.2 An example of English work arising from a chosen text
Source: Birmingham LEA Primary Planning Programme (1996)

Planning for efficiency

Efficiency is a key factor in successful schools and is specifically evaluated by an Ofsted inspection. Where planning is effective, all the resources available to a teacher, including time, are being well used. Time is probably a teacher's most precious commodity and needs to be tightly planned if quality teaching and learning are to take place.

The teaching of English should occupy around 20 per cent of the timetable. From 1998, every class teacher has to teach one hour of literacy per day, on top of any quiet reading or extended writing.

The challenge when allocating time to areas of the English curriculum is to ensure a healthy balance between depth and quality while providing a wide range of literacy experiences. In order to plan effectively, teachers plan the curriculum along three timescales, for the long, medium and short term.

- *Long-term planning* usually refers to plans or schemes of work covering one or two years, or even a whole key stage (see Figure 5.3).
- *Medium-term planning*, term-by-term, attempts to 'flesh out' the long-term plans, providing detail and a specific timeframe. This level of planning may include topics, mini-projects or blocked work.
- *Short-term planning* is the responsibility of the class teacher. Short-term planning tends to focus on monthly, weekly and daily planning .

Long-term planning: key stage and year plans

Designing an English scheme of work or key stage plan for a whole school is a formidable task, usually tackled by a school's language specialist or coordinator, with colleagues. Some schools prefer therefore to adopt or adapt a scheme of work prepared by local authority advisory teams.

It is common, when drawing up a scheme of work, to separate the three strands, Speaking and Listening, Reading and Writing, and to plan, separately, areas of specific focus, such as drama, information and communications technology (ICT), poetry, use of language, spelling, or poetry.

Long-term planning: starting from the programmes of study or NLS objectives

Long-term plans need to identify the areas in each strand which teachers propose to cover. (See Figure 5.5.)

Within each strand, we find the following framework with three sections: Range, Key Skills, Standard English and Language Study.

Long and medium-term planning: the SCAA model

Guidelines published by SCAA in 1995 suggested that teachers should consider planning for English on three different levels: continuous, linked and blocked (see Chapter 4).

Planning continuous work

The first level identifies the English activities which are continuous or regular. These activities occur every day or several times a week and may take a routine format, for example the uninterrrupted, sustained silent reading (USSR) or quiet reading time, which many schools operate on a daily basis. These times can become so routine and unchallenging that they lose their effectiveness, unless they are planned thoughtfully.

Planning linked work: teaching English through topics

Until recently, most primary teachers used topic webs for planning, but a topic web has no timescale so it cannot suggest progression or ensure continuity across a key stage. A web can still be helpful in the initial stages of planning or in the planning of a blocked unit of work, for example a 'module' on a text (see Figure 5.2) or on reading or writing non-fiction. (See NLS 1998, Module 6, *Reading and Writing for Information*.)

Many teachers plan cross-curricular links using a matrix (see Figure 5.4). There are two purposes to this:

- to make the most of the language-teaching opportunities that will arise through other subjects
- to be aware of the language demands placed on the children by activities planned across the curriculum.

	Reception	Year 1	Year 2
Autumn	Focus on stories and lists letters turn-taking Role-play toy area = shop, post office Alphabet *Themes: SHOPS, SHAPES, XMAS*	S+L POS 1a: describing events POS 2a: understanding needs of listener R POS 3b: vocab for specific occasions POS 1d: folk stories (re weather) POS 2b: syllables 3c: story features W POS 1a: writing as a record – weather 2b: writing poems, lists – different forms 2d: word families *Themes: AUTUMN, WEATHER, ELECTRICITY*	S+L POS 1a: giving reasons for opinion POS 2b: building on previous speaker POS 3b: storytelling devices R POS 1d: playscripts/poetry POS 2b: alliteration POS 3c: textual features of poems W POS 1: identify purpose for writing POS 2c: commas and question marks POS 2d: letterstrings *Themes: TRANSPORT, GEOLOGY*
Spring	Focus on poems and rhymes Retelling a story Role-play area = doctors and hospitals Initial blends *Themes: HOSPITALS, MYSELF*	S+L POS 1a: predicting outcomes POS 2b: asking and answering questions POS 3b: word games R POS 1b: using dictionaries 2a: alphabetic awareness 2b: reading non-fiction W POS 1a: observations 2b: collaborative writing 3a: verbs and verb endings *Themes: SPACE, GROWTH*	S+L POS 1c: what makes a good listener POS 2a: detail in explanations POS 3b: words – similar and opposite R POS 1b: reading non-fiction 2a: print around us 3: features of texts W POS 1c: writing for different audiences 2b: organising factual writing 3c: punctuation, commas *Themes: HEALTH, ROMANS*
Summer	Focus on non-fiction, books about sea Expressing and justifying opinion Role-play, pet-shop, educational zoo, yellow submarine and island Digraphs *Themes: PETS, THE SEA, HOLIDAYS*	S+L POS 1a: learning poems by heart POS 2b: detail in descriptions POS 3a: differences in written and spoken English R POS 1: reading diagrams 2b: prefixes 3c: characteristics of fiction/non-fiction W POS 1a: written non-fiction 2c: capital letters 3a: word order *Themes: COLOUR, MINIBEASTS*	S+L POS 1: discussing possibilities POS 2a: presenting to different audiences POS 3a: dialect/accent R POS 1: characters, settings, plots 2b: suffixes 2b: phonic inconsistencies W POS 1: writing diaries 2c: punctuation – review 3a: sentences – links connectors *Themes: OUR SCHOOL, WATER*

← CONTINUOUS WORK IN ENGLISH →

Figure 5.3 A Key Stage 1 plan for English

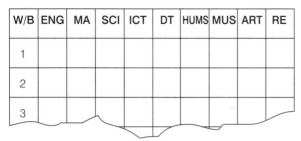

W/B	ENG	MA	SCI	ICT	DT	HUMS	MUS	ART	RE
1									
2									
3									

Figure 5.4 A cross-curricular planning matrix

Planning blocked units of work

Teachers often plan modules of a few weeks. They list the weeks and plan what they can realistically achieve in each week, taking into account all the other events that occur in a school year, such as the school concert or a visiting puppeteer.

For these situations, blocked units of work can be very useful. For example, if there were a puppet performance planned for a year group, it would make sense to deviate from the syllabus for a week or two, in order to exploit the stimulus of the puppet show, for instance acting out in drama or writing an imaginative story about a puppet who comes alive, like Pinocchio.

Examples of blocked work for English, for anything from a week to half a term, might include the study of an author, such as Allan Ahlberg or Philip Pullman.

Medium-term planning : planning schemes of work

A school's key stage plans for English will form the basis for a more detailed scheme of work for each teacher. Medium-term planning provides more detail and may specify activities and assessment opportunities. It sets out to translate the content of the longer-term plans into a realistic time frame, for example a scheme of work for one term (Figure 5.5) or a half-termly overview of interrelated English skills.

The National Literacy Strategy and the literacy hour

First piloted in 1996, the National Literacy Strategy has been introduced to raise literacy standards, achieving specific literacy targets for each LEA, by the year 2002.

To raise the profile of literacy nationwide, the NLS and DfEE:

- designated 1998/99 as a national Year of Reading
- recruited approximately 200 LEA literacy consultants
- decided to use a number of schools and teachers as good literacy teaching models
- required that, in 1999, all schools devote two INSET days to literacy
- identified four cohorts of schools in need of extra support from literacy consultants and the LEAs
- stipulated that, from September 1998, all schools, unless granted exemption through the LEA, will have to timetable one hour a day for each class to focus on literacy.

The NLS sets clear expectations for what should be covered each term and half-term. A medium-term planning framework has been provided, which focuses upon continuous and blocked work. The NLS is dedicated to the teaching of English as a discrete subject within the literacy hour. (See DfEE 1998, Section 3, p. 58.)

The content of the Framework is set out, in the ring-binder, under three interrelated elements:

1 phonics, spelling, vocabulary (word-level work)
2 grammar and punctuation (sentence-level work)
3 comprehension and composition (text-level work)

The literacy hour is made up of four phases (see Figure 1.2, p. 8):

- 10–15 minutes of text-level work, e.g. whole-class reading or writing
- 10–15 minutes of word-level work, e.g. phonics, spelling (KS1 and 2) or sentence-level work (KS2)
- 25–30 minutes of guided or independent group activities (the teacher works with at least one group and probably two groups)
- a plenary session to reflect on and share learning outcomes.

Following the literacy hour structure, however loosely, should ensure lessons are well paced. Learning not to attempt too much in one session is important. It is helpful to organise and explain clearly to the children the systems by which they can check, share and hand in completed work, so that they work in as independent a way as possible for their stage of development.

Practical guidelines about managing the literacy hour, teaching children to work as groups,

YEAR:6	SPEAKING AND LISTENING	READING: LITERARY RESPONSE	READING: NON FICTION	WRITING	USE OF LANGUAGE	IT
TOPIC	Feeling/colours association survey interviews Y1 + Y2/3 + 4	Class novel: Bridge to Terebithian / Group reading: 1. Rose Blanche 2. The Big Pink 3. Red Poetry Books 4. Play scripts / SEN Winnie the Witch / Look through the Window / Bookshare – Y5	Biography Logie Baird Escher Leonardo da Vinci / Research-jigsaw groups to make books about a colour and an artist / Dewey system patterns	Story patterns (1c) / Write different verse patterns / Biography of artist	Use of thesauruses description of lines, tones and colours (1b) / Patterns in poetry – verse forms / Alliteration / Dialect – Rhyming slang patterns / Standard vs dialect	Spellstring collections on database / Close texts-rhymes / CD-ROM – ENCARTA (1b) / Individual poems – word processing
Colour and pattern	Description of pictures – guess the painting-in pairs					
Focus themes	Assembly-gallery Assembly-poetry-festival					
RANGE	1a) explaining ideas sharing opinions enacting poems / 1b) different year groups as audiences and whole school / 1c) media = paintings artist visiting / 1d) playscript cameos Gallery drama – paintings come alive	1a) independent and shared reading / 1c) variety of structural features – stories, poems / 1d) variety of cultures and traditions	1b) reading sources not designed for children (e.g. art catalogues and organisational)	1a) varied purposes / 1b) varied audiences / 1c) commentaries, explanations, notes Letters to artists	READING 3 Introduce terms to enable class to discuss texts they've read / Comparison of biography and 3rd person novel	4 different examples of English software / Individual groups of 2/3 plus graphics package to generate patterns
SKILLS	2a) making exploratory tentative comment / 2b) re-present talk / 2c) questioning others for clarification and extending/following up ideas	2a) phonics and graphic knowledge – more complex patterns, e.g. TION, UAL, ON, EOUS, PH, PSY / 2b) Inference and deduction and evaluation of texts	Non-fiction reviews / 2c) pose question – What do I want to know about . . . / 2d) catalogues and Dewey system	2a) formality of catalogues / 2b) revision – publishing process / 2c) patterns in punctuations e.g. in dialogues / 2d) spelling / 2e) handwriting	WRITING 3a) writing down dialect (e.g. cockney slang) 3b) paragraphs chronological writing 3c) use of thesauruses to aid description	Word processing • info retrieval • prediction • identifying spelling patterns • designing patterns

Figure 5.5 A scheme of work for one term: Key Stage 2, Year 6

with a teacher or independently, and sample activity plans can be found in the Literacy Training Pack (NLS 1998). Each of the three levels of work, outlined above, has a module of materials. There are also modules on Shared and Guided Reading and Writing and on Reading and Writing Non-Fiction.

The NLS guidelines suggest that teachers should have three connected levels of planning:

- *the Framework* (given): What should I teach?
- *medium-term planning* (termly or half-termly): When should I teach it?
- *short-term planning* (weekly): How should I teach it?

Weekly planning

To start planning a week, teachers may now use the NLS planner provided in the Framework (see DfEE 1998, Section 3, p. 59). Whole-class work, guided and individual group work and the plenary can be planned, in some detail. It is essential to plan for the other adults who may be coming into the classroom to support individual children or independent group tasks. Some teachers use a planning sheet (see Figure 20.1, p. 191) for their auxiliary colleagues and volunteers. Planning ICT into the week's literacy teaching is important, arranging a rota system to ensure equal access to the computer. Assessment schedules are helpful, ensuring that the areas or individuals to be assessed through the week are clear (see Figure 5.6).

Daily agendas

Many teachers share their agenda with the class and write it out on a sheet or on the board. Key Stage 1 teachers sometimes use a wheel or chart with visual prompts.

To start on a daily plan, it is useful to:

- prepare a sheet with the blocks of time in the school day
- identify which activities each group will do
- add a message, challenge, spellstring or phoneme (see Glossary) of the day
- show children which activities they can move on to if they finish early or if the weather is bad at play or lunchtime.

An agenda like this (Figure 5.7) is useful as an aide-mémoire for the teacher and can also serve as a guide for classroom assistants or parent helpers.

Short-term planning: English activities

Some sample Activity Resource Sheets are included in the Literacy Training Pack, within the relevant modules (see for example Figure 5.8).

These sheets offer suggestions for class, group and plenary activities, but teachers still need to adapt them and many still use traditional planning formats to plan lessons.

A detailed lesson plan would include the information given in Figure 5.9. This example was favourably commented upon during an Ofsted inspection.

The quality of English lessons, from the child's perspective, is primarily decided by the quality of planning, teaching style and classroom management.

The Ofsted Handbook (1995) supports the need for clear planning of objectives and detail. Laar (1996) suggests that an Ofsted inspector would look for:

- clear objectives
- transparent links with the National Curriculum/NLS
- reference to longer-term plans
- differentiated tasks and/or outcomes
- organisational planning and good resourcing
- assessment opportunities identified.

Occasionally, teachers confuse their general aims for the learner with educational objectives. For example, 'To become a confident writer' is more of an aim than an objective. It would be very difficult to claim that a lesson had fulfilled such a wide-reaching aim. It would also be difficult to assess such an aim.

However, 'To write shopping lists in imaginative play' would be a more specific objective for an early years class whose role-play corner had been turned into a farm shop. 'To write and lay out vertically a list of books, using capital letters' or 'To write lists horizontally using commas' are further examples of objectives related to the writing of lists, suitable, this time, for older children. All of these educational objectives are assessable, so learning objectives can be matched to learning outcomes.

In general, it is important to ensure that the children are clear about the purpose and pursuit of any English task:

Class:
Year Group(s):
Term:
Week Beg:
Teacher:

	Whole class – shared reading and writing	Whole class – phonics, spelling vocabulary and grammar	Guided Group Tasks (reading or writing)	Guided Group Tasks (reading or writing)	Independent Group Tasks			Plenary
Mon	Introduce story and read through extracts on Resource sheets to decide on sequence.	Discuss use of adjectives; draft range of adjectives showing scales of intensity.	Group A Activity 1. Identify commonly used words and suggest more interesting alternatives, using thesaurus. (T)	Group B Activity 2. Read first paragraph, omitting adjectives and discuss effect on description. Use adjectives in own sentences. (OA)	Group C Activity 3. Skim test for clues about where Seymour lived, then write short passage describing it. (I)	Group D Activity 4. Children think about age-group the story was intended for, and draft a picture version of story for young children. (I)		Review Group C's work, inviting constructive comments.
Tues	Read chapter 1, encouraging children to think about how we know Seymour's world is an imaginary one.	Develop work on adjectives to teach about comparative adjectives.	Group B Activity 1. Identify commonly used words and suggest more interesting alternatives, using thesaurus. (T)	Group C Activity 2. Read first paragraph, omitting adjectives and discuss effect on description. Use adjectives in own sentences. (OA)	Group D Activity 3. Skim test for clues about where Seymour lived, then write short passage describing it. (I)		Group A Activity 5. Children use word search to find and spell frequently used words. (I)	Ask groups B and C to explain Activity 2 to the class, and encourage others to ask questions.
Wed	Discuss how attitudes and emotions can be conveyed in writing, and identify any parts of the text that are emotive, and why. Refer to text for answers.	Develop work on comparative adjectives, using them in sentences.	Group C Activity 1. Identify commonly used words and suggest more interesting alternatives, using thesaurus. (T)	Group D Activity 2. Read first paragraph, omitting adjectives and discuss effect on description. Use adjectives in own sentences. (OA)		Group A Activity 4. Children think about age-group the story was intended for, and draft a picture version of story for young children. (I)	Group B Activity 5. Children use word search to find and spell frequently used words. (I)	Recap on work on comparative adjectives, using them in sentences.
Thur	Look at descriptive language in text, and ask comprehension questions based on story. Children to answer in complete sentences.	Work on word definitions.	Group D Activity 1. Identify commonly used words and suggest more interesting alternatives, using thesaurus. (T)		Group A Activity 3. Skim test for clues about where Seymour lived, then write short passage describing it. (I)	Group B Activity 4. Children think about age-group the story was intended for, and draft a picture version of story for young children. (I)	Group C Activity 5. Children use word search to find and spell frequently used words. (I)	Review Group B's work on picture books.
Fri	Recall main points of story, and write up. Predict what might happen next, referring to text.	Handwriting practice, using the prediction drafted in text work session plus a sentence from the text.		Group A Activity 2. Read first paragraph, omitting adjectives and discuss effect on description. Use adjectives in own sentences. (OA)	Group B Activity 3. Skim test for clues about where Seymour lived, then write short passage describing it. (I)	Group C Activity 4. Children think about age-group the story was intended for, and draft a picture version of story for young children. (I)	Group D Activity 5. Children use word search to find and spell frequently used words. (I)	Verbal book review of Seymour story.

T = Teacher   OA = Other Adult   I = Independent

Figure 5.6 An example of a weekly plan
Source: *Stanley Thornes Primary Literacy Year 4 Teacher's Book*, Stanley Thornes (Publishers) Ltd

MONDAY 15th NOVEMBER

8.55: register – JS and PK – show and tell

Class circle time: Focus on what we like about our friends – pairs and whole class

9.20: Change for PE / Read poems

9.30 – 10.00: PE in Hall – ball skills carousel/mirroring pairs – reflections

10.00: Change and Mental Arithmetic

10.30: Break (Maths games if wet)

10.45 – 11.45 LITERACY HOUR:

15 mins: Whole class: Shared text – Extract from 'Smith' by Leon Garfield.

Let's think about describing people's characters

15 mins: Whole class: Focused sentence work – descriptive phrases

20 mins: Group work: Group A – Group reading and discussion – with me

Group B – Writing phrases about people (faces from magazines)

Group C – Writing a cameo description of a character

Group D – Comprehension – with Mrs G

Group E – Adjectives activities – with me

10 mins: Whole class: what have we learned today?

> Today's challenge:
> How many -tch words can we find?
>
> witch, catch …

Figure 5.7 Extract from a daily agenda

- Can the children appreciate *why* they are doing it?
- *Who* is the audience for any writing they may do?
- *When* does the work have to be completed?
- *Where* are the resources they will need?
- *How* should they work? Individually, independently, in silence? In groups – able to discuss their ideas? In pairs – sharing solutions with other pairs?
- *How* will the transitions between activities be managed to avoid disruption?
- *Who* will be available to work alongside groups and individuals and *how* will they be informed?
- *How* will the children be supported and the tasks differentiated for individual needs?

Planning for differentiation

There are several categories of children for whom teachers need to make special provision in their planning.

Children who display challenging and distracting behaviour
These may need to work in particular groupings or settings or have tasks broken down into several small and achievable elements. They may respond to particular kinds of resources, responsibilities, encouragement, incentives and praise, for example setting targets for achievement or behaviour.

Children who are 'invisible'
These children are quiet and 'appear' to understand even when they are unsure.

Children for whom English is an additional language
(See Chapter 16.)

Children who have learning difficulties
(See Chapter 20.)

Children who have some physical challenge
Children with visual or hearing difficulties will need to be seated in the optimum place for each activity. Teachers need to check for understanding and ensure they are able to cope with the task. Appropriate aids may be required and teachers may seek professional advice and further training.

Children who are very able
Very able children are seldom given access to adult helper support but such children deserve individual planning and support. Too often, differentia-

NLS Activity Resource Sheet

Year	3
Term	1
Strand	S1

Objectives

To use awareness of grammar to decipher new or unfamiliar words, e.g. to predict from text, read on, leave a gap and return; to use these strategies in conjunction with knowledge of phonemes, word recognition, graphic knowledge and context when reading.

Activities

N.B.
Support and teaching strategies:
Always aim at helping the reader towards independence. Rehearse strategies with the children. e.g. *Six things I can do if I get stuck before asking the teacher.* Make a chart of the strategies. Rehearse with them how much they know already.

Class
• Through Shared, Guided, Group and Independent Reading:

- mask out a word and keep going. Then go back and guess the word from context *(syntax and context)*
- go back to the beginning of a sentence and take a run at it - read back and read on *(syntax and context)*
- use initial and final sounds and blends *(phonics)*
- find words within words, compound words, etc.
- practise onset and rime: (*If I know zip, I know blip, skip, ship (phonological knowledge, graphic knowledge)*
- investigate common letter clusters *(phonological knowledge, graphic knowledge)*
- make use of sight vocabulary from other sources: Where have I seen it? *(graphic knowledge - logographic)*
- use root words, prefixes, suffixes and inflections *(grammatical knowledge)*
- use picture information *(pictures - context)*

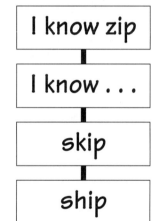

Group
• During Shared Reading, model strategies, e.g. masking words, cloze procedure and re-assembling cut-up sentences or words on cards.
• Provide wall charts, e.g. simple flow charts, or some prompt cards for children to keep in their reading diaries, to cover a range of procedures that help readers use cueing strategies.

Plenary
• Practise with a new shared text the strategies from the class chart.

Relevant published materials/resources

First Steps Reading Resource Book (Heinemann). **Independence in Reading.**
Don Holdaway (Ashton Scholastic).

Figure 5.8 NLS Activity Resource Sheet
Source: NLS 1998

Teacher	Mrs Robinson	**Lesson**	Book Talk	**Date**	26/11
Year group	Yr 4/5	**Number in Class**	33	**Location**	Rm 9

Learning objectives	To extend the children's knowledge of different genre. To develop critical awareness of the range and quality of reading resources. To enable children to articulate their experiences of and attitudes towards literature.
Introduction	Introduce the book 'The Elephant Trunk' to the children. Ask them to comment on what they think the book is about before we read it. Does the cover appeal to them? Would they buy it from just looking at the cover? Why?
Development	Give the children a brief introduction to the book, consider the layout and what it is going to tell us.
Core activity	Read the first half of 'The Elephant Trunk' to the children – what do they think of it? How is it appealing? Do the words alone tell the story? What do the pictures do to enhance the story? What is 'unsaid'? Who would it appeal to? Is there a message in the book? What do children think of the story?
Support	By having a class discussion all children will have the opportunity to draw from each other.
Extension	
Conclusion	Discuss the real story. Now how do they feel, what does it make them want to do? What is the author's intention? Is he successful?
LSA	N/A
Teacher input	total
Curriculum links	
Resources	The Elephant Trunk
Assessment	Can the children contribute effectively to the class discussion? Can they draw anything from the book?
Evaluation	*Children liked the book, were able to make predictions and seemed genuinley interested in the story. They picked up on the suspense.* *Must find time to finish the story.*

Figure 5.9 A plan of a lesson which was highly rated by an Ofsted inspection team
Source: Claire Robinson

tion for the more able only means writing a longer poem, reading more books, i.e. differentiation by outcome.

The able child needs more challenging questioning or a different task, involving research or problem-solving. A personal project, where children investigate a subject of interest to them and make a book or file about it, is a good example of an ongoing extension activity on which children can work at their own pace.

Differentiation by outcome
A teacher may wish the children to attempt the same task but have different expectations of the results and quality of work. It is important that a teacher does not convey the impression that he or she holds low expectations of an individual because it may lower children's expectations of themselves. However, it is inevitable that a task

given to 30 children will lead to a wide range of standards of achievement.

Differentiation by task
This is not only valuable for the more able. Children with moderate learning difficulties sometimes just need a more personalised approach, or more opportunity to understand concepts and time to practise skills. Children who find abstract concepts difficult to grasp will need concrete examples, materials and visuals. Teachers may have to simplify concepts and the language or resources they use.

Figure 5.10 is an example of a young teacher who considered resources, strategies and outcomes for children with special needs in her planning. This teacher gave the class a diagnostic writing task. The less confident writers were supported by the learning support assistant (LSA). The teacher then

Less able child
This piece of work was produced with close support from the LSA … Some meaning was established. Large printed letters, little punctuation, spelling uses single consonant phonic strategies. The work took almost an hour and was very intensive.

Strategies
- Cloze passage work
- Use of writing frames to structure ideas
- 2-letter spelling blends
- Use of sentence maker (Breakthrough to Literacy – 1978)
- LSA support
- Diagrams and pictures to support in topic/geog/DT
- Use of word bank for new topic-related words

Middle-range ability
Work shows use of full sentences in terms of units of meaning. There are some linking strategies such as use of 'but' and 'and'. However, most sentences do not follow on from each other. Full content with wide range of info. Some punctuation but sporadic. Inconsistent cursive style.

Strategies
- Punctuation work
- Correction passages
- Handwriting support
- Spelling patterns, especially double consonant blends, e.g. church/runner/shirt

Very able child
Work shows full cursive script – clear and legible.
Capitals and punctuation are correct. Content is interesting and varied.
Some spelling errors evident, e.g. 'writing'.
Little conscious organisation of content. Writer has engaged in editing process to correct majority of surface details.

Strategies
- Spellings of words using prefixes and suffixes
- Organising work into units of meaning – paragraphs
- Full use of drafting procedures to organise work and correct errors
- Identifying important points within writing

Figure 5.10 A young teacher's plans following a diagnostic writing task
Source: Cara Hills

analysed the writing and decided to highlight certain strategies to encourage each child's English development. These extracts are taken from the annotations on the pieces of writing, which were later stored in the children's individual portfolios.

When teaching writing to struggling writers, teachers may provide keywords, partially complete sentences, writing frames (Wray and Lewis 1998) or concept keyboards to support them and provide what Bruner (1986) called 'Scaffolding'.

Concluding the lesson: a plenary session

When the lesson is over, teachers need to ensure the children gather together. The NLS (1998) says plenary sessions are particularly important because:
- They provide opportunities for pupils to reason and discuss their work.

- They give the teacher a chance to monitor and evaluate the work of the class and to assess the work of some pupils.
- They enable pupils to reflect on, explain, justify, etc., what they have learned.
- They help to develop an atmosphere of constructive criticism and appreciation of other pupils' work.
- They enable the teacher to spread ideas, encourage and praise pupils in front of their peers.

Some teachers make use of what is known as the 'response sandwich'. Between the slices of specific praise about two things that were good, these teachers include, as the sandwich filling, a helpful suggestion about an area for improvement. The written feedback given to a child can have a marked impact on their progress. Research by Black and Dylan (1998) suggests that it is a teacher's suggestion for improvement that makes a real difference to the quality of a child's future work.

Lesson evaluation

At the end of the day, teachers reflect on their teaching and evaluate the following:

- Which learning objectives were fulfilled? What did the children learn?
- Did the children achieve high standards?
- Were the lessons appropriate to the children's interests? Were the children motivated?
- What did I learn? What would I change?
- What will the children do next? (implications for future planning).

SUMMARY

The introduction of the literacy hour has, for many teachers, radically altered the way they plan for English. In some respects, teachers can now share in a nationwide debate about the teaching of literacy and have improved access to in-service opportunities and a wealth of published material and guidelines. There is much advice about planning for English in the NLS training pack (1998). This chapter has tried to focus on key principles which underpin planning:

- Careful planning ensures coherence, continuity, progression and efficiency, through long, medium and short-term plans.
- English may be taught in groups alongside other subject areas or it may be taught to the whole class in the concentrated or discrete form, e.g. in a literacy hour.
- Detailed lesson plans, with a clear definition of the learning objectives and outcomes, are vital if teachers are going to be able to monitor children's achievements and progress in English.
- Planning is closely linked to assessment.

References

Birmingham LEA (1996) *Primary Planning Project: English*, Birmingham LEA
Black, P. and Dylan, W. (1998) *The Power of Feedback*, King's College, London
Bruner, J. (1986) *Actual Minds, Possible Worlds*, Harvard University Press
DfEE (1997) *The Implementation of the National Literacy Strategy*, DfEE
DfEE (1998) *The National Literacy Strategy: Framework for Teaching*, DfEE
First Steps (1999) Literacy Development Continuum, Ginn Heinemann Professional Development
Laar, W. (1996) *The TES Guide to Surviving School Inspection*, TES/Butterworth Heinemann
NLS (1998) *Literacy Training Pack. Modules 1: The Literacy Hour, 2: Word Level Work, 3: Sentence Level Work, 4: Shared and Guided Reading and Writing KS1, 5: Shared and Guided Reading and Writing KS2, 6: Reading and Writing for Information*, DfEE
Ofsted (1995) *The Ofsted Handbook: Guidance on the Inspection of Nursery and Primary Schools*, HMSO
SCAA (1995) *Exemplification of Standards in English* (DfEE)
SCAA (1997) *Use of Language: A Common Approach*, HMSO
Wray, D. and Lewis, M. (1998) *Writing across the Curriculum: Frames to Support Learning*, University of Reading

Further reading

Kyriacou, C. (1998) *Essential Teaching Skills*, 2nd edition, Stanley Thornes
An excellent and clear overview of teaching and classroom management skills. There is useful advice on planning, preparation and presentation.
Tann, S. (1992) *Developing Language in the Primary Classroom*, Cassell
This clearly written and logically structured book provides guidance in all areas of language development. Particularly challenging and useful are the questions which help the reader develop an increasingly reflective and professional stance towards her own practice.
Whitebread, D. (1996) *Teaching and Learning in the Early Years*, Routledge
This is an accessible and comprehensive collection of practical guidelines for and perspectives on planning the early years curriculum.

6 Assessment and record-keeping in English

OBJECTIVES

By the end of this chapter you should be able to:

- understand the close relationship between the assessment of children's language attainment and the progress they make
- plan assessment opportunities for English
- keep useful records of children's achievements and progress in English.

Key principles of assessment

Before considering how we can assess children's work in English, it is important to consider some general principles:

- Teachers need to form sound judgements based upon their systematic evidence, observations and analysis of children's work. They need to use the information in their planning.
- Clear records provide evidence of children's attainment and can be used when summarising children's progress, e.g. in end-of-year reports.
- Assessments need to be linked to the National Curriculum programmes of study and the level descriptions.

There is unease among teachers that time spent on assessment is time lost for teaching. It is very true that 'measuring a tree will not help it to grow', and teachers need to concentrate on the quality of their teaching. However, time spent assessing children's attainment, needs and progress is likely to contribute to more effective learning.

The report of the Task Group on Assessment and Testing (1987) stressed that assessment should be the servant not the master of the curriculum, and went on to say: 'It should be an integral part of the educational process, continually providing both

"feedback" and "feedforward".' Feedback tells teachers what and how the children have learned. 'Feedforward' means that judgements about children's learning will feed into teachers' future plans.

Assessment, therefore, can take place before, during or after learning.

Before: Recently, there has been much interest in 'value added education', whereby children are assessed on entry into the school system (SCAA 1997). At classroom level, it is important to find out what the child knows before teaching new skills and concepts.

During: Through observation and interaction, teachers are involved in making judgements about the way a child is learning while actively engaged in teaching. Teachers need to diagnose difficulties, assess progress and record development.

After: Teachers need to monitor standards achieved by children, matching their attainment against lesson objectives and comparing them with National Curriculum levels of attainment. To do so, teachers use three main kinds of assessment: formative, diagnostic and summative.

Different kinds of assessment

Summative assessment

The purpose of summative assessment is to identify the level of achievement the child has reached after a unit of work or period of time.

Summative assessment is designed to provide a snapshot of a child's abilities at a given point in time. It cannot always provide a clear or comprehensive picture but it is helpful to measure progress at regular intervals, for example by teacher assessments and SATs (standard assessment tasks). Such tests enable comparisons to be made between previous achievement and current

51

performance. In English, the weekly spelling test represents another example, though it could also be used formatively, identifying which spelling patterns and families are causing difficulty for a child.

Norm-referenced assessment

When raw scores are standardised according to the mean or average and adjusted to fit a curve of normal probability, the assessment is norm-referenced. This kind of assessment relates the child's performance to the work of others of the same age range. In education, we use norm-referencing a great deal, for example when placing children in positions 1st to 30th, grading work A–E and calculating percentages in tests. In English, standardised reading and verbal reasoning tests are examples of norm-referencing. (See Chapters 9 and 10 on Reading.)

Criterion-referenced assessment

In this kind of assessment, teachers measure a child's competence against criteria and assess a child's level of competence when performing specific tasks. In English, for example, it would be possible to say whether a child *can* or *cannot* form letters accurately. National Curriculum level descriptions provide criteria against which teachers can measure attainment; for example: 'Sequences of sentences extend ideas logically and words are chosen for variety and interest' (Attainment Target 3: Writing, Level 3 description).

Formative assessment

Formative assessment is most closely related to the planning process. It is developmental and occurs over time. It is like a video camera, constantly scanning a moving object. It could be nicknamed '*in*formative' assessment because its main purpose is to *in*form a teacher's planning for the next stage of the children's learning.

An example, for English, is regular marking of the children's written work. In addition to feeding back to the child, orally or in writing, a teacher may make a notes of writing skills which need more teaching or practice.

Diagnostic assessment

Diagnostic assessment is closely related to formative assessment and is designed to analyse learn-

ing difficulties. A teacher will use diagnostic assessment, designing an informal or formal test or specific task, to identify a child's specific learning needs.

In English, a Running Record can be used to ascertain with which reading strategies a child may need further help. Diagnostic assessment is like the zoom on a camera, focusing on specific details in order to improve understanding of the whole.

Where to start with assessment in English

At the beginning of a school year, a primary teacher is faced with the challenging task of identifying the language skills and learning needs of a large number of children.

Before the children arrive, it is essential to establish, by consulting previous records, what it is that the children have already learned in English, what they know and what they can do. Otherwise, it will be very difficult to provide for progression.

Every task planned for English will generate some useful information and evidence about a child's current levels of achievement in literacy and oracy.

The following example describes the way a young teacher responded to her initial assessments of her new class:

She recorded in her journal:
'I made various diagnostic assessments as to the nature of the children's speaking and listening skills through observing them interacting in groups. Features I identified were:

- Problems in formulating reasons or arguments
- Poor collaborative group skills
- Problems in listening to complex instructions.'

She then planned some strategies to overcome the problems she identified:

- Group activity identifying requirements for successful group functioning. To be used as guidelines for assessment of children by each other.
- Activities to encourage children to listen for key points (interviews, tapes, etc.)
- Activities enabling children to take on another person's point of view
- Children to give instructions to each other.

Some of these strategies could be used within her planning for continuous work in English, while others she may decide to focus upon in a blocked unit of work. (See Chapters 4 and 5.)

Teacher assessment

Teacher assessment is primarily diagnostic. Close observation of the children is crucial.

Many teachers find the most practical way to record their observations is to keep a notebook or file with a page for each child. Some teachers find it helpful to focus on three children in depth each day. However, this does not preclude them from making notes about significant achievements of other children. A page divided into four areas, with each quadrant representing the academic curriculum – English, Maths, Science, Other subjects – can be useful. In the English quadrant, a teacher can record any language incident which represents a benchmark in a child's development.

On the reverse of each child's page, there might be two divisions, one for *Social* and the other for *Successes/Self-esteem*, so that a teacher could record any extra-curricular achievements or incidents which relate to friendships and attitudes.

In a large and busy classroom, it is possible for some children to become almost 'invisible'. Regular record-keeping helps teachers to ensure that individual children are not neglected. By keeping this kind of record, updating it as necessary or once every half-term, teachers can build up a rounded picture of each child.

Teacher–child interaction

In English, a teacher, through interaction with children, tries to:

- find out whether they appreciate that certain forms of language are used in certain contexts
- identify the fluency with which children can express their ideas, and the qualities of reasoning and reflection behind those ideas
- discover their attitudes to reading and writing and their understanding of the purposes, audiences and forms of literacy.

According to Fisher (1990) there are five main strategies which teachers can use in interaction with children in order to discover what they have learned and how they think. These strategies, which also serve to extend children's thinking through discussion, are:

- *pausing:* allowing a child adequate time to think about the question
- *accepting:* acknowledging an idea by restating it and building upon it in some way
- *clarifying:* encouraging the child to elaborate on an idea and to provide more detail
- *facilitating:* keeping the channels of communication and enquiry open
- *challenging:* provoking deeper thought, asking for explanations, beliefs or justification for a point of view.

In order to encourage children to interact, teachers need to avoid asking too many 'closed' questions in favour of more challenging, open-ended questions (Kerry 1982). For example, instead of asking a literal question about a story, such as 'What did so-and-so do next?', opinions could be sought and children could discuss the story in pairs: 'Why did so-and-so do that? Was it right that he acted thus? Would it always be right for someone to act that way? How might this action have affected the other characters?'

Marking children's written work

Marking a child's written work enables teachers to:

- assess the child's writing competence
- assess the child's understanding of curriculum content
- assess the child's use of language and vocabulary
- assess the child's level of handwriting and presentation skills.

Marking is therefore a professional duty which carries a great deal of responsibility. Teachers can respond to a child's written work on two levels: the secretarial or surface features level (e.g. the punctuation, spelling, handwriting) and the compositional level (e.g. the ideas, values and meanings which the writer wants to convey). (See Chapters 11 and 12 on Writing.)

The teacher's response to ideas

When marking a piece of writing, therefore, it is essential to respond first to the content and ideas; for example, 'Your report helped me to imagine the way people must have felt in the fire.' Sometimes, a teacher's comments can help the young writer appreciate the need for more context or detail. A teacher might write: 'You need to explain more clearly why your hero lost his nerve.'

The teacher's response to surface features (spelling, punctuation, presentation)

The presentation, layout and handwriting are probably the first things a reader notices. Sometimes a teacher will comment on one of these; for example: 'Your writing's *much* neater – well done!' Alternatively, points of grammar may need attention: 'Look at speech marks in your reading book. Let's talk about these.' If the child is at a very early stage of writing development, which is independent of the writer's age, it is customary for a teacher to respond only to the ideas and effort made but to note down the writing skills which need further work.

It is certainly not advisable, at any stage, to try and correct every mistake because a child who is struggling with his writing will only grow demoralised. Where schools encourage children to be reflective and independent, teachers encourage the children to self-correct before handing in work.

If a child has spelled 'rocket' incorrectly, a teacher might write in the margin two more words with the same spellstring (see Glossary) or pattern, such as 'pocket', 'socket'. Here assessment is combined with teaching. At the same time, if several children have made a similar error, the teacher knows that this is a spelling pattern she should highlight in the near future, during word-level work.

At drafting and redrafting stages errors can be corrected, but redrafting also offers children a valuable opportunity to change their ideas and the structure of their writing as well.

Group and whole-class tasks in English

It is obviously more economical in terms of teacher time to discover, through whole-class or group tasks, what the children know or whether your teaching has been effective. The danger is that some children may fail publicly. It is advisable to assess, separately and diagnostically, individuals or groups of children who might be unable to cope with a group task.

Examples of group assessment in English might include:

- a group dictation or spelling test, to assess spelling competence and identify phonic work for the future
- observation of a group to identify features of speaking and listening development
- a quiz of knowledge, e.g. parts of speech
- a visual dictation, where children listen and draw what they hear, to assess listening skills
- a cloze test (a text with certain words blanked out which children have to fill) to assess awareness of verb tenses

- a standardised reading test, to identify reading strengths and difficulties or to provide reading ages, however inaccurate these may be
- National Curriculum SATs, e.g. running reading records or writing tasks (KS1) or a reading comprehension test where all children at KS2 read through a booklet or poem and answer questions.

Designing assessment tasks in English, based on the National Literacy Project

Taking a sample objective from the National Literacy project in the range of *Non-fiction: Instructions* we see that it suggests that, in Year 2, Term 1, Task 15, children should be taught 'to write simple instructions, e.g. getting to school, playing a game'.

The assessment task

Each child is given a Kinderegg surprise toy, in pieces. They have to piece it together and write instructions for their partner.

Assessment questions the teacher might ask could include:

- Do the children understand what instructions/directions are?
- Do they appreciate the need for sequence, for clarity?
- Can they give clear oral/written directions/instructions to others?
- In pairs, can A read B's directions and achieve the intended result?
- Are the instructions legible, well written and well illustrated?

Standardised assessment

The SATs for English change their format and range from year to year but each year, an informative Teacher's Handbook is provided with the test materials. It describes how teachers should administer each test so that children can perform at their best. 'The child should feel relaxed and free to browse and to talk about the choice of the book' (Teacher's Handbook, KS1, 1998).

When assessing children with standardised testing, there are some points teachers can follow:

- Make sure the children are not overawed by the idea of testing, because they will not perform well.
- Try to encourage the children to see the test as an experience rather than an ordeal.

- Be clear with instructions and speak slowly enough for those who find listening comprehension difficult.
- Give warning that time is running out, if the test is timed, and encourage children who seem 'stuck' to move on.
- Practise working in test conditions beforehand and try to give the class some practice of answering test-type questions.

To provide an idea of what the SATs involve, let's look at some recent SATs.

SATs for Key Stage 1

Speaking and Listening
These involve teacher assessment only, measuring children's competence against the level descriptions for the relevant key stage.

Reading
The reading task consists of a running record from a choice of picture books. Some of the books are identified as being suitable for the visually impaired (VI) child, available in Braille (B), or appropriate for children learning English as an additional language (EAL). Using an overlay, teachers record children's reading accuracy on a specified page of text, using miscue analysis techniques (Clay 1985). (See Figure 6.1.)

A reading assessment record is then completed, for Levels 1 and 2, with possible comments from the teacher describing, for example, the child's ability to discuss the text's features, such as structure, characters and style.

For Levels 2 and 3, there are comprehension tests. For Level 2, the comprehension booklet usually contains a story in picture-book format and a non-fiction text. At Level 3, children have to read a 16-page booklet and then answer questions about the text.

Writing
Each child has to complete a writing task, based upon the text chosen for the running record. For example, the child could produce a piece of informative writing, such as a leaflet or fact sheet .

The teacher then assesses the writing, against the descriptors provided in the Handbook.

A writing assessment record is filled in. Later, each child's levels are recorded with the other children's on a class record.

The writing evidence from the SAT task can include whether the child:

- communicates meaning
- engages the reader
- uses imagination and clarity
- displays characteristics of different forms of writing
- uses effective organisation and layout
- writes grammatically correct sentences
- uses punctuation accurately
- is beginning to spell following patterns and conventions
- has handwriting which is legible.

Spelling
Children working at Levels 2 and 3 have to be given a spelling test; this is optional for Level 1.

SATs for Key Stage 2

Reading
For children between Levels 3 and 5, there is a reading comprehension test, in booklet form. The children record their answers in an answer booklet. Some of the tasks involve mapping or filling in a matrix, instead of answering in full sentences (see Chapter 10 for fuller description).

Writing
Children have to produce one extended piece of writing, choosing from:

1 A piece of information writing, following prompts provided in the information and planning booklet. Children's notes, in preparation for their pieces of writing, are not marked.
2 A story, choosing from three titles.

Spelling and handwriting
Children listen to a passage read by the teacher and write in the missing words, spelling them correctly. For handwriting, they have to copy a short passage in joined-up and legible handwriting.

Optional Year 5 tests
For those schools who wish to test children halfway through Key Stage 2, some optional test material is provided.

Level 6 extension tests
For those children who are very able readers there is a more challenging comprehension and composition test, lasting 60 minutes, with its own answer booklet.

Billy's Beetle

										Strategies Used
Suddenly	the	sniffy	dog	stopped	digging					
and	took	off	like	a	rocket!					
'Look	at	him	go!'	said	the	man				
'He	can	smell	Billy's	beetle!'						
But	the	sniffy	dog	had	not	smelled	Billy's	beetle.		
He	had	smelled	sausages.							
'Leave,	sniffy	dog!	'Leave!,	said	the	man.				
So	the	sniffy	dog	grabbed	the	sausages,				
and	left!									
Now	there	was	Billy,	the	girl,	the	hedgehog,			
the	sniffy	dog,	the	man	with	the	sniffy	dog,		
and	the	woman	without	the	sausages,					
all	looking	for	Billy's	beetle.						
(And	a	polar	bear	who	had	joined	in	for	fun)	

T = told   O = omitted   Sc = Self-corrects

Strategies   Ph = phonic   G = graphic   S = syntactic   C = contextual

Figure 6.1 An example of a running record
Source: *SATs Teacher's Task Handbook*, DfEE 1998
Text from *Billy's Beetle*, by Mick Inkpen, Hodder Children's Books. Reproduced by permission of Hodder and Stoughton Limited

Standardised assessment: other tests

As well as the reading assessment made by the SATs, many schools continue to use other standardised reading tests, for example tests in Year 4, to monitor standards over time in relation to the same instrument of measurement. Sometimes, this is demanded by the local authority. Verbal reasoning tests are also administered, in many authorities, to help select children for transfer to secondary schooling.

Other forms of assessment

Peer assessment

Involving children in assessment is helpful to the busy teacher but can also benefit the children since they can learn a great deal for themselves while assessing each other. The following examples illustrate this.

- *Speaking and Listening:* Children rehearse a presentation about a personal project with a partner, who has a checklist of speaking and listening criteria for a presentation, which the class have drawn up in a whole-class session. Each partner listens to the presentation and ticks the criteria fulfilled, then feeds back to the presenter before swapping roles.
- *Writing:* Children read through, discuss and correct each other's writing drafts before handing them in to be marked.
- *Spelling:* Children test each their on their weekly spellings, in ability-matched pairs. Child A incidentally learns Child B's words and vice versa.
- *Reading:* Children read and discuss each other's books and book reviews.

Self-assessment

Most teachers find it helpful to be honest with children about their strengths and weaknesses.

In some schools, children are encouraged to identify areas where they need to try harder, perhaps setting specific targets for themselves, for example to improve handwriting, write longer pieces of writing, take turns in discussion, listen to others' points of view more willingly, and so on.

Children respond very positively to being involved in the assessment of their work because they feel a greater sense of control and ownership. The self-assessment records are then added to the child's individual profile and are kept with the child's other records.

Monitoring children's progress

When planning assessment opportunities for English, it is helpful to use a range of approaches to assessment and recording which enable a child's progress in English to be carefully monitored. These include:

- Observation and listening: either observing children informally and making notes or using structured observation schedules (see Figure 6.2, for example).
- Discussion and interaction: planning opportunities for discussions with children about their work and asking open-ended questions.
- Individual conferences: the National Literacy Project (1997) suggests a literacy conference with each child every half-term where, in a ten-minute discussion, a teacher agrees with the child on a reading target and a writing target to be achieved by the next conference.
- Self-assessment: some teachers have translated the National Curriculum level descriptions into language which is meaningful to children.
- Peer assessment, e.g. in writing conferences where children comment on each other's drafts.
- Group or whole-class tests and tasks: assessing a number of children simultaneously.
- Alternative approaches to assessing understanding through written work: devising alternative ways for the children to record their understanding or knowledge, e.g. a diagram or map.
- Marking, analysing and annotating written work: looking for evidence of learning in written work and identifying learning need. The quality of teachers' comments on children's work and their identification of specific ways to improve have the most impact on children's progress (Black and Dylan 1998).
- Keeping examples of work to demonstrate progress and building up a profile book, portfolio or record of achievement.
- Keeping records of the child's performance in school-based or standardised tests, e.g. reading tests, SATs, copies of school reports.
- Making a miscue analysis or running record of a child's reading strategies.
- Using published reading scheme reading inventories, e.g. *Sunshine Readers, Oxford Reading Tree*.
- Using published class or individual reading or phonics records, e.g. *First Steps* (Heinemann) or NLS assessment proformas.

ACTIVITY	SUBJECT(S)				DATE
Speaking and Listening Objectives	1) 2) 3) 4)				
NAME	1	2	3	4	Implications for future learning
A					
B					
C					
D					
E					
F					

This group needs practice in:

Expressing feelings	Telling stories	Hypothesising	Analysis
Persuading	Retelling stories	Predicting	Giving instructions
Expressing opinions	Describing in detail	Summarising	Presenting to others
Contradicting	Supporting	Questioning	Formulating rules
Justifying opinions	Listening to others	Interviewing	Discussing
Explaining	Reflecting on learning	Role play	Arguing a case
			Reasoning

Figure 6.2 Observation schedule for talk: a group record

Keeping useful records

Teachers probably make over a thousand professional decisions a day. Many of these are assessment decisions which will affect what they note down about children in their records. Most of the records may never be shared with others, though they may be summarised for parents or colleagues. A child's record of progress can be passed on from teacher to teacher so that a clear picture of attainment over time can be achieved.

Class records for English

In English it is advisable to keep separate class or group records for:

- Speaking and Listening, with different contexts shown (Figure 6.3)

CLASS	SOCIAL GROUPINGS			In school With an adult	On visits With visitors
ACTIVITIES	Whole class	Small group	Pair		
Literacy hour					
Reading for pleasure					
Role play					
Story telling					
Shared writing					
Research for information					
Plenary					
Show and tell					
Problem solving					
Investigative maths					
Art and craft					
Craft/DT					
ICT					
Science					
Humanities					
PE					
Music					
Assembly					

Figure 6.3 Contexts for language experience: a class or individual record

- *Writing* (divided perhaps into word level, sentence level and text level, based upon the NLS literacy hour, or range, purposes and skills, based on the National Curriculum)
- *Spelling:* showing spellstrings taught, test results or spelling difficulties to be worked on
- *Handwriting:* showing which joins have been mastered
- *Reading:* many teachers like to keep a class record of reading skills covered across the curriculum over the year.

On whole-class records a teacher might record English tasks and activities or monitor groupings and language opportunities (Figure 6.3). A tick-sheet to monitor completion alone will not really help inform future planning.

Some teachers use symbols to indicate progress

on individual records. For example, they indicate experience, understanding and application:

Experience: Child has experience	/
Understanding: Child has completed task and understood	x
Application: Child can apply understanding	⊗

Individual English records

Speaking and listening tapes/oral records

Making a cassette offers children a valuable opportunity to make choices and to evaluate their performance (see Chapters 7 and 8 on Speaking and Listening). It is unlikely that the child's next teacher would have time to listen to the cassettes of the whole class, but they can access them for individual children.

Phonics records

Key Stage 1 teachers systematically record which phonemes a child has been taught and can use confidently and correctly in their writing. (See Figure 6.4.

Spelling records

Schools use a variety of ways to track children's spelling. Children can keep a personal dictionary. Some teachers use a system of two envelopes where children keep a) words they wish to learn and b) words they have learned. When a word is learned, it can be transferred to an individual word book.

Other schools use a 'Look, Say, Cover, Write, Think and Check' book as a record of spelling development. Teachers often use diagnostic dictations, with texts which include spelling families taught, to assess spelling. They can keep these as evidence of spelling progress.

Reading records

Many schools use a reading log or journal to record the books a child reads and to monitor reading progress. Teachers also use informal and formal reading assessments, such as running records or miscue analysis, to understand more deeply the strategies which children need to develop. Through discussions about books the teacher also probes children's understanding and their attitudes to reading.

Writing samples

Teachers tend to monitor the range of writing opportunities a child has experienced over the year. This is important if children are to develop their abilities to write for different audiences and purposes. Teachers who want evidence of a child's writing development may keep some of the drafts in a child's writing portfolio.

Records of achievement or pupil portfolios

Many schools ask teachers to collect examples of each child's work in a portfolio, record of achievement or profile. The profile for each child contains records of SAT results, standardised tests, teacher assessments and observation schedules.

For English, the contents of the profile might include:

- an example of a child's handwriting
- a story, which includes the first draft or drafts and the final version or best copy
- a poem
- different types of writing, e.g. non-fiction writing: reports, letters, lists, reviews, captions
- other written work which has been significant, across the curriculum
- the most recent reading journal which records the child's reading and the dialogue between parents and teachers
- examples of spellings mastered (e.g. an end-of-year spelling test or diagnostic dictation)
- NLS record sheets
- a phonic record sheet
- a book made by the child.

Can identify initial sound	Cannot identify initial sound	Can identify final sound	Can identify medial vowel

Figure 6.4 A class record form for the identification of phonemes

Annotating work

At Key Stage 1, it is usually the teacher who decides to keep a piece of work for a child's profile or record of achievement. By Key Stage 2, many teachers like to involve the children in choosing samples of writing. However chosen, it is helpful to date and briefly annotate the work. This may seem time-consuming but it provides valuable evidence of progression and will be useful in teacher assessment and moderation when allocating each child to a certain level.

Target setting

Targets are closely related to learning objectives. They describe the intended achievements of pupils and provide:

- a steer for planning
- a focus for teaching
- criteria for monitoring teaching and learning
- evidence of achievement to share with parents and others.

LEAs have been set targets for Literacy and teachers have been encouraged to convert school targets into year group and individual pupil targets, including those set by the children themselves. An example, taken from the 'Leading on Literacy' (NLS Conference, 2000) illustrates this process, which has been called the breaking down or 'layering' of targets.

- A year 1 target:

'Children can write a recount or narrative, beginning to break up the series of events with connectives other than 'and'.'

- A termly target (year 1, term 3):

'Children can write simple recounts linked to topics of interest/study or personal interest, using the language of texts read as models, in which the time sequence is clearly signalled by words such as 'first', 'next', 'after', 'when', etc.'
(NLS Framework, Text Objectives 18 and 20)

- A pupil's learning target:

'My stories and recounts show the order in which things happened.'

It can be very helpful to share the learning targets for an English task or session with the children before they start work. Sometimes, as a teaching strategy, a teacher may prefer to see whether the children can identify the objectives of the activity later on, employing problem solving. The plenary session and teacher feedback, however, should focus on the learning achieved in relation to the targets.

Reporting to parents

Reporting to parents about their child's progress can be done informally as they collect or deliver their child at either end of the school day. At parents' evenings the feedback is more formal, supported by evidence in the form of the child's written work. It is much easier to describe a spelling or handwriting issue with relevant pages open on the table. Using Post-its to earmark certain pages can be helpful, and having up-to-date records is vital.

Parents will receive a written report about their child, at least once a year. Parents are interested in their child's levels of attainment in English and it helps to be specific in telling them what progress their child is making. Teachers often find writing reports very difficult because space is limited and it is sometimes hard to avoid using educational jargon. Teachers need to remain positive and constructive. They can do this by identifying children's achievements in terms of their learning skills, their language development and their attitudes. Where problems exist, it is always helpful to suggest ways in which parents can work with their child to overcome them.

SUMMARY

In this chapter we have explored the key principles behind English assessment. It is important that teachers are clear about how they intend to assess children's language at the planning stage.

- Assessment should be primarily formative or diagnostic so that each child can be helped to move along a developmental continuum of language knowledge and use.

- It is important to keep evidence of each child's progress in English, e.g. in a portfolio.

- Systematic record-keeping is important to monitor children's progress in English. Records need to be as simple and accessible as possible. They should reflect the strands of the National Curriculum and the NLS objectives.

References

Black, P. and Dylan, W. (1998) *The Power of Feedback*, King's College, London

Clay, M. (1985) *The Early Detection of Reading Difficulties: A Diagnostic Survey with Recovery Procedures*, Heinemann

DfEE (1998) *The National Literacy Strategy: Framework for Teaching*, DfEE

Fisher, R. (1995) *Teaching Children to Think*, Stanley Thornes

Kerry, T. (1982) *Effective Questioning: A Teaching Skills Workbook*, Macmillan

SCAA (1997) *Baseline Assessment Scales*, DfEE

Task Group on Assessment and Testing (1987) *The National Curriculum: Report and Digest*, DES

Further reading

Barrs, M. (1988) *Primary Language Record*, Centre for Language in Primary Education
Although devised prior to the National Curriculum, this practical approach to the assessment and recording of language development still has a great deal to offer teachers in the formation of their own English records.

Bearne, E. (1998) *Making Progress in English*, Routledge.

Chambers, A (1993) *Tell Me: Children, Reading and Talk*, Thimble Press
This lucidly written exploration of the role of interaction in the teaching and assessment of reading provides useful models of teacher questions which will help to develop children's responses to literature.

Clemson, D. and Clemson, W. (1996) *The Really Practical Guide to Primary Assessment*, 2nd edition Stanley Thornes.
This book makes the principles behind assessment clear and offer teachers very useful approaches to assessment and record keeping.

Drummond, M. (1993) *Making Assessment Work: Values and Principles in Assessing Young Children*, National Children's Bureau.
A school-based INSET resource which looks at important issues and practical approaches to assessment in the early years.

Gipps, C. (1995) *Intuition Or Evidence? Teachers and National Assessment of Seven-Year-Olds*, Open University Press.
Based upon a three-year research study into the impact of National Curriculum assessment at the end of Key Stage 1. The researchers look at the ways in which teachers' assessment practices were affected by the standardised tests at age seven. They also look at the impact on teachers' teaching and classroom organisation.

QCA/99/391 (1999) *Teaching, Speaking and Listening at Key Stages 1 and 2*, HMSO.

Sainsbury, M. (1996) *Tracking Significant Achievement in English*, Hodder and Stoughton.

7 Speaking and listening at Key Stage 1

OBJECTIVES

By the end of this chapter, you should be able to:

- discuss the central role of speaking and listening at KS1

- identify different types of talk and levels of listening

- consider different contexts for speaking and listening activities

- consider how to plan and resource speaking and listening activities

- plan appropriate methods of assessment, recording and reporting.

The centrality of oracy at Key Stage 1

During the last 25 years, there has been a steady growth in the recognition that the prominent place of oral language in society should be reflected proportionately in the work of the classroom. Spoken language is central to what it means to be human. It is pivotal to all our communication and is a constantly functioning process throughout most people's lives. The skills of speaking and listening are usually referred to as 'oracy'. The term is intended to counterbalance the word 'literacy', which is used to mean reading and writing. At Key Stage 1, oracy should be central to all that takes place in the classroom for two main reasons.

1 Using and understanding oracy skills
As children gradually learn about language diversity in all its richness, they should see eventually that they can use many language forms, all of which have equal value but different functions and places in their lives. Speaking and listening skills need to be planned directly from the English pro-

grammes of study, and applied right across the curriculum, so that an increasingly wide repertoire of talk can be developed for different purposes and audiences.

2 Wider learning through oracy
The valuable processes which link talking, thinking and understanding assist children's learning in ways which are developmentally appropriate. The child who seems to be talking to herself as she plays with a fire engine is in fact practising roles and language, and externalising quite sophisticated thought processes. The talk helps to structure the thought and consequently the understanding. Likewise, the group of children who are discussing their observations of materials and their reactions to water are theorising, sorting, ordering and reasoning with their ideas – a process which positively assists conceptualisation.

Teacher talk and the importance of reflective listening

Prior to starting school, children have been used to a much smaller child-to-adult ratio, ranging from the 1:1 of the child who has stayed at home with a parent, through the 1:4 of the child cared for by a child minder, up to the 1:10 of a child who has been to a playgroup or nursery. In any event, it is unlikely that children will have been used to sharing the main adult with approximately 30 other children! A major adjustment of starting school is that they will have less 1:1 interaction with an adult, and the main consequences of such a change are:

1 They will experience less personal undivided listening from an adult.
2 They will hear less personal direct speech from an adult.
3 They will have to take turns to speak.
4 They will have to listen for longer periods.
5 They will spend more time speaking and listening with peers.

This can have a big impact on a young child, and so the way in which you structure the speaking and listening into your classroom needs to reflect an ethos which is encouraging and supportive of every individual child. This includes your own speaking and listening as well as that of the children!

Your own oracy skills are of paramount importance if you are to maximise the potential of all your pupils. You need to be aware of the impact your talk can have, both negatively and positively, upon the children in your care. Negative responses to the child's home language can alienate and prevent learning, leading to loss of self-esteem and retarded progression. If children are going to learn to speak clearly and effectively to a wide range of audiences they need to develop confidence, and this needs to start from where they feel familiar in an environment where they feel supported and valued. The set of key questions in Figure 7.1 offers you some guidelines for reflecting on your own practice.

Unplanned opportunities

One of the most difficult things for student teachers to learn is how to maximise the language potential of every encounter with children. In other words, how to make positive influences on children's spoken language in the playground, in the cloakroom, in the classroom before school starts, in the corridors on the way to assembly, and so on.

You should never underestimate the influence you will have on your pupils. You are one of the key adults in their lives and your responsibilities lie above and beyond the planned lessons! Your talk is not only a model for the children but it can also initiate fruitful talk opportunities at most times during the school day. There are many natural approaches to this, but the following list will give you some ideas which you might like to consider.

- initiating talk through your open-ended questions
- offering lots of opportunities for the children to ask questions

Figure 7.1 Key questions for teachers in reflecting on their own practice

- using spontaneous opportunities for rhyme and rhythm word play
- always showing that you value their ideas
- asking their opinions about the classroom
- involving them in displays
- tidying, organising, rearranging the classroom
- spontaneous discussions about class problems
- reminiscing about previous activities in school
- showing an interest in children's lives outside school
- talking about your own life outside school
- telling jokes.

Planning for oracy at Key Stage 1

The National Curriculum provides specific descriptions of the opportunities which pupils should be given to develop their abilities in speaking and listening, but you might find it useful to regard those within the six overarching objectives, listed in Figure 7.2, which acknowledge and build upon the language learning which the child brings to school from home.

A well-planned oracy curriculum
should enable each child to...

...extend vocabulary
...extend the range of types of talk
...adapt talk for widening range of audiences
...develop an understanding of language variations
...extend the range of listening levels
...develop social skills of speaking and listening

Figure 7.2 Key objectives for oracy at Key Stage 1

Within a framework such as this, the National Curriculum can be planned more systematically, and the gradual widening of skills and knowledge within each of the six categories enables the monitoring of progression.

Types of talk

Effective planning for oracy depends on a sound understanding of the complex nature of talk. There are many different types of talk. If you take a break from reading this book for a moment and stop to think about all the different reasons you have had for talking during the last 24 hours, you will find that you have talked to different people in different tones, different formats, different moods, and so on, for many different reasons. These might range from ringing your bank manager to request an overdraft (formal explanation and request) to telling a close friend about a party you went to last Saturday (informal description, reporting, expressions of delight), and so on! You are able to switch in and out of different speaking modes according to what you know is expected. Young children have little or no experience of this and so need practice through play and other learning activities which offer them contexts for using different types of talk.

Figure 7.3 lists the types of talk required by the National Curriculum at Key Stage 1 plus two additional suggestions at the end. Each variation has been illustrated with an example.

The literacy hour

The literacy hour includes discussion and exploration of written language at word, sentence and text levels. This can be planned so that oracy as well as literacy objectives are being achieved. Indeed, if you are planning a group activity where discussion is taking place you need to structure it carefully, setting clear guidelines, goals and outcomes which provide evidence. As one example of this at Key Stage 1, a group investigating rhyming analogies from a set of starting words could discuss ideas, then make a tape of their list. This would provide clear evidence of their literacy understanding, but also require them to speak clearly for a purpose. It would also ensure that their ideas were not limited by the extent of their spelling skills.

Type of talk	Example
storytelling	retelling a known story to a partner
imaginative play and drama	role-playing a shopkeeper in the role-play area
reading aloud	role-playing a parent at bedtime in the home corner
reciting poetry and nursery rhymes	whole-class recitation
exploring ideas	problem-solving in science
developing ideas	group story-planning
clarifying ideas	answering questions about the group story
predicting outcomes	discussing effects of a new supermarket building
discussing possibilities	discussing ways to help each other (RE)
describing events	describing a personal piece of news
describing observations	describing leaves during science
describing experiences	feelings in the swimming pool
explaining choices	evaluating a model built in technology
giving reasons for opinions	saying why they do/do not like wearing uniform
giving reasons for actions	explaining why they made a technology model in the way that they did
asking relevant questions	clarifying what to do after teacher explains
answering questions	after reading their own story to the class

Young children might also be encouraged to *give instructions* and *evaluate*.

Figure 7.3 Types of talk required at Key Stage 1

Finger games, puppets, masks, role play and drama all have a valuable part to play in the literacy hour. Sequencing key story events, separating sentences, exploring character motivation, etc., are all learning experiences which can be enhanced by such interactive oracy contexts. Chapters 17 and 18 give specific examples of oracy activities within the contexts of drama and media studies which can be purposefully used to teach effectively during the literacy hour.

Talk across the curriculum

When planning the English curriculum for your class, you should not only be considering individual English activities. Language is 'happening' during every minute of the day, and by considering the opportunities for teaching English throughout all curriculum areas you can multiply the language-learning potential many times over. However, in order to do this effectively you need to plan carefully. It is not enough to assume that just because the children are engaged in a practical science experiment the 'right' sort of talk will happen; you need to structure the activity so that it *does* happen!

There are different models for planning speaking and listening across the curriculum. One of the most effective ways is to plan key oracy themes (for example predicting outcomes – the use of the

future tense) across a two- or three-week period. The theme is then applied across every curriculum area. In this way you can reinforce vocabulary extension, and provide opportunities for certain types of talk over and over again but within different curricular contexts.

Repetition is a crucial component of language development. As you will know yourself if you have ever tried to learn a foreign language abroad, hearing a word once is rarely enough to cement it into your memory! So to set up a situation where the children are using a certain type of talk which is itself the subject of discussion can work in very positive ways. Figure 7.4 illustrates this approach by applying the theme of describing observations to geography and art.

The key vocabulary indicates the words which you would repeatedly use when talking about talk, as shown in the examples in Figure 7.5.

By modelling the language yourself, you will be providing the children with repeated examples of meaning within different contexts and will find that they eventually start to use the same vocabulary when speaking to you and to each other. Other reasons for using this themed approach across the curriculum include:

- Repetition assists understanding and memory.
- The application of the same themes in different contexts assists consolidation.

KEY THEME:	describing observations		
KEY VOCABULARY:	observe, observation, explain, explanation, describe, description		

	Subject:	**Geography** (Shops in Our Town)	**Art** (Wallpaper designs)
Activity:		After looking at photographs of several main shops in the town they work in pairs, taking turns to describe a selected shop while the other draws it as fast as they can. (Egg timers can be a useful way of keeping them on task!) They count the number of things described as recorded in the drawing, and discuss the accuracy of the observations.	Having looked at and discussed several contrasting designs they then design and paint their own. During whole-class time, use two telephones to 'role play' ringing a wallpaper shop. You are the customer enquiring about their new design which you heard about on the radio. Can they describe it to you? After modelling this with four children, let the rest of the class make a phone call in pairs, describing their own design without letting their partner see it. (Sitting back to back can be an effective way of organising this.) The enquirer must decide if they would like to place an order, having asked as many questions as they can about the paper.
Social focus:		Explain clearly and patiently	How do shop assistants talk on the phone?
Audience variation:		Peer	Adult role play
Listening focus:		Listening in order to carry out an instruction	Listening in order to make a decision

Figure 7.4 **Examples of an oracy theme across two curriculum areas**

- It is easy to organise because you are focusing on specifics.
- It provides many opportunities to focus on particular skills for assessment.

Information and communications technology

Much useful talk takes place at the computer. Usually, children are highly motivated when working with technology. There are many types of software which provide contexts for reading and writing, and talk plays an important part in this work when children are using the computer in pairs. Other types of software are designed specifically for different types of talk such as:

decision-making
planning
discussion
sequencing
evaluation

responding/answering questions
description.

These might operate as part of the function of the program; for instance, the children might be working interactively with a CD-ROM which requires speaking and listening responses. Alternatively, the programme might offer ways for you to structure talk into the activity. For instance, editing a story in pairs offer opportunities for description, suggestion, correction and explanation. This is covered in more detail in Chapter 19.

Bilingual learners

Children for whom English is the second language and who are still in the early stages of developing spoken English require lots of opportunities to work interactively within English-speaking groups so that they can:

- hear the vocabulary and constructions
- repeat and imitate what they hear

'How many things did you **observe** in the photograph, Darren?'

'How did Gemma begin her **description** of the weather?'

'Stacey made four really useful **observations** about colours when she described her wallpaper.'

'Kulraj, can you **explain** to the class why you decided not to buy Ben's paper?'

'Leanne, your **explanation** of how you wanted to redecorate your bedroom was very clear.'

'Who can **describe** how they feel when they are very hungry?'

Figure 7.5 Modelling key vocabulary

- practise their responses
- ask and answer questions
- gain additional clues from the body language of speakers
- be helped and corrected by others in the group.

Working in isolation is of little value to their language development, and can sometimes lead to frustration and a sense of failure. Audio and visual aids such as tapes, models, toys, pictures, puppets, masks and texts can add to the quality of the learning as they provide a further sensory dimension to assist understanding.

It is also important that the child's first language should be valued at school, and, wherever possible, used as a foundation on which to build skills in the new language learning. The main reasons for this are:

1 Existing linguistic knowledge can help the child to conceptualise the new language.
2 The first language is a central part of the child's identity, and disregard for this can lead to feelings of insecurity and loss of self-esteem.
3 All children need to explore the diversity of

language if they are to learn about how language works.

Levels of listening

Arguably, listening is the single most constant process in the classroom as it is integral to every aspect of communication, and yet it is also the most difficult to measure. Listening has an ephemeral quality because it is so very personal to the listener. A group of children gathered on the carpet where the teacher is reading a story may, to an observer, be 'listening beautifully' because they are sitting quietly and still. In reality, some may be listening and responding to what they hear by thinking thoughts and questions about the story, others may be listening to the story without such responses, some may be dreaming in another world where they merely hear the sounds of the teacher's voice as noises but do not register their meaning, and others will not even hear the sounds but be in a trance world.

We can divide listening into four levels which we all use at different times according to the situation:

- *selective listening:* tuning in and out between focused attention and trancing
- *passive listening:* where attention is paid but no response given
- *responsive listening:* where the listening leads to a response such as following an instruction, answering a question, and so on
- *interactive listening:* a more prolonged process in which the listener engages with one or more other speakers to develop an organic discussion which might change according to what is said.

The National Curriculum focuses on the following Key Skills for listening at Key Stage 1:

- attention
- concentration
- appropriate response
- effective response
- asking appropriate questions based on what has been heard
- remembering
- taking different views into account.

However, whilst these can guide you in your planning, it is vital that you also consider the evidence for listening. For instance, how do you know if a pupil is 'listening carefully'? (Level 2, Attainment Target 1: English). They might be looking studious whilst dreaming about their birthday party that is about to happen at the end of the day! The need for evidence reinforces the view that planning and assessment are inextricably linked, so when planning listening activities for your children you might need to ask yourself these two helpful questions:

1 What sort of listening do I expect from this activity?
2 How will I know that such listening has taken place?

The box below shows an example of how this might translate:

In this example, you would need to consider that

Listening focus: paying attention and remembering
Activity: drawing a scene which the teacher describes only twice
Evidence: how many details has the child remembered which can be counted from the drawing (e.g. The house had a green roof and the chimney was blue. There were five windows and one was round, etc.)

---

you are also assessing the child's sequencing skills and short-term memory.

Resources

Most children have a natural inclination to talk, and because of this it can be tempting to assume that no additional resources are needed to assist and encourage. This is very far from the truth. There is no doubt that children will chat away from morning till night (see classrooms during wet playtime!), but if we are to structure the talk so that it is extending and developing their repertoire we need to plan activities which will ensure that the talk is not merely 'chat'.

Helping to structure the talk

Resources can assist greatly in structuring activities in ways which will steer the talk in the required direction. Resources for oracy fall into three categories: stimulus resources, support resources and recording resources. *Stimulus resources* are those which provide something for the children to talk about, for example two photographs of the same street 100 years apart to discuss the historical changes. *Support resources* are those which structure the activity and provide an organisational framework for the talk, for example an egg timer against which the children might race to say rhyming words. Finally, *goal resources* are those which provide a target or focus for the talk by requiring the children to write, draw, tape, film, etc., the outcomes of their talk. Further examples of each type of resource are listed in Figure 7.6.

Stimulus resources	Support resources	Goal resources
photographs	speaking shell	chart
stories, poems	instruction sheet	list
video	rule card	brainstorm chart
visitors	egg timer	picture
artefacts	clue cards	tape
drama	clock	score chart
children's work	rota	graph

Figure 7.6 Examples of different resources

Adults are also a valuable resource, of course, and they can fit into all three categories. Good questions can provide a stimulus, clear rules and boundaries can provide support, and a range of adults can provide audiences which might be the focus for the talk.

Role-play areas

Role-play areas provide opportunities for children to explore different types of language through their play. However, the nature of the talk and the usefulness of the play can depend very much on the quality of the provision. In other words, it is simply not enough to direct three children into a sparse and untidy home corner with nothing new to stimulate their invention.

Some teachers change their role-play area half-termly, sometimes to integrate the language and play into their topic work (e.g. a space station as part of a science topic, a dentist's surgery as part of a health-care topic, etc.). However, even where the home corner remains for a longer period, the inclusion of new 'props' on a regular basis can provide a remarkable springboard for the talk. This might mean providing items which relate to a story you have told, or perhaps changing the cultural tone of the home. Figure 7.7 shows some examples of particular props which might encourage different types of talk.

Theme	Props	Talk about
Home corner	wok, chop sticks	Chinese cookery
Three Bears' House	wooden bowls	stealing
Greengrocer's	money	mathematical language
Bat cave	batcape costumes	gender roles violence
Staffroom	report forms	behavioural issues
Cafe	menus	decision-making
Police station	forms	questioning/ answering

Figure 7.7 Props and talk in the role-play area

Assessment, recording and reporting

Building up a bank of evidence about a child's speaking and listening can provide a profile of their development and help you to plan for their learning needs. It is quite feasible to assess speaking and listening within the context of many different activities right across the curriculum. Some of these might be incidental, such as your observations of a child's increased willingness to answer questions during story time, and others might be during planned assessment tasks, such as the child's retelling of a story within a small group situation.

As with all types of assessment, it is important that the children know what is being assessed. If you say to a group 'I am going to sit and watch you during your discussion and I want to see how carefully you are listening to each other', they are actually 'in the know' about what is expected of them, and that is part of the teaching process.

Objectivity and evidence

Good assessment always requires objectivity and evidence, and because oracy has such an ephemeral quality it can sometimes be difficult to plan in ways which encompass tangible information. It is therefore important to be clear about what you are assessing and what you will need to see as evidence. The SCAA video and accompanying booklet *Exemplification of Standards. English: Speaking and Listening* (1995) provide some good examples of situations in which children's oracy can be assessed and the types of observations which count as evidence.

Objectivity includes consideration of points such as:

> Was the child named to answer the question or was it open to the whole group?
> Was the question answered spontaneously or prompted?
> What was the size of the group?
> Am I assessing talk or the knowledge?

Records and their uses

When recording the evidence of assessments you need to be mindful of why you are recording. Records need to be useful and clear to others, otherwise there is little point in investing all the time which it inevitably takes. Different types of records can serve different purposes.

Notebook
Some early years teachers find it useful to have a notebook handy at all times to jot down the unexpected observation which can later be transferred to that child's profile.

File cards
A box of file cards with one card per child can be a useful way of rotating your observations systemat-

ically. Taking the front two out each day, you then focus on those particular children and make notes. This will include different contexts such as assembly, PE, going into lunch, etc., as well as actual activities. The two cards go to the back of the box at the end of the day, so each child has a close observation approximately every two to three weeks. If you miss a day it doesn't matter because the system allows for this, and it also means that you will pinpoint all children including those 'invisible' children that are sometimes in danger of fading into the walls.

Tick sheets

These can be useful for keeping track of specific criteria, but need to be supported by evidence.

Profile

This might include tapes, photographs, records of your observations, the children's own self-evaluations, comments from parents, plus transfers from any of the records listed above. One tape per child might be used repeatedly to gather evidence, and involving the child in this (for example letting them decide when they have something worth recording which they are proud of) can take some of the time-management problems away.

Don't forget to report to the child!

You will know that reporting takes place for a wide audience, but don't forget that the person who needs the feedback the most is the child! Telling them what they have done well will encourage them to do better. Talking about speaking and listening in an evaluative way will help the child to learn that it is an important part of their learning and not merely a social sideline.

The reflective spiral

A reflective approach towards your practice can provide a sound underpinning to all you do. The way in which you reflect upon assessments should be seen as a spiralling process which moves in a progressive way, repeatedly around through planning, activities and assessment, and upwards through new levels of learning. In this way, assessment should never be seen as a stand-alone or bolt-on occupation which has to be done at the end of a piece of work, but instead it should be regarded as an active part of the teaching process which assists in the planning and progression of children's learning.

SUMMARY

In this chapter, we have explored the central role which oracy has to play in the curriculum at Key Stage 1. Planning for oracy should reflect the prominence which speaking and listening play in our society, and four key principles should underpin this:

- Children need to be provided with opportunities not only to continue developing their own oracy skills, but also to learn through the kind of activities where the talk is helping the conceptual understanding.

- This requires you to plan oracy into the curriculum both as a discrete English activity and as an appropriate tool for learning across the curriculum.

- There are many kinds of talk which can be used for different purposes. Children learn about these, and how to use them, by being provided with meaningful contexts for using them.

- Planning oracy activities should be part of a reflective spiral in which your observations and assessment of the children's speaking and listening skills provide the basis of what their next stage learning needs are within the context of National Curriculum requirements.

Further reading

Andrew, M. and Orme, D.(1997) *Curriculum Bank: Speaking and Listening Key Stage One – Scottish Levels A–B*, Scholastic
This is a book packed with useful ideas for activities which also include suggestions for extension, support, IT, displays, assessment and performance. Some of the activities are accompanied by references to appropriate resources (e.g. particular poetry anthologies), some are accompanied by

photocopiable sheets, and the Overview Grid which relates the activities to objectives provides an accessible frame of reference to planning.

Edwards, V. (1995) *Speaking and Listening in Multilingual Classrooms*, Reading and Language Information Centre, University of Reading
An excellent book which all teachers should read. It sets the context of spoken language generally before going on to discuss diversity. The book explores how multilingualism can be of benefit to all children, and important issues are sensitively explained. Suggestions about the types of activities teachers can plan are made in general terms.

Fidge, L. (1992) *The Essential Guide to Speaking and Listening*, Folens
This is an ideas book which is arranged into useful sections built around different categories of spoken language. The section on the teacher's role and organisation, including assessment, is particularly helpful.

Norman, K.(1990) *Teaching, Talking and Learning in Key Stage One*, NATE
Originally produced by the National Oracy Project for the National Curriculum Council, this excellent book is now distributed by the National Association for the Teaching of English (NATE). It underpins many useful practical suggestions with a sound rationale for oracy, and deals with differentiation and individual needs in a particularly helpful way.

8 Speaking and listening at Key Stage 2

OBJECTIVES

By the end of this chapter you should be able to:

- discuss the complexity of talk
- identify discrete English themes for developing oracy skills
- consider speaking and listening across the curriculum
- understand the relationship between assessment and planning.

The place of oracy at Key Stage 2

In Chapter 7, it was established that oracy has an important part to play in young children's learning. It is now widely recognised that the oracy curriculum continues to be a valuable component of the learning process for older children. Not only are the skills a major part of the English Order for the National Curriculum (Attainment Target 1) they also provide a framework for teaching and learning in other subject areas. Likewise, speaking and listening are embedded into cross-curricular issues such as gender, and moral development.

There is sound evidence to show that 'children who talk, question, and actively discuss get higher scores and grades' (O'Keeffe 1995). The spoken word is the means by which we encode thought. In other words, thoughts, ideas and responses become reality when we frame them into sentences. By engaging in discourse with others we are able to adapt, revise and extend those thoughts and ideas so that they are continually being developed and challenged. In this way we integrate knowledge and concepts into our minds. For example, if children are to understand that there might be a range of views on a particular issue (e.g.

reducing the number of cars on the roads), it is not enough for you to simply tell them. If they role-play different perspectives, discuss and debate the issues in groups and express their own views at the start and end of these activities they are likely to have a much greater depth of understanding than if they sit in silence for 40 minutes listening passively to your explanations. They will also remember it for longer! This doesn't mean that you should never explain things. Your input provides important information for them to consider, but they must be allowed time for reflection and discussion – it is part of the learning process.

However, speaking and listening do not exist in some kind of 'key stage vacuum'. Teacher training is now based upon government expectations that all primary teachers should have a full knowledge of both key stages, regardless of the age they teach. The foundation years are crucially important to children's language development, and as a professional learning expert you will need to understand the whole picture. The two chapters on oracy are intended to be read as a pair, so items and terminology introduced in Chapter 7 will be used in this chapter without repeated explanations.

The functions of talk

Talk helps us learn in many ways. Its many contexts, constructions and presentations provide a complex network for human communication. Figure 8.1 illustrates the major functions of talk.

Talking and thinking

Talking modifies thinking. This is a powerful tool for learning when applied across the curriculum. If children can develop high levels of language this will have a direct impact upon their levels of thinking. Consider the dynamics which take place when a group of children are engaged in a discussion. Figure 8.2 illustrates this in the simplest terms.

73

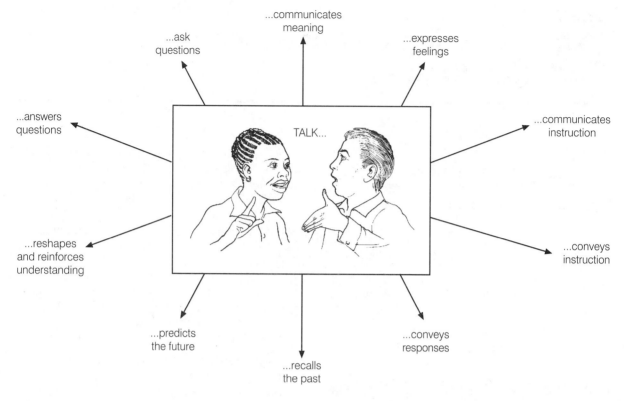

Figure 8.1 The functions of talk

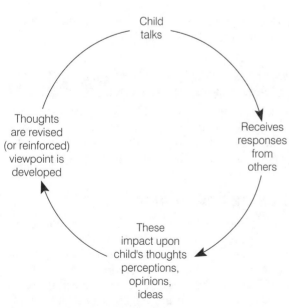

Figure 8.2 Expansion of talk in groups

A comment or idea is put to the group. This receives response and/or feedback, such as an alternative opinion or modified agreement. This alters the perception (though not necessarily the opinion) of the first speaker and broadens the horizons of the subject matter. In the light of this, revisions are made to the speaker's thinking and further comments are made. These may be a persistence with the original idea but with additional supporting arguments. On the other hand it might be an adaptation of the first idea in the light of the feedback. And so the cycle continues. It is important to bear in mind also that the cycles of each individual are inextricably linked into a much more complex three-dimensional model in which many dynamics are affecting each other.

Types of talk

If you are to provide opportunities for children to engage in a wide range of talk tasks you need to be aware of the different types of talk. Figure 8.3 provides a model to illustrate one way in which talk can be categorised.

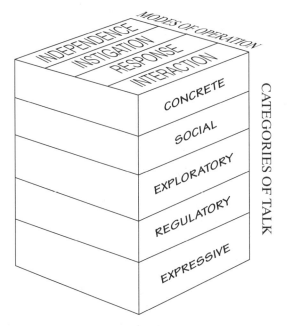

Figure 8.3 Categories of talk and the four modes of operation

The model is three-dimensional, because each of the categories can be operated on four levels, described here as the modes of operation. These are:

Independence	**talking alone**
Examples	asking oneself questions as one solves a problem
	role-playing with toys
Instigation	**where one initiates the talk**
Examples	asking someone else a question
	giving information
Response	**where one talks in response to** another's talk or actions
Examples	answering a question
	disagreeing with a proposal
Interaction	**where the talk develops and** changes as a result of exchanges
Examples	debating a topical issue
	justifying an idea in the light of another's opposition

Whilst this is only one model of many, it serves the purpose of enabling you to think analytically about the complexity of talk and its contexts.

The National Curriculum states that pupils at Key Stage 2 should have opportunities to develop the following types of talk:

- exploring, developing, explaining and sharing ideas
- sharing insights and opinions
- planning, predicting, investigating
- reading aloud, telling stories, enacting stories and poems
- presenting to an audience, live and on tape
- commenting, evaluating, questioning, qualifying, justifying
- extending and following up ideas
- opposing points of view
- using standard English.

You should also consider providing opportunities for pupils to:

- announce
- demonstrate
- entertain
- hypothesise
- instruct
- interpret
- report
- speculate
- summarise.

These lists are useful because they give us indica-

The model identifies five categories of talk:

Concrete	types of talk which relate directly to concrete experiences
Examples	describing another person
	relating an event which has happened
Social	types of talk which are for relationship purposes
Examples	asking if someone wants a cup of tea
	expressing anger with someone
Exploratory	talk which helps to solve problems or make new discoveries
Examples	asking questions
	commentary to problem-solving
Regulatory	talk which controls the actions of others
Examples	giving instructions
	giving warnings
Expressive	talk which expresses ideas, feelings or emotions
Examples	predicting what might happen next in a story
	describing responses to a painting

tions about the purpose of the talk as well as the type. Nevertheless, having access to such comprehensive lists of talk types is only a starting point, and can only be translated into good practice if you can provide credible contexts within which the talk takes place. This means designing activities which:

- have a worthwhile and interesting reason for taking place
- have sufficient content for children to have something to talk about
- have a specified intended audience.

Creating a productive oracy environment at Key Stage 2

If the value of talk is to be developed to its full potential at Key Stage 2 it has to be given status. The children must recognise its importance, value its uses, and respect the fact that talk is a valid part of their work. As the person responsible for creating such well-informed attitudes you will need to adopt the following habits as part of your everyday practice:

- talk about speaking and listening
- comment specifically on the children's oracy skills
- give rewards for oracy achievements
- encourage the children to reflect on their own talk and that of others
- develop and maintain clear guidelines for speaking and listening which takes place in your classroom – involve the children in this decision-making, it is their classroom too!
- plan some areas of work which are explicitly about talk
- provide a wide variety of role models from outside school (e.g. visitors, visits, TV, radio)
- show that you respect and value what children have to say
- teach children new modes of speaking through modelling and interaction rather than negative correction
- never 'talk down' to children – you will receive more mature responses if you offer mature models of discourse
- provide a wide variety of talk activities
- provide a comfortable and supportive environment where it is safe to 'take risks' with talk
- don't dominate the talk
- respect and show an interest in the children's home language whether it be dialect (e.g. Scouse) or another language (e.g. Spanish)

- involve the children in planning and discussion about their work
- consult the children about problems in the classroom or decisions which have to be made.

The role of the teacher

The teacher's attitude towards children is probably the single most significant factor in the ethos created in your classroom. The atmosphere and working values will be reflected by:

Your spoken language: *Which is better and why?*
a 'I was particularly impressed with the way Sean listened to Jason and helped him along by asking prompting questions when he got stuck'; *or*
b 'Sean was listening nicely, wasn't he, children!'

Your body language: *A child is having a problem with a maths activity. You want her to explain what she has done so far so that you can gain an understanding of her thinking strategies. Do you:*
a stand on the opposite side of the table facing her with your arms folded; *or*
b pull up a chair to sit alongside her at the same level?

Equal opportunities: *When you are working with the whole class on the carpet and they have their hands up to answer questions, do you:*
a ask the noisy wriggling boys to quieten them down; *or*
b make sure that everyone always has a fair chance?

Your listening skills: *When a child is explaining something do you:*
a jump in to prompt quickly if she seems to be stuck for words; *or*
b encourage by nodding, leaning forward, maintaining eye contact and leaving plenty of time for the child to think of what she needs to say?

Your questioning skills: *Ben is stuck with his story writing. Which of the following two questions might help Ben most and why?*
a 'How are you going to end your story, Ben?'
b 'How many different things might happen to your character, Ben, now that he is in the castle?

Your tuning-in skills! *When a child is talking, to what extent do you use information from what they say to formulate your next question? Alternatively, do you already have a set of questions prepared regardless of how the child responds?*

Your feeding-back skills: *Which of the following comments is most likely to influence the children's future work?*

a 'I liked the way that the Badger Group referred to each other as they were presenting their design. This really showed that they were working as a team and everyone knew what everyone else had to say.'

b 'Well done, Badger Group. That was a good presentation.'

The needs of the audience

Understanding the needs of an audience is a sophisticated type of knowledge but one of which children should be aware. Planning for the audience can help children to understand why in some situations it is necessary to change their own speech to standard English, or why they are working on dynamics of language such as speed, volume, intonation, pausing, providing opportunities to ask questions, and so on.

Talk across the curriculum

Different areas of the curriculum lend themselves to different modes of teaching on different occasions, and they all offer opportunities for talk. Figure 8.4 gives examples of some types of talk which might take place for each area of the curriculum. There are many more examples which you will be able to think of for yourself, but this is intended to get you started and raise your awareness of how oracy can be planned into activities which have another subject focus.

Talk topics in English

Discussions about language are an ongoing part of good classroom practice. While children are working on a mathematical problem-solving activity you might draw their attention to the language they are using. However, it is also important to plan specific English topics which are *about* speaking and listening: for example, learning about the role of talk, different types of talk, talk in the media (see Chapter 18), talk in the work place, and so on. The children should be involved in active language processes if they are to learn effectively, and should have opportunities to reflect on the language they are using if they are to learn *about* those processes.

Drama

Drama enables children to develop key oracy skills in meaningful and active contexts. It provides a vehicle for producing 'audiences' and different simulated talk situations within which children can use a wide range of talk for different purposes. There are many different forms which drama can take. These are covered in more detail in Chapter 17, which should be used as a guide for planning drama into your English schemes of work.

Learning about language

If children are capable of learning about historical, scientific and geographical issues then they are also capable of learning about language issues. They should be learning how to discuss and analyse language, as well as actually using it. Each of the three attainment targets includes a section called 'Standard English and Language Study'. This makes explicit the need to teach children about language.

Categories of speech

If you are going to teach language studies competently you must ensure that your own knowledge is wide enough. For instance, what is the difference between accent and dialect? How familiar are you with the following terms and why do you think it is important to distinguish between them?

- *accent*: the pronunciation of sounds; for example, 'bath' is pronounced 'barth' by some, 'baath', by others and 'bayth' by yet another group!
- *dialect*: regional features of grammatical construction (e.g. 'I never did nothing') and vocabulary (for example, snickett, jitty and ginnel are all names for a narrow alleyway)
- *standard English*: the central English dialect based on 'rule book grammar' as taught to foreign students on TEFL courses
- *received pronunciation (RP)*: the standard accent, traditionally spoken by BBC announcers
- *bilingual*: able to speak two languages
- *biliterate*: able to read and write two languages
- *multilingual*: able to speak more than two languages.

Vocabulary extension

Clearly, when you are considering vocabulary extension, some words will relate to work in other areas of the curriculum, some will relate to general knowledge, but some will also need to relate to language itself. A metalanguage is a language

Subject area	Context	Types of talk
Maths	In pairs: working out a shopping list for a family of four to last a week on a specified budget. All meals need to be planned and prices calculated from supermarket shopping price guide.	questioning suggesting planning speculating
Science	In fours: planning a health education campaign to encourage teenagers to care for their teeth. Information to Include the functions of teeth and the importance of dental care.	explaining retelling information presenting decision-making evaluating
Design and technology	In pairs: Compare and evaluate two vacuum cleaners which you have brought into the classroom for children to examine, test and report on.	comparing describing expressing views evaluating
Information and communications technology	In pairs: reorganise a story which you have typed into the computer in a muddled order.	ordering discussing decision-making evaluating
History	Whole class: observe, discuss and arrange into chronological order a set of lighting implements (e.g. candle, oil lamp, torch, electric lamp, gas light)	debating comparing describing justifying speculating
Geography	Whole class: role-play debate about the proposed building of a new out-of-town mall in a rural area. Pupils represent various groups.	presenting views giving evidence opinions disagreement summarising
Art	Individual: reflect on a painting they have completed and answer questions from the class.	describing evaluating answering questions
Music	In fours: listen to two contrasting pieces of music and discuss their differences.	describing comparing justifying expressing opinion
Physical education	In fours: one group at a time splits up to visit another group in order to instruct them how to perform a newly designed movement piece.	instructing describing answering questions feeding back
Religious education	Whole class: debate about crime and punishment.	reasoning speculation opinion

Figure 8.4 Talk across the curriculum

about language. Such a vocabulary enables you to discuss and analyse language at a range of levels. This can range from discussing gossip in the playground in Year 3 to comparing generalisations with hypotheses in Year 6. The lists included in Figure 8.5 are only a starting point. However, given that the lists are cumulative, in other words the words in Year 3 will continue to be used in Years 4, 5 and 6, and so on, they provide a sound base for developing a useful metalanguage which children can use regularly. The vital thing to remember is that we do not extend our vocabulary by merely being told what words mean. They have to be used repeatedly by the teacher and eventually by the children if they are to become firmly fixed.

Planning for progression

In order to build a classroom environment where it is common practice to talk about talk, it is necessary to plan for progression of learning. Figure 8.5 illustrates an example of how the focus on oracy might progress through the four Key Stage 2 years. It includes a topic focus for each year, and also a list of oracy vocabulary. It helps enormously to have such a list because if you are going to extend children's vocabulary you need to be absolutely clear which words you need to introduce, why you need to introduce them, and when this will take place.

Management and organisation

Children's motivation depends very much upon interest level, and they tend to stay on-task for longer if the activity is meaningful and enjoyable. However, good management is essential to the smooth running of even the most enjoyable activities, and this can be achieved by careful grouping, considered time management, appropriate resourcing and clear targets.

Groupings

The composition of a group can make an enormous difference to the dynamics. For instance, in a pair there is equal responsibility whereas in a trio it is possible to withdraw. Younger children tend to work more effectively in groups of four rather than six, and are less troubled by mixed-gender groups than older children. Mixed-ability groups can

result in a range of different skills and the less able learn from the more able (and sometimes vice versa!). Ability groups on the other hand help you to address differentiation more effectively. Bear in mind that groupings according to oracy ability might be very different from the groupings for writing or maths, and recognising this can have a positive effect on the self-esteem of children who are used to failing in other areas but who are good at talking.

It is fairly obvious that you can select groups of different sizes, and sometimes you will work with the whole class. Beware of creating working groups which are too large (even six is too large sometimes) for children whose oracy and social skills are not very far advanced. Perhaps more importantly, you need to develop a repertoire of 'devices' to ensure that the children stay on task. Here are some examples:

- After working in pairs ask the children to change partners and take turns reporting to their new partner what has just been discussed with the first partner.
- In trios, one child acts as observer, making notes on the performance of the other two, then gives feedback.
- Generic to expert groups: in a group where everyone has a different 'responsibility' (e.g. the illustrator, the editor, the marketing manager and the typesetter) they can be required to move into expert groups (i.e. all the editors together), perhaps for some specialist input from you. They then report back to their generic group.
- Asking for evidence of discussions (e.g. brainstorming list, tape, diagram) helps the children to stay focused and gives a clear goal.
- Asking groups to report back to the whole class also provides a target for the work. Using support resources such as an overhead projector or flip chart can help to make this task particularly appealing to children!
- Reporting to you also provides a focus, but you need to be time-specific (e.g. 'I'll come back in five minutes and will expect you to show me your three ideas').
- Asking the children to fill in a talk evaluation sheet gives the talk importance and can help them to focus their awareness on particular skills.

Timing

Too long on an activity can be a threat to productivity! Be realistic in your planning and never allow

YEAR 3	YEAR 4	YEAR 5	YEAR 6
Topic	**Topic**	**Topic**	**Topic**
Looking at the children's own language	Looking at other languages	Regional differences in Britain	Language in the world of work
Activity example	**Activity example**	**Activity example**	**Activity example**
After discussions about how we change our language according to whom we speak, role-play situations in pairs as: • friends in playground • parent and child • teacher and child Make tapes or perform. Discuss differences and possibly write scripts or draw cartoons as an extension.	Ideally using the mother tongue of pupils in the class, look at different foods and compare the names. Experiment with pronunciation. Compare with English. Make posters. Include a discussion about nouns. Shop role-play, asking for foods.	Look at three short TV clips of soap operas: • Coronation Street (Manchester) • East Enders (Cockney) • Brookside (Liverpool) Look at the areas on a map. Identify nouns which are local. Discuss the meaning of dialect and accent and introduce the concept of standard English as a dialect for specific purposes.	After a class discussion about the different types of language used by different professions ask the children to prepare a 'documentary' for the rest of the class about language in the work place. This should include examples of three different jobs, e.g. supermarket checkout, dentist and washing-machine repair engineer. Make sure each group works on different occupations. When the class watch the end products they should make notes on the features of each type of talk, e.g. specialist vocabulary, functions of talk such as questioning, explaining, etc.
Metalinguistic vocabulary for the year	**Metalinguistic vocabulary for the year**	**Metalinguistic vocabulary for the year**	**Metalinguistic vocabulary for the year**
slang chatty gossip communication discussion explanation instruction comparision noun verb	adjective adverb tone expression translation similarity pronunciation accent mother tongue bilingual	standard English dialect accent formal informal persuasive debate presentation regional diversity	sentence construction presentation vocabulary purpose interview generalisation speculation hypothesising body language metalanguage

Figure 8.5 Talk topics across Key Stage 2

too long. It is also worth considering 'chopping time up' into chunks. For example:

● five minutes' brainstorming
● you give brief feedback on their performance so far
● five minutes with a partner from another group to compare ideas
● return to groups and summarise onto a chart
● groups show charts to whole class.

In this way there is little time to become distracted.

Resources

Ensure that there are useful resources to support the talk. If children are going to talk they need something to talk about! This might include pictures, books for information, cue cards with situations or questions, etc. Chapter 7 includes a more detailed discussion of the different categories of resources.

Targets

Children should always have clear targets so that they know what is expected of them. These should relate closely to the time limits described above. For example:

- 'In five minutes I shall want to see your brainstorming webs.'
- 'I shall be watching this science group today to see how your listening skills are improving!'
- 'The presentation should only be three minutes long so here is an egg timer to keep a check. I am looking for quality rather than quality so you will need to keep reviewing and changing what you do so that you are constantly improving it.'

Assessment

The assessment of speaking and listening can seem a daunting task. The ephemeral quality of talk means that one minute it is here and then it is gone. However, don't forget that you can assess oracy during all curricular activities, and this maximises the chances available to record children's progress. It should be an ongoing part of everyday classroom practice, and there are a variety of ways in which it can be undertaken.

Unplanned observations: Making notes about unexpected incidents can build up into a useful bank of reference data. The file card system outlined in Chapter 7 is excellent for this.

Planned observations: These might be taped activities, or your observations of the children working on a specific task. You may or may not choose to tell the children what you are doing. Both ways serve useful purposes at different times. For example, if you say to a group: 'Now while you are planning your model I am going to watch you to see if you are taking turns, listening to others, and making sure that everyone pulls their weight! I want to see how good you are at holding a proper discussion', it becomes clear to them that the talk is important and that you have high expectations about their performance. On the other hand, there will be some occasions when you want to see how they perform without knowing that you are assessing them.

Interviews: these should be enjoyable occasions which provide children with a chance to experience individual quality listening time. You may want to ask them about how they are getting on with their work, where they would like more support from you, etc., or you might ask them to talk about a particular interest. It is probably best not to refer to these as interviews as this could seem quite threatening to some children. 'One-to-ones' is quite a user-friendly term, popularised by telephone advertising!

Peer assessments: In a trusting and open environment it is possible to ask children to assess their peers. Again this can be done in a variety of ways, such as observing then reporting ('fly on the wall game'), giving feedback in turn to partners, discussing everyone's performance after a group discussion, and so on.

Self-assessments: By reflecting on their own work in a context which is safe and supportive, children can develop critical skills which build constructively into their learning. They might report back orally or use an evaluation form.

Assessment questions

It can help your assessment procedures enormously if you have clear questions in your head during planned assessment. This helps you to be more objective about what you are observing and less influenced by other factors such as accent, personality or ability.

Examples of such questions include:

- Does the child wait her turn to speak?
- Does the child disagree and defend her arguments when necessary?
- How does the child support others when they are speaking?
- Does the child answer questions during whole-class discussions?
- Can the child switch to standard English for appropriate purposes?
- Can the child order her material logically during a presentation?
- Does the child speak clearly so that she can be understood?
- Can the child explain the meaning of accent and give examples?

Evidence

By developing clear assessment questions it

becomes simpler to collect the evidence. For example, during a presentation you might make notes on the order in which the child talks about her topic. These notes could be placed in her profile, perhaps along with a tape recording of the presentation. Collecting evidence helps us to be more objective. It is too easy, and not very useful, to make a hollow remark such as 'Emma spoke very well during the assembly'. It is much clearer to write something like: 'Emma read her poem aloud during assembly for the parents. She spoke loudly and slowly and could be heard by those sitting on the back row.' However, if you are building up such a store of precious information it is important to organise it in a way which is easily accessible and clearly communicated to others. The profiling approach is ideal for this.

The profiling approach to recording

A profile normally includes a wide range of different examples of evidence. Over a period of time a clear pattern of progress should be noticeable and this in itself can be a highly motivating factor for a child. An ongoing tape is ideal for this. Ideally a summate proforma should also give an overview of what the child has achieved in order to assess her current level of competence. The profile should be an open document which is available to parents, outside agencies and most importantly to the child herself. Looking at and talking about her profile can help to give the child a sense of progression and also raises the status of speaking and listening.

Informing your planning

As well as feeding back on what has gone before,

assessment should feed forward into what is needed next by your pupils. If we are to develop children's potential in an ongoing and rigorous way our assessments should be used to identify the needs at every stage of the way. Assessment and planning are part of the reflective cycle in which the good practitioner constantly acts upon her observations of her pupils in order to achieve the most appropriate levels of learning. An example of this could be where you have observed that a certain group are constantly interrupting each other and not listening to individual contributions. In response, you might talk to them about this and introduce an activity where a large shell is held by each speaker in turn. This could be followed by your asking them about the contributions made by their peers.

SUMMARY

In this chapter we have discussed how oracy continues to play an important part in children's learning at Key Stage 2. In addition to all the important and equally relevant points made in Chapter 7, we have examined how:

- older children should continue to be developing knowledge about oracy as well as learning and practising oracy skills

- this should be planned across the curriculum and be integrated into a continuous process

- discrete oracy activities are a statutory requirement of the National Curriculum for English at Key Stage 2, and should continue to be a part of your planning.

References

O'Keefe, V. (1995) *Speaking to Think. Thinking to Speak*, Heinemann

Further reading

Andrew, M. and Orme, D. (1997) *Curriculum Bank: Speaking and Listening Key Stage Two – Scottish Levels A-B*, Scholastic
    Key Stage 2 version of the book described in Chapter 7.
Holderness, J. and Lalljee, B.(1998) *Frameworks for Talk: An Introduction to Oracy*, Cassell

An excellent book which underpins practical ideas with sound theoretical bases. The chapters are organised helpfully into different themes; the drama chapter is particularly useful.

Norman, K. (1990) *Teaching, Talking and Learning in Key Stage Two*, NATE

Key Stage 2 version of the book described in Chapter 7.

See also Edwards (1995) and Fidge (1992), as described in Chapter 7.

9 Reading at Key Stage 1

OBJECTIVES

By the end of this chapter you should:

- understand the ingredients needed in order to read

- understand the importance of reading aloud to the class

- be able to plan and implement activities to develop a sight vocabulary

- be able to plan and implement activities for developing phonological awareness

- know how to diagnose and assess children's reading ability through hearing them read aloud

- understand the importance and role of parental support.

Introduction

The debate over the 'best' way to teach reading has rumbled, and occasionally erupted, ever since it was recognised as imperative that every child should learn to read. All teachers knew that children need to recognise words easily and rapidly in order to comprehend what a text is about; however there was considerable argument over whether this was best taught through teaching letters and their sounds or teaching children to recognise words on sight and as 'whole' units. It was not until the 1980s that these approaches were challenged; the central role of ensuring that children understood the purpose of reading was perceived as the vital ingredient and the skills of reading were seen to support this understanding rather than lead the way. What teachers were constantly saying was that they could teach a child to read but they could not ensure that the child remained a committed reader.

The importance of pre-school experiences

From 1870 to 1970 teachers in the reception class often assumed that children coming to school had roughly uniform experiences that would underpin the teaching of reading. However, the growth in numbers of children with reading difficulties and the obvious differences between children's ability to learn to read was highlighted during the 1980s and 1990s. The good pre-school literary experiences enjoyed by many children were recognised as the seed bed of reading.

As a result of these observations the School Curriculum and Assessment Authority (SCAA) published a list of 'Desirable Outcomes for Children's Learning on Entering Compulsory Education' (1997). These are described in Chapter 2. They now form the baseline which the teacher can use to assess what prior knowledge children have when they enter the reception year. It is essential that these pre-school experiences are offered to all children, and those who have not had them need to have time set aside to ensure that this knowledge is firmly in place.

What beginner readers need to know

It is now generally accepted that there are two main ingredients that will set children along the path to becoming readers.

1 Story knowledge

It is essential that children understand the purpose of reading, that they are provided with experiences in the classroom (and hopefully outside the classroom) that show them that reading is purposeful, meaningful, useful and enjoyable. Sharing stories with children and talking to them about the content is the easiest and most productive activity that both introduces children to print conventions and shows them the purpose of reading.

Activities to develop children's understanding of the purpose of reading
Establishing story knowledge through reading aloud to children

> The single most important activity for building the knowledge and skills eventually required for reading appears to be reading aloud to children.
>
> Marilyn Jager Adams (1990)

Teachers have long known that reading aloud to children plays an important role in preparing children for reading; however it is only recently that the real value of this activity has become recognised.

When teachers read aloud to the class they are promoting the following range of responses:

- By hearing a complete story children begin to assimilate story structure.
- Children begin to understand the written form of our language.
- Through talking about the story children begin to make connections between what they hear and their own life experiences.
- Children begin to assimilate the need for sequence and in turn begin to tell their own stories with more logic.
- Children begin to associate the words printed with the words as spoken.
- Through talking about the story children learn how to reflect upon events.
- Children hear how stories are read with intonation and expression.

Establishing story knowledge through discussion and debate
Children need to become inventors of stories and to respond to the characters and events in the stories they hear read to them. In return the teacher needs to encourage storytelling and retelling. Teachers, asking the children to predict what they think will happen, what they would do in the same situation and modelling the retelling of stories, help the children to place the purpose of reading firmly in their thinking. This ensures that when they are having to concentrate upon the decoding skills they retain the purpose behind these activi-

ties. This form of teaching now takes place in the initial reading time in the literacy hour, where the teacher shares a text with the whole class and is able to involve all the children in discussion and analysis.

2 Print knowledge

> Only if your ability to recognise and capture the meanings of words is rapid, effortless and automatic will you have available the cognitive energy and resources upon which comprehension depends.
>
> Marilyn Jager Adams (1990)

The acquisition of word recognition is vital to the beginning stages of reading. The work of Linnea Ehri and others has shown that this skill has developmental stages and that children need help in order to move through these stages.

Stage 1: Visual clue reading
The first evidence that children are aware of the importance of print often emerges when they look at a word in the environment and accurately pronounce what it says. However, it is unlikely that they are defining individual letters. What seems to happen is that the child memorises visual, contextual or graphic features of a word. Many children, long before they come to school, can confidently identify 'McDonald's' because the 'golden arches' of the letter 'M' and the context of the environment enable them to link this to the word. At this stage children rely solely upon such clues. They do not use letter-sound correspondence.

Activities to develop 'visual clue readers'
Text-level activities

- Use big books to read aloud to the class to model reading behaviour using both fiction and non-fiction texts. Show the children where you are starting to read, the direction of the print and the reading from top to bottom of the page.
- Encourage the children to learn by heart repeated phrases from the story and to join in the reading when these occur. For example: 'Run, run as fast as you can, you can't catch me, I'm the Gingerbread man.'

Sentence and word-level activities

- Point out the environmental print, notices on the classroom walls, alphabet friezes, labelled parts of the classroom. Ask the children to replace the labels in the correct places.

- Write notices for the classroom and talk to the children about what you are doing and why.
- Play rhyming games with the class. Ask them to tell you if you are saying rhyming words, e.g. frog, log, door, floor. Then ask the children to tell you the two words that rhyme from a selection of three, e.g. goat, coat, frog.
- Teach rhyming poems, songs and nursery rhymes. Ask the children which words rhyme.

Stage 2: The rudimentary alphabetic stage

Readers in this stage of development begin to use letter-sound correspondence to read words but they only process some of the letters and sounds in words. This is most commonly initial and final letter sounds. They can only guess at unfamiliar words from the context because these 'phonic cue' readers lack the sounding out and blending skills to accurately figure out unknown words. These readers are able to remember words far more accurately than the 'visual cue' readers because they are using a phonic cue system to support their memory. Knowing the alphabetic system greatly facilitates the task of finding and remembering relevant connections between the written words and their pronunciations.

Activities to develop children in the rudimentary alphabetic stage
Text-level activities

- Story knowledge: Continue to show and model pre-reading behaviours using big books.
- Read aloud story books and picture books. Ask the children to retell the story in sequence after they have heard it several times.

Sentence and word-level activities

- Sight word recognition: Write sentences for the children and say the words as you write them. Make a second sentence and cut up the words. Ask the children to match the words in the sentence and to say the words as they place them under the original sentence.
- Remove the sentence strip and shuffle the individual words. Place these face up on the table. Ask the children to tell you any word they can recognise. Finally ask them to find words that you select.
- Phonological awareness: Play rhyming games and alliteration sentences, e.g. Jane jumps just like a jelly. Freddie frog finds fish frightful.
- Teach initial letters of the alphabet. Select letters that can be clearly enunciated, e.g. vowels, and f h l

m n r s v w. Ask children to group pictures that start with the same sound or to find the odd one out from a tray of objects.
- Play 'Granny went to market and she bought …'. The children then have to think of something that starts with the chosen letter sound.
- Link handwriting formation and letter sounds together when teaching initial letter sounds.

Stage 3: Mature alphabetic stage

In this stage children have a much clearer idea of how the alphabetic system symbolises speech. They are able to sound out and blend unfamiliar words. They have an increasing sight vocabulary of high-frequency words. These words are those that are common to most texts and become stored in the memory. As the number of these words increases so children are more able to use context to help them predict unfamiliar words, and the fluency rate of the reading increases.

Activities to develop children in the mature alphabetic stage
Text-level activities

- Story knowledge: Continue to use 'big books' to show the children voice to word matching. Point out familiar words on the page and ask them to 'read' them with you or to you.
- Continue to read aloud fiction and non-fiction texts. Begin to demonstrate how to use non-fiction books. Show the children the contents page and talk about how it is used. Read aloud non-fiction texts and ask them to reflect upon the content. 'What did we Know? What do we Want to know? What have we Learnt?' (This is called the KWL approach as advocated by the National Literacy Strategy.)

Sentence and word-level activities

- Sight word recognition: Use environmental print displayed on the classroom walls and ask the children to 'read' the notices with you. Point out familiar words, for example 'the', 'a', 'Here', and ask the children to find other examples of these words in different notices.
- Write down a sentence that the child suggests using a highlighter pen or light-coloured crayon/pencil. Show the child how each word is represented and draw attention to the spaces between the words. Ask the child to go over the words in pencil. Finally cut up the sentence and see if the child can place the sentence into the correct order, and then shuffle the sentence and ask if the child can recognise any of the individual words.
- Encourage the child to write high-frequency core

words from memory. Start with simple single letter words 'I' 'a' and then select words that the child is reading in their reading book, e.g. 'the', 'said', 'come'.

- Phonological awareness: Continue to play rhyming games.
- Ensure the child knows all the initial letter sounds, plus the four main digraphs (*sh, ch, th, wh*)
- Move into teaching consonant clusters. Select from the following list as appropriate: *br, cr, fr, tr, bl, cl, gr, fl, sl, st, sc, sn, sm, sp, sw, dr, gl, pl, pr, tr*.
- Play 'Snap' using consonant clusters as the common denominator.
- Ask the child to pick up a picture card starting with the consonant cluster card that you show them. The child must first say the consonant cluster, e.g. *sl*, and then select a picture card, e.g. 'slug', 'sledge', 'sleeve'.

- Offer the child three words and ask them to tell you the words that start with the same consonant cluster, e.g. 'sleep', 'snail', 'slope'. Finally ask the child to tell you the consonant cluster that began the words.

Hearing children read

Every school should have a clearly stated policy on hearing children read. This should include how often the teacher is expected to listen to the children in the class and how the teacher is to record this reading.

Many teachers consider hearing children read as the most important component of good practice. However, it is now recognised that just hearing a

The following 12 words account for approximately 25 per cent of all the words we read:

a	and	he	I	in	is
it	of	that	the	to	was

The following 20 words account for about a further 10 per cent of all the words we read:

all	are	as	at	be	but
for	had	have	him	his	not
on	one	said	so	they	we
with	you				

The following 68 words account for another 20 per cent of all the words we read:

about	an	back	been	before	big
by	call	came	can	come	could
did	do	down	first	from	get
go	has	her	here	if	into
just	like	little	look	made	make
me	more	much	must	my	no
new	now	off	old	only	or
our	other	out	over	right	see
she	some	their	them	then	there
this	two	up	want	well	went
were	what	when	where	which	who
will	your				

Figure 9.1 The 100 most frequently used words

child read is not teaching the child to read. Time needs to be spent listening to a child read but this time must be used in a diagnostic way, and action that will help the child develop their reading should be as a direct result of the diagnosis undertaken while listening to them. This inevitably brings up the problem of how often the teacher can reasonably be expected to hear a child read in an individual session.

Research has now clearly shown (Southgate *et al.* 1981) that hearing children on a daily basis for two minutes at a time did not give the teacher a chance to assess or diagnose the child's strengths or weaknesses. It is far more productive to spend five to ten minutes listening to the child read once or twice a week. This problem has been addressed in the literacy hour with its emphasis upon 'Shared' and 'Guided' reading.

Shared reading

This is the term given to the time a teacher spends sharing a text with the whole class. In Key Stage 1 this is generally a big book, where all the children can see the text. The teacher uses this text to demonstrate and teach the conventions of print, discuss story content and highlight words, punctuation and spellings.

Guided reading

This is generally undertaken in small groups (usually six children). The groups are selected according to reading development and the teacher uses this time to support and encourage the development of reading strategies appropriate to the needs of the group. Each member of the group has an identical text and the group are asked to read the text at their own pace. The teacher observes and aids children as they read and often discusses a common problem with the group after they have all finished reading. Although teachers may hear individual children read aloud during the day, the 'guided' reading time is perceived as the main time set aside for the specific teaching of reading.

When children are first introduced to a book with the teacher it is essential that they understand what the story is about. Many teachers read the story to the children and then encourage them to join in. As most beginning reading books have

simple repeated text it is possible for the readers to 'know by heart' the text. At this stage they should be consolidating the skills of voice to word matching and reading from left to right. In order to turn the memory of the words into recognition of those words it is essential that the follow-up work should offer activities which link the reading to writing and which encourage the readers to learn the individual words (see 'Sight word recognition' activities on page 86).

Getting going with books

As children take over complete responsibility for a text it is quite usual for them to concentrate so hard upon the decoding that they lose the story. It is essential that children are not given books that are too difficult for them. It is suggested that a child needs a text which is 95 per cent known and which then enables the child to decode the remaining 5 per cent. This proportion ensures that the meaning of the text is retained and the decoding does not overwhelm the story. The teacher needs to observe and record those aspects of the text which cause any problems and to devise activities to help the reader overcome these problems. In the literacy hour this form of diagnosis and remediation takes place in the 'guided' reading time.

Taking a running record

Teachers may diagnose a child's problems just by listening to them read, but a more permanent record does need to be undertaken once or twice during a term. This can take the form of a running record.

- Tick every word correctly identified.
- Put a letter 'T' over any word you have to tell the child.
- Put the letter 'O' over any word omitted.
- Write 'sc' over any text that was self-corrected.
- Write 'PH' over any word that was phonically decoded.
- Write 'S' when a substitution is syntactically sensible.
- Write 'C' when child offers a contextual substitution.

Action and diagnosis for common errors

See Figure 9.2.

Diagnosis	Action
1 Limited sight vocabulary	• Find an easier book • Look for texts with repetition • Play sight word games • Present child's sentence in 'own book'
2 Over-dependent on 'sounding out'	• Play sight word games • Let child find sight words in newspapers
3 Waits for teacher to read word	• Check and teach letter sounds • Tell child to re-read sentence from beginning and predict word • Ask child to read on and think what word should be written
4 Limited phonic knowledge	• Play rhyming games • Teach onset and rime • Teach all letter sounds/digraphs/consonant clusters
5 Not reading for meaning	• Talk about story before reading • Read with child before encouraging them to read alone • Offer sequencing activities • Encourage group reading and discussion
6 Ignores punctuation	• Draw attention to punctuation in big books • Ensure child reads in group and 'hears' punctuation • Undertake 'group writing' and stress place of punctuation
7 Slow, robotic read	• Prepare the story beforehand • Encourage child to read easy books to younger children • Let child practise reading to younger children
8 Fails to use picture clues	• Share pictures before reading • Point out how pictures support text • Cover noun and ask child to look at the picture for a clue
9 Over-uses picture clues	• Play snap with word and picture noun cards • Read text to child and ask for suggestions for next word • Stop child guessing too frequently and draw attention to word written • Check child is using more than first letter clue
10 Guesses wildly	• Talk through story before reading • Provide easier text with repetition • Provide opportunities for reading with partner • Provide group reading sessions • Play sight word games • Check phonic knowledge

Figure 9.2 Action and diagnosis for common errors

Taking off with reading

The more children read the more they learn to read. As they acquire a large sight vocabulary and become more confident with ways to decode words they do not recognise, they become more engrossed with books and suddenly find they do not need to say the words aloud. It is very easy to think that when this occurs it is unnecessary to spend so much time with the reader. The danger is that children's decoding skills may outstrip their understanding, and without discussion and reflec-

tion undertaken with either an adult or a peer there is a chance that the child will select more and more difficult books and be content to say the words in their head without worrying about what they mean.

Suggestions for discussion prompts

The following questions can help the children to reflect upon what they have read.

Which part of the story did you like best?

What would you have done if you had … ?

Did you find anything sad or funny in the story?

Would you like to read another book about these characters/by this author?

Could this story have really happened?

Who would you have liked to have as a friend in this story?

Who would you not like to meet?

Who do you think would enjoy reading this story?

If this book did not have pictures would you still like it?

Why do you think this book is called … ?

What do you think would happen if… . ?

Keeping reading records

Schools tend to vary considerably as to how they keep careful records about a child's reading progress.

However, all school records should clearly indicate the titles that the child has read, any problems that the child has encountered and what action the teacher would like to be undertaken as a result of this diagnosis. Many schools also have a 'Home–school' book in which they encourage the carer and the child to comment (see Figures 9.3 and 9.4).

Date	Book Title, Author and Genre	Strategies including knowledge about Language and Study Skills — Response – personal, critical	Summary of Development Forward Planning
7/4 10/4 18/4	Bulls-Eye! Pip and the Little Monkey ORT sparrows Adam goes shopping ORT. The Grumble goes for a walk.	Page 14 needed some support, new words in green book. she has read this book before but she said it was new to her. Read well – obviously needed this familiar book for confidence. We discussed how to work out unknown words – a combination of looking at initial sounds / pictures / sense. (She did not know 'th' sound) This is easy – aim to build confidence – try more challenging texts next week. Could discuss and predict well.	Aim to build confidence in her own ability – make it a positive experience. • Not too challenging texts – storywords? • Systematic revision of phonics – initial sounds / consonant clusters.

Figure 9.3 Sample of school reading record

Date	Book Title, Author and type of reading material	Response and comments
13/3	The Little Red Hen,	Read extremely well, very enthusiastic about this story. Only had trouble with the word "threshed". Enjoyed and understood what the moral of the story was – well done! JV
14/3	John Brown, Rose and the midnight cat.	15.3. Read well, stuck on a few words. Enjoyed the story. JV

Figure 9.4 Sample of home–school reading record

Assessing reading

The Standard Assessment Tasks at the end of Key Stage 1 (Year 2)

Standard Assessment Tasks (SATs) for Reading take place in the summer term at the end of Key Stage 1. There are very clear guidelines provided by the DfEE on the administration and form of this assessment. (See Chapter 6 for more information about the SATs for Reading.)

Reading Level 1: Children are asked to look at specified books, to select one and to comment on their choice. They should recognise some letters in the title and be able to say how many words are in the title. The teacher reads the book to the child and the child reads independently wherever possible.

Reading Level 2: The child is offered a selection of titles and chooses one of them to read aloud. The teacher starts the reading but the child reads independently at a specified point. The teacher then takes a running record of this section and marks any errors or attempts. The teacher notes the overall independence and accuracy of the reading and assesses pace, fluency and expression in the reading aloud.

A group written comprehension task is also undertaken. The children are asked to answer questions which are set on each page of the story.

Reading Level 3: If the teacher thinks the child is showing considerable confidence with their reading then they can be entered for Level 3. This is a comprehension booklet with more difficult text and the questions are set at the end of the story and the non-fiction text.

Organising and displaying reading resources

The organisation of reading resources can vary between schools and even between classes within a school. The way a school displays and organises its books should be clearly stated in the school policy document. Many schools provide a 'book corner' in the classroom and have carpet and cushions for the children to sit on while they browse or read from the resources displayed.

Some smaller schools have a central resource to which all children have access as this provides a wider range of choice rather than sharing the resources between classes. Whatever the way it is essential that all teachers and children understand how the resources are organised and how to help children make the best choice from these resources.

If children are to become independent readers who are able to make informed and appropriate choices then they need access to as wide a range of material as possible. This should include not only fiction and non-fiction but also magazines, comics, catalogues, dictionaries and reference books.

There is no obvious right or wrong way to organise early reading books but the following questions should be taken into consideration.

Questions to consider about book organisation

- Does the organisation of the books help the children to make good choices?
- Does any very obvious grading on the books cause anxiety to either the child or the parent?
- Does the grading encourage a competitive attitude to the books or help children to choose more easily?
- Are the books displayed at a height that small children can manage?
- Is there a range of books that will suit all readers?
- Can the books be easily returned to the correct place?
- Is the area where children can sit and browse comfortable and inviting?
- Are there taped stories for children to listen to?
- Is there a range of illustration within the book selection?

Encouraging children to become responsible for keeping the book corner and shelves in order also ensures that children become familiar with the range of resources in the classroom or school.

The role of parents

Teachers should take account of the important link between home and school and actively encourage parents to participate and share in their child's reading.
DES/Welsh Office, *English in the National Curriculum*
(1989)

Parents have a legal right to be involved with their child's education, and now it is acknowledged that they can play an important role in supporting their child with reading. Schools have been encouraged to have a clear policy on the way in which they wish parents to support their work. What works in one school might be inappropriate in another. However, where schools and parents do work together the results are happier children, parents and teachers.

In order to ensure that the parents/carers support the school policy, clear guidelines need to be produced so that both teachers and parents work together. The following questions could form the basis for these guidelines.

- How long should the parent spend listening to their child read?
- What should they do if the child cannot read a word?
- What should they do if the child refuses to read to them?
- Are they expected to hear every book that is sent home?
- What should they do if the child has already had the book?
- What should they do if the child says they do not like the story?
- How can they help if they are uncertain about hearing their child read?

- How often is the child allowed to change their book?
- Are they allowed to choose a book to read with the child?
- What should they do if they think the book is too hard or too easy for their child?

Parents and carers are probably the most valuable resource that a school can call upon, but they do need help and encouragement provided on a regular basis.

SUMMARY

This chapter has discussed:

- what beginner readers need to know
- ways of hearing children read
- the standardised assessment at the end of Key Stage 1
- the importance of parents.

Reference

Southgate, V., Arnold, H. and Johnson, S. (1981) *Extending Beginning Reading*, Heinemann

Further reading

Adams, M. J. (1990) *Beginning to Read: The New Phonics in Context*, Heinemann
This book offers a precise review of the research about the teaching of phonics. The author places phonics within the field of learning to read but recognises that it is only a part of the reading process.
Browne, Ann (1996) *Developing Language and Literacy 3–8*, Paul Chapman
This is a very useful overview of the teaching of reading. It is a practical and comprehensive guide to teaching and learning in the early years.
Clark, Margaret (1994) *Young Literacy Learners and How We Can Help Them*, Scholastic
This book provides a useful overview of the teaching of reading. The author describes how recent thinking has changed the approaches to the teaching of reading and how the best innovations can be used to meet the requirements of the National Curriculum.
Roberts, Geoffrey (1994) *Learning to Teach Reading*, Simon and Schuster Education
This is a very readable text. It outlines the main processes and approaches to reading, clearly defines the link between reading and writing and suggests basic principles upon which the teaching of reading rests.

10 Reading at Key Stage 2

OBJECTIVES

By the end of this chapter you should:

- be able to help children to become fluent and committed readers
- understand the demands of reading non-fiction
- understand how to help children to read poetry
- monitor and assess reading development
- promote the ongoing partnership with parents.

Introduction

By the age of seven most children have made a promising start with reading. Their early years experiences will have provided them with a basic knowledge of the conventions of print, they should be able to tell the difference between stories and information texts and they should have a basic knowledge of many sight words and be able to use letter sounds effectively. Above all the early years curriculum will have introduced them to the pleasure of reading. Although all children will have made progress throughout the early years there is likely to be a wide range of differing abilities and enthusiasm by the time they reach the end of Key Stage 1.

The range of reading ability

Some children will enter Year 3 avid readers who always seem to have their nose in a book. These children seize every opportunity to read, they talk about what they are reading and often have a list of books that they intend to read. These children frequently visit the public or school library and choose books suited to their needs. Such children appear to need very little support from the teacher, but these characteristics can easily decline if they are not nurtured by the teacher and supported by parents. A common failure is to forget to praise these children or to keep a watchful eye on them and ensure that they read a wide variety of both fiction and non-fiction.

Other children are able readers but they need encouragement and support with their choice of reading and many opportunities to discuss what they have read. These children often perceive success to lie in attempting thick and difficult books, and they are more concerned with their 'image' as a reader than with gaining pleasure from what they read. They need careful observation and record-keeping to ensure that they are provided with suitable texts that they can read with ease and which they want to share with their peers.

Some children enter Key Stage 2 uncertain about the reading process. Some of these children will need specialist help and they still need all the experiences given to children in Key Stage 1. (See Chapter 9.) Other children have made a tentative start with reading but they are unable to decode many of the words in the books they are reading with any speed or fluency. They often consider themselves poor readers and they derive very little pleasure from their reading. These children need texts that they can manage with 95 per cent accuracy and which offer them a satisfying experience. Some books have been published with a lower reading age but a higher interest age, and these texts are often more suitable for these children, who then begin to change their self-image if they realise that they are successful and that reading is both pleasurable and worthwhile. The teacher needs to treat these children in the same way as those more able readers rather than singling them out for extra 'practice' in reading aloud. These children must be offered achievable goals and lots of praise when they reach them. They need to browse in book corners, talk about what they have read, join in group reading and be shown that they are making progress so that they come to believe they will be readers.

All children whatever their ability deserve the best resources a school or school library can provide. They need experiences with books that are both challenging and satisfying. They need constant and genuine praise and plenty of opportunities to talk about what they have read so that they become critical and committed readers.

Reading fiction at Key Stage 2

The National Curriculum (1995) requires that children at Key Stage 2 'should be encouraged to respond imaginatively to the plot, characters, ideas, vocabulary and organisation of language in literature'.

For many children entering Key Stage 2 this seems an impossible experience to give them. Their reading skills are not quite ready to move away from decoding and understanding a simple story line; however, the teacher can read aloud texts to the class which provide all the children with stories which capture their imagination and which are rich in language, irony and characters and contain more complex plots.

The introduction of the literacy hour has provided a very clear list of literacy ingredients that children are expected to have received during their primary schooling. An 'hour a day' has to be set aside for the specific teaching of reading and writing. The division of the hour into different sections is entirely at the discretion of the teacher, but guidelines are provided and many schools will use the model described in Chapter 1.

Developing reading through reading aloud to the class

Reading aloud to the class may take place at a convenient time during the day or be part of the literacy hour. Whatever is chosen, time needs to be set aside to model for children both how to read a text aloud and how to interrogate the text.

By sharing a worthwhile text with the whole class and ensuring that there is time to discuss the story with the children, a teacher is able to model for all the children the way competent readers respond when they read for themselves. Children need to see that as we read we reflect upon what has happened, question what might be about to happen and often link this to experiences or concerns in our own lives.

Through this kind of 'running commentary' we deepen our understanding of the text and this in turn prepares us for reading the next book. The more we bring to a text the more we are likely to get from it. In the same way children need to become critical readers who reflect, predict and relate to a text.

Activities for reading aloud to the class
Text-level activities
Many of the activities will involve the teacher asking the children about the story – to look at the development of a character through the story and to discuss with the class how the plot is unfolding. Before embarking on reading aloud to the class it is important that the teacher reads the story first and devises questions that will encourage the children to make predictions which are based upon what they have heard, questions that ask them to reflect upon the story and to make links with their own experiences or to other books that they have read.

Examples of open-ended questions
- What kind of a book did you think this was going to be?
- Could the story have really happened?
- Were there any parts you particularly liked/disliked?
- What would happen if the order of events was changed?
- Can you think of a different ending to this story?
- Which character did you like the most/least?
- Who are the most active characters in the story?
- Does this book remind you of any other story or film you have heard or read?
- Do you feel the same about the character now as you did at the beginning of the story?
- Who would you give this book to?

Sentence and word-level activities
From this broad discussion it is possible to move to sentence and word-level work; for example, you might ask the children: 'What punctuation made you read the text in a certain way?' 'Did the author literally mean what was written or was the author using irony to help the reader respond to the situation?' As children become more secure in looking at the sentence levels of texts it is possible to start to show them how we understand what kind of story we are reading through the language used by the author. For example, how did we know this was a mystery story? What language did the author use that enables us to deduce that we were reading a specific genre? Children need to be able to recognise these features in text shared with them before they can start to include this in their own writing.

Finally, they could discuss why the author has chosen certain specific vocabulary, or look, for example, at compound words or verb tenses.

Criteria for choosing books to read aloud

- How long will it take to read the book to the class?
- Does the book raise any issues you wish to discuss?
- Does the book link with an ongoing topic?
- Is the book by an author you wish to introduce to the class?
- Is the book acceptable to both boys and girls?

Useful authors for Key Stage 2

Most authors write in many different genres and across many age ranges. The following is a short list of outstanding authors and an indication of the genre with which they are generally associated.

Allan Ahlberg	fantasy stories
Joan Aiken	myths and legends
Bernard Ashley	modern realistic stories, often set in a school or urban setting
Nina Bawden	modern realistic stories, often set in the countryside
Gillian Cross	modern mystery adventures
Anne Fine	modern stories which raise strong issues
Nickolas Fisk	science-fiction
Jamilla Gavin	multicultural settings and characters
Dick King Smith	humorous animal stories which raise issues
Penelope Lively	historical
Margaret Mahy	supernatural stories
Jan Mark	humorous modern stories
Michael Morpurgo	mystery and adventure, often set in other countries
Jill Paton Walsh	historical
Rosemary Sutcliff	historical
Robert Swindells	modern adventure stories

Classic stories

Frances Hodgson Burnett	*The Secret Garden*
Lewis Carroll	*Alice in Wonderland*
Kenneth Grahame	*The Wind in the Willows*
A.A. Milne	*Winnie the Pooh*
Mary Norton	*The Borrowers*
Selina Hastings	A selection from *The Canterbury Tales*
Charles Dickens	*The Christmas Carol*
Leon Garfield	*Shakespeare Stories, Animated Shakespeare Tales*
Jonathan Swift	*Gulliver's Travels*, adapted by Victor Ambrus

Developing reading through 'guided reading'

It is now recognised that when children work in groups they enhance their own knowledge and comprehension. Group work fell into disrepute because although children were sitting in groups they were undertaking individual activities and perceived these to be in competition with their peers.

In order to give children opportunities to discuss and reflect upon texts teachers have found it productive to ensure that all children experience 'guided reading'. Groups of up to six children are provided with a common text which they read to themselves in the group. The teacher may punctuate this reading by asking the children to predict what might happen or to discuss a common reading problem or an issue, or by looking at specific vocabulary. The group are generally chosen by ability and this guided reading takes place in the literacy hour.

The importance of guided reading

- It enables children to discuss a book in more detail.
- It encourages children to share interpretations and through this to deepen their understanding.
- It encourages children to talk about characters and plot.
- It enables the teacher to 'hear' more children read aloud.
- In talking about a book with others children come to absorb book language, e.g. 'I liked the ending', 'I liked the style …'.
- It is possible for weaker readers to be part of a mixed-ability group and to hear how other children read aloud and interpret texts.
- It allows children with similar interests to share a read that reflects those interests.

Activities for guided group reading
Text-level activities

Provide the children with a set of questions which encourage both prediction and reflection. These will be very similar to those asked by the teacher when talking with the whole class (see p. 94).

Sentence and word-level activities

- Ask the group to select a part of the story that has considerable dialogue and to discuss the use of punctuation. Ask them to find examples of different kinds of punctuation and to explain why these were used.

- Remind the group about the different parts of speech and ask them to find ten (nouns, verbs, adverbs, adjectives) and see if they can think of alternative words which either retain the sense of the sentence or change the meaning of the sentence.
- Select a spelling pattern from some of the words used in the story and ask the group to skim through the book and collect as many words as possible that contain this pattern, for example *-ight*, *-ough*, *-ious*.
- Ask the group to collect groups of words, for example 'verbs used instead of said'. They should skim through the book and see how many different verbs they can find and list these.
- Ask the group to find ten words that they think might be difficult for younger readers to understand. Ask them to try to devise a definition to help younger children and then to check their definitions against a dictionary.

Developing reading through individual reading

Most reading that children do is individual. Those children that are hooked on books will take every opportunity to find time to read either at home or in school time, but others need encouragement to settle with books and to be given sufficient uninterrupted time so that they can really get into the story. Silent reading times endeavoured to provide this, but few teachers could really claim that this time was used very effectively. In order for children to either become or remain readers we need to ensure that they are provided with books for individual reading which they can read without too much of a challenge and which fire their imagination.

Organising books in the book corner or library

Many schools have tried to grade the books in their classrooms in order to help the children to select books that are within their reading ability. They may do this by putting a coloured sticker on the cover or by marking the books in some way. The problem with this is that parents and children often wish to get to the top level without reading for pleasure. They believe that they must be seen to be a good reader, and conversely the poor readers become even more aware of their own lack of ability because they are on a low level. There is no easy solution to the problem of ensuring that children select a book at an appropriate level. How-ever, teachers have found that most children are quite capable of selecting books that suit their needs so long as adults are not trying to force the pace! Children are more likely to choose a book that is within their grasp or even easy for them than to deliberately select something far too hard. For individual reading, easier texts enable children to practise their reading skills. If this activity is balanced with challenging guided reading and discussion then children make good progress and enjoy the activity.

Ensuring a range of genres in private reading

Some children (and adults) find an author or a genre that they really enjoy, and read all the titles by that author or look for books from the one genre. Although this is quite acceptable out of school, within school hours we need to try to ensure that children attempt different kinds of texts and become familiar with the features of the different kinds of texts so that they can turn with ease to the demands of the various forms. Some schools have tried to raise awareness about genre by organising their stock of fiction titles according to genre bands. They have then asked children to ensure that they select from the different fiction genres and keep a record, not only of the title of the book that the child is reading but also into what main genre category the book falls. Keeping a chart of the different reading experiences is very important. It is all too easy to think that the child who reads lots of books and who is obviously engrossed in a book is receiving all the necessary experiences that will enable them to succeed with all types of texts. This is unfortunately not the case.

Reading non-fiction at Key Stage 2

Most people will read far more non-fiction texts during their lifetime than fiction. Historically it was assumed that if children could read fiction well then they would also be able to read non-fiction texts, and little attention was given to showing children how to read non-fiction texts.

Fiction, marvellous as it is as an art form, is poor training for reading non-narrative. The story carries the reader along and stimulates the understanding of a text without too much

conscious effort. When those pupil readers hit a text explaining facts or arguments they expect the same thing to work and are disappointed and baffled when it does not.

(Marland 1981)

We need to model for children how to read non-fiction texts just as often as we model reading stories aloud. Non-fiction requires a broken and reflective read. As adults we select the appropriate chapter or page that we hope will give us the information we seek. We then read the passage and reflect upon the new knowledge it has provided. We may then decide that we should continue to read on or realise that the text is not providing what we sought. We might then skim through the rest of the section to confirm this analysis and possibly see something we wanted to know, or we might turn to the index and try to find other references. Reading non-fiction is rarely undertaken by reading from the beginning to the end of a book. If we want children to learn how to read non-fiction then we must make non-fiction part of our reading aloud sessions and we must make plain what, why and how we are reading.

What skills are needed for reading non-fiction?

Children need to be able to find the appropriate section, chapter or pages that will answer their question when looking at non-fiction texts. They need to see when it is appropriate to skim through the chapter headings and when it is more useful to turn to the index. In order to use an index effectively they need to know alphabet order. They also need to try to think of the different headings that the author may have used in the index. For example, it might be of little use to look up 'Gladiators' in a general book about the Romans, but the information they seek might come under 'Games' or 'Pastimes' or even 'Christian slaves'.

Having found the appropriate pages the children need to understand the relative importance of the main heading to subheadings. They need to become confident with the different typographical devices used by the author: for example, what the author is trying to indicate by the use of italics or bold print. Readers also need to recognise the importance of the charts and diagrams. A picture may be glanced at but a graph or chart is integral to the information and needs to be interpreted carefully.

Activities to help children become familiar with non-fiction textual devices

The following activities are suited to the whole class.

Text-level activities

- Read aloud short sections of non-fiction text to the class. Explain why you have chosen the passage and how to read the text. Give a running commentary as you read, pointing out the parts of the information that you already knew and reflecting upon the information that is new.
- Give the class a topic and ask them to tell you what they already know about the topic. Then ask the children to help you compose five questions about things they would like to know. Write the questions on the board and demonstrate how you would select appropriate books and how you would access the information through the contents and index pages.

Sentence and word-level activities

- Write a question on the board. Read the contents page out loud and ask if any of the chapters sound as if they might answer the question.
- Use a big book and show the children the different headings and layout of the page. Talk to them about how this helps the reader. Explain the use of italics and bold.
- Use a big book to demonstrate the different charts and graphs. Explain how these displays help the reader to gain information at a glance. Show how easy it is to compare and contrast information through diagrams.

The following activities are more suited to small groups of children.

Text-level activities

- Give each group a non-fiction book. Ask the group to evaluate the presentation of a text. They should award marks for overall presentation, the clarity of the contents and index pages, the use of headings and side headings, and the glossary. Ask each group to tell the rest of the class their conclusions.
- Give each group a different aspect of a given topic to research. They should start by making a list of the relevant pages in the different books by using the contents and index pages. Explain that they must decide how to relay the information they find to the rest of the class. They could do this through charts, notes, a lecture, etc.
- Provide each group with a set of questions and ask them to see how quickly they can scan and skim

through the books to find the answers.

- Provide information in written form and ask the group to decide what graphic form would enable the reader to gain the information more quickly. For example, you might write a short passage describing how the children in the class get to school. This could then be converted into a Venn diagram which would be a much faster way of gaining the information.

Developing the reading of poetry

At its best, poetry helps children to become vigorous, adventurous and graceful users of words.
Jack Ousby (1988)

In order for children to become confident readers of poetry it is essential that poetry becomes a central and regular part of classroom reading activities. Many children find reading poetry hard because of the demands made upon the reader to pay particular attention to punctuation, pauses, rhymes and metaphor. The teacher needs to demonstrate how to read the different poetic forms by reading poetry aloud to the class and following this up by telling the children how she knew how to read the verses. Children need to revisit poems many times and to learn some by heart. As they become more familiar with the different forms of poetry so they will become more confident readers of poetry. Ted Hughes (1963) wrote: 'What matters most, since we are listening to poetry and not prose, is that we hear the song and the dance in the words.'

If we want children to enjoy both reading and listening to poetry then it must be provided on a regular basis and it is essential that the teacher shares her enthusiasm with the class. It is rare that a poem receives immediate understanding and appreciation. Children need to hear the poem several times and the teacher needs to tell the children both why the poem was selected and how the poem works for her. Careful planning is essential if poetry is to play more than a peripheral part in the primary curriculum.

Just as children need to read from a wide range of genres so they also need to be introduced to the many different forms of poetry. In order to ensure that children have access to the various forms it is important that many different kinds of poems are

found in the book corner and on the library shelves. There are collections of stimulus poems, experience poems, pattern poems, narrative poems, humorous poems, family poems, animal poems, war poems, old poems and new poems, general collections of poems some of which are set round a theme while others are a personal collection selected for different age ranges. There are poems that rhyme and poems that don't rhyme. The list is endless but if the teacher enjoys poetry and allows children to return to the poems again and again then she will be providing the best environment that will ensure a love of poetry by the children in her class.

Activities for developing the reading of poetry
Text-level activities

- Read a poem to the class through twice. Talk to the class about the poem and why you selected it. Ask the children to say what they think about the poem. Read the poem again and if the poem is suitable ask the children to join in with any part they can remember.
- Read a poem to the class once. Read it again but this time leave gaps in the reading. Ask the children to try to provide the missing word. Discuss with the class when their words are appropriate or not appropriate. Talk about rhyme and rhythm if appropriate.
- Make a poetry display. Ask each child in the class to select their favourite poem and to write this on to A4 paper. They may illustrate it with either a border or a picture. Display these poems on the classroom wall.
- Show the class a collection of poetry books and make a list of their titles. Ask the children why they think the title was chosen. Let the children work in pairs and look at a different book each and see if they can decide why the poet chose the title.
- Show the children that poetry is often indexed by title and first line. Discuss why the first line is helpful in identifying a poem. Discuss how much the first line of a poem makes you want to continue reading the whole poem. Ask the children to work with a partner and find an opening line to share with the class that they found interesting.
- Read a poem to the class and omit the title. Ask the children to suggest titles. Write the titles on the board and discuss why they thought of the titles. Finally disclose the author's title and discuss why they think this was chosen.
- Find a poem with either a story line or a definite sequence. Cut up the verses and give them to the group. Ask them to decide on the order of the

verses. Show them the author's order when they have made their final selection.

Sentence and word-level activities

- Provide a group with a poem in which you have deleted some words. Ask the group to suggest words to fill the gaps. Finally ask each group to read out their poem and ask the rest of the class if they think the 'new' words work.
- Give a copy of a poem to the group and ask them to select the ten most interesting words used by the poet.
- Ask the children to each select a poem that they enjoy. Suggest that they make a word collage from their favourite poem and display this on the wall.
- Ask the group to read a poem and then to make a list of the feelings they had when reading the poem.
- Select an appropriate poem and discuss with the group the use of simile in the poem. Suggest they then try to write in the same style as the poet. For example, 'Shall I compare thee to a summer's day?' (William Shakespeare) could be changed to 'Shall I compare you to a football match?'.

Monitoring and assessing reading

Effective teaching depends on the cycle of assessment – diagnosis – remediation – assessment. (See also Chapter 6 for further information on this process.)

Why assess reading?

- To assess the effectiveness of teaching
- To attempt to diagnose children's difficulties
- To identify children with reading difficulties
- To monitor children's mastery of specific reading skills

In order to ensure that we offer children the best teaching suited to their needs it is essential that the teacher keeps accurate and informative records of a child's progress and regularly assesses the progress that the child is making. This information should be built upon previous records and information and should lead to a planned programme of activities to ensure progress. This is turn needs to be assessed for its effectiveness, and so the cycle of assessment goes on throughout the children's education.

As children become silent and fluent readers it becomes increasingly difficult for the teacher to easily monitor the reading progress of the children

in her class. There are three main types of reading assessment:

1 norm-referenced tests
2 criterion-referenced tests
3 informal assessment.

Norm-referenced tests

These tests compare children with the norm. The reason for these tests is to demonstrate the differences between children, and the results of these tests are often expressed as 'reading ages'. These tests may help schools to see how their pupils compare to others in the country but they provide very little information that will inform teaching. It is very possible that two children could have the same result on these tests but have a very different attitude to and enthusiasm for reading. Such tests tell you who is better than whom but only rarely what they are good at. The most famous of these tests is the Schonell reading test, which is a list of words graded in difficulty which the child is asked to read aloud. Many children may be able to read this line of words: 'physics, campaign, choir, intercede, fascinate' and receive a reading age of 9 years 11 months, but no check is required to see if they understand these words!

Examples of popular norm-referenced tests

Salford Sentence Test (1976) Hodder and Stoughton
Primary Reading Test (France) (1979) NFER
Suffolk Reading Scale (1987) NFER

Criterion-referenced tests

These tests compile information on children's specific ability to succeed at a specific set of skills. The criterion is set and the results show how far the child has attained the skill. This kind of assessment reflects more closely the development of literacy and it is incorporated in the level descriptions in the National Curriculum.

Example of popular criterion-referenced tests

Edinburgh Reading Tests (1977, Hodder and Stoughton) are a battery of tests starting with word recognition and progressing through completing gaps, sentence and word order, speed-reading passage and comprehension questions.

Some tests are both norm-referenced and criterion-referenced. This means the score can be compared with a criterion level and it can be compared with a set of norms.

Informal tests

These tests include checklists, running records (such as those used for assessment at Key Stage 1), monitoring and observation. This kind of assessment can appear to be time consuming and it lacks the spurious authority of the statistical evidence of other tests, but it can offer the most informative type of assessment because it is closely linked to classroom practice. Such tests can reflect the way children have been taught, and consequently the pattern of teaching/learning/assessment can be drawn together. Probably the most informative of the informal tests is Miscue Analysis or Running Records (see Chapter 9). Here the teacher listens to the mistakes a child is making when reading aloud. From this sensitive observation a teacher can determine what reading strategies a child is using and plan the teaching using this knowledge. As children become generally silent readers it is possible for a teacher to gain this insight when listening to a group of children reading aloud (see pp. 95–6).

The national assessment of reading at Key Stage 2

If teachers assess children as unlikely to achieve Level 3 in the Key Stage 2 Standard Assessment Tasks then these children are assessed in the same format as for Key Stage 1 (see Chapter 9, p. 91).

If children are expected to achieve a Level 3, 4 or 5 then they are given a booklet of readings which may contain all or some of the following: a short story or story extract; a non-fiction text; a poem; an advertisement. An answer booklet is provided and the skills assessed are: understanding through the retrieval of specific words or retrieval of explicitly stated information; features of the texts such as plot, character, the effects of the choice of words, the layout and organisation and the conventions of the text/genre; and response to the texts such as whether the text is fitted to its purpose, whether the text achieves its purpose, the personal view of the reader and an appreciation of the text as a whole.

Some children may be entered for Level 6. This is a separate paper and is of the same standard as GCSE grade C. This paper contains both reading and writing. The main booklet contains several forms of texts and the writing prompts are given at the end of the booklet.

Assessment through book talk

In order to assess whether children have really understood what they have read a teacher can assess comprehension through book talk. This discussion might take place in a group situation after a group has completed a story or in an individual talk with the teacher. The teacher needs to assess whether a child has reflected upon their reading, is able to make predictions about the story, and has responded to the story and drawn out personal interpretations. We need to help children by guiding their responses and this can be done through effective questioning (see p. 94 for possible questions).

The role of parents

When children first come to school many parents seem obsessed with worry over whether their child will learn to read. They may take an overpowering interest in the acquisition of every word and become very concerned if their child is not making obvious progress. However, when children enter Key Stage 2 this interest seems to disappear. They are happy that their child can read and the interrogation that took place in the early years of schooling disappears. In reality this role needs to be reversed. Intense pressure on children who are learning to read can put many children off and cause unnecessary anxiety, but once a child has learnt to read the parent can play a vital role in encouraging the child to remain a reader.

What parents can do to help

- Encourage their child by showing an interest in what their child is reading – either by continuing to hear them read or by talking about the story they are reading.
- Continue to show their child how important reading is to their lives – using the telephone directory, consulting a recipe book, using a bus timetable.
- Continue reading to their child. Sharing reading by reading to all the family and talking about the story shows children the importance they put on reading for its own sake.
- Encourage the use of the school and public library. Many librarians are very happy to help parents and children find books that are suitable both in content and in reading level.
- Buy books for their child. Children who own books and who re-read favourite books have been shown

to be children who read for pleasure and remain readers.

- Provide a book allowance for their child. This may be part of their pocket money but directing their money in this way elevates books and shows the child the importance the parent places upon reading.

SUMMARY

This chapter has:

- discussed ways of ensuring that children become committed and confident readers during Key Stage 2

- suggested ways to encourage discussion of fiction texts

- discussed the reading requirements for reading non-fiction texts

- discussed what teachers need to do to encourage the reading of poetry

- looked at the different forms of assessment

- suggested ways in which parents can support their children with reading in the primary years.

References

DfE (1995) *English in the National Curriculum*, HMSO

Hughes, Ted (1963) *Poetry in the Making*, Faber and Faber

Marland, Michael (1981) *Information Skills in the Secondary Curriculum*, Methuen Educational

Further reading

Karavis, S. and Davies, P. (1995) *Progress in English: Assessment and Record Keeping at KS1 and 2*, Reading and Language Information Centre, University of Reading
This booklet describes the rationale for assessment and the important changes that have taken place in recent years. It suggests ways of collecting evidence of progress and provides photocopiable pages to support teachers' record keeping.

Mallett, Margaret (1994) *Reading Non-Fiction in the Primary Years: A Language and Learning Approach*, NATE
This brief booklet succinctly summarises the different genres in non-fiction and suggests practical ways of encouraging all children to read non-fiction. It offers classroom examples of lessons and evaluates what the teacher and children learnt from the lesson. An extension of this work can be found in Mallet's *Making Facts Matter: Reading Non-Fiction 5–11* (Paul Chapman, 1991).

Phinn, Gervase (1995) *Touches of Beauty: Teaching Poetry in the Primary School*, Roselea Publications
This is an excellent book which clearly describes the different forms of poetry and then provides many examples of how children responded by writing their own poem in the designated form. A very useful publication.

Reid, D. and Bentley, D. (1996) *Reading On! Developing Reading at Key Stage 2*, Scholastic
This looks at all the aspects of reading at Key Stage 2. It traces the development of reading from children who are able to recognise most words to those who are able to analyse and evaluate texts. Each chapter addresses a different genre and suggests practical activities to enhance the children's understanding of that genre.

11 Writing at Key Stage 1

OBJECTIVES

By the end of this chapter you should:

- understand the developmental stages of writing at Key Stage 1

- understand the relationship between supported and unaided writing

- have a clear idea of practical ways to teach writing in the early years classroom.

The demands of writing

Many adults describe writing as 'an effort' or 'a chore'. They may appreciate its role as an essential form of communication but they are also aware of the effort required to achieve a successful piece of writing.

For young children the task can seem impossible. They may know nothing about the function of writing in a literate society; they find it very difficult to achieve the fine motor control required to make accurate marks on paper; and they find the complexities of the English spelling system a nightmare.

The National Curriculum expects children of seven to:

- use writing as a means of remembering, communicating, organising and developing ideas and information
- identify the purpose for which they write
- write for a range of readers
- write in different forms, e.g. narratives, poems, notes, records and messages.

This represents a real challenge to young children who just over two years before may have had little sense of what writing is, let alone how it is done.

The skills of writing discussed in this chapter will concentrate upon the composing/creative aspects of writing; the performing/secretarial aspects – pencil control, handwriting and spelling – are dealt with in Chapters 13 and 14.

How was writing taught in the past?

In the past, little distinction was made between the two aspects of writing, and it was generally assumed that until children had a degree of mastery over the skills of handwriting and spelling they were incapable of expressing themselves in the written form. The focus of teaching was on the 'product' – the final outcome of the writing task – and the priority was to make this as near perfect as possible at the first attempt. Children were discouraged from experimentation and were rarely offered the chance to redraft or rethink a piece of writing. It was expected to emerge from the end of the pencil correctly written and correctly spelled. Recent research has stressed the importance of valuing the 'process' of writing and has recognised that how we set about the task and modify our writing as we reflect upon it (just as real writers do) is something that children too should experience. The work of writers like Donald Graves (1983) has encouraged teachers to view children's early mark-making not as imperfect forms of 'correct' writing (and therefore of no value) but instead as a step towards the correct form and, as such, to be celebrated. If we as teachers discourage children from feeling in charge of the writing process, if we constantly point out the discrepancies between their best efforts and correct forms of writing, then we run the risk of two things happening:

1 We will convince children that 'good' writing is primarily neat writing with no spelling mistakes and not a form of communication through which they convey their thoughts and feelings.

2 We will put children off writing and it may be very difficult to persuade them of its value even though they may have good spelling and handwriting skills.

Stages of development in writing

The most effective way to teach writing is to have a full understanding of the stages of development in the writing process (shown in Figure 11.1) so that one may best support and help children at any particular stage. In the early phases of writing the secretarial skills tend to dominate, and so in many respects the stages of development at the beginning of writing are similar to the developmental stages of spelling (see Chapters 13 and 14).

Spelling stages	Writing stages*
Preliminary	*Role-play writing* Experimenting with marks on paper
Semi-phonetic	*Experimental writing* Child understands that writing is speech written down; some attempt to link sounds heard in words with letters making those sounds.
Phonetic	*Early writing* Many words can be deciphered by the teacher; child writes simple, often repetitive text.
Transitional	*Conventional writing* Writer selects form to suit purpose and uses a variety of sentence types.
Conventional	*Proficient* Writer develops ideas and attempts to meet audience needs.

*Stages of writing as described in *First Steps* (Dewsbury 1994)

Figure 11.1 Stages of development in writing

Motivating young writers

Linking writing to classroom activities

How can we foster an attitude towards writing that gives children confidence in their own efforts? The priority for the teacher in the early years classroom is to give children plenty of opportunities to incorporate writing alongside playing and working activities so that they see writing as a natural development of play. For example:

- Place a pad of paper by the toy telephone so that children can 'take messages' when using the telephone. This is an example of writing nearly all children will have witnessed in their own homes and so it is very meaningful to children as it relates to their lives.
- Incorporate writing into play situations such as doctors and patients, when the 'doctor' can write out a prescription for the patient, or encourage children to write shopping lists before visiting the play shop.
- Have a notice board in the classroom where children can send and receive written messages.

Encouraging experimenting with writing: setting up a writing corner or a writing box

Although space is often at a premium in the early years classroom there should be an area where children can experiment with writing implements and writing equipment. If an area cannot be made available then a plastic box of writing materials will suffice. Allow children access to the box as and when appropriate and allow them the freedom to experiment with the effects of different pens and pencils. Although when formally teaching the skills of handwriting you may be insisting upon the use of certain pencils, using pencil grips and writing on particular paper, children should also be given the opportunity to feel how different writing implements react with different papers.

Contents of a writing box

- Variety of paper in different textures, colour and sizes
- Card and cardboard
- Mini-blackboard and chalks
- A variety of pens and crayons of different colours and thickness

Whole-class work: shared writing

An effective way to support young children's writing is for the teacher and the children to create a story together. This activity can be undertaken with the whole class. The teacher might suggest a topic and invite the children to consider a suitable story opener. Children volunteer parts of the story and the teacher writes it down on a flip chart or white board. The teacher needs to keep re-reading the story as it unfolds to aid continuity and to stress the importance of events impinging upon one another – an aspect of writing that young children find hard to master, and typically their own 'stories' are a chain of relatively unconnected events.

Shared writing enables the teacher to offer the following learning opportunities:

- the opportunity for the whole class to share a creative writing experience
- the opportunity to discuss story language
- the opportunity to develop aesthetic language beyond the everyday transactional language
- the opportunity to introduce aspects of language study, for example discussing appropriate adjectives, adverbs and carefully chosen verbs; children can offer alternatives and then decide which words are most effective in the particular context
- the opportunity to read and re-read a story that children almost know by heart by the end of the session
- the opportunity to introduce simple notions of genre.

Classroom organisation

- Each whole-class writing session should take approximately 25–30 minutes.
- Don't be afraid of keeping the story on track – even if that means turning down one child's suggestions.
- Inevitably some children will contribute more than others. Invite the more reticent children to supply a word here or there or to decide between two given options. Once these shy children get used to the idea of contributing in a safe environment their confidence should build.
- Keep re-reading the story as it unfolds and encourage everyone to join in with the reading. Point at the text as you read, much as you would when modelling reading using a big book.
- Incorporate some sound-letter knowledge as you transcribe the dictated story: for example 'Who knows what letter is at the start of the word "tiger"?'
- Possibly re-read the story at the usual end-of-the-day story slot, thereby giving it the status of a published story.

This arrangement fits comfortably into the structure of the literacy hour where the teacher will be working for 10–20 minutes with a group of children organised in ability groupings. This smaller group size ensures the involvement of all participants, which can be difficult to achieve in whole-class writing.

When the story is completed ask the children to resequence it orally into key events. Ideally break the story down into a number of events which matches the number of children in the group. Invite each child to choose an event to illustrate. Some discussion needs to accompany the illustration to ensure continuity of character depiction. Give each child a sheet of A3 paper and mark a pencil line five centimetres from the bottom of the page. This allows space for those children who are able to write some caption of their own to accompany the picture. While the children do their pictures you can check through the story to make sure it has no errors. Some teachers like to write out the group story again taking more care with handwriting and presentation, which may not have been possible while the story was being created. Invite any children who quickly finish their illustrations to illustrate a cover design or to help you to list authors on the back cover. Use A3 sugar paper for the cover. As a group decide upon a title for the story and write this on the cover. Finally staple together the pages of the transcribed story interleaved with the children's illustrations and have a final joint read of the story. The book should then be stored in the class library for other children to enjoy.

Advantages of guided group writing

- It enables the teacher to demonstrate all the ingredients of sustaining a continuous narrative.
- Children enjoy the freedom of composing at length without being frustrated by presentational skills.
- It forges strong links between reading and writing.
- It will influence the children when they write individually, providing them with the experience of how stories are structured.

Group work: guided writing

On occasions it is very beneficial if a group of six to eight children can construct a story with a teacher.

Planning for writing

Most professional writers spend a considerable amount of their working day planning and redrafting their writing. We should not expect inexperienced writers to be able to formulate ideas for writing and to simultaneously assess the needs of the audience for that writing. All these complex components of the writing process will take considerable time to evolve. As teachers we should share with children the necessary planning which must precede most writing tasks.

Decide on a topic for children to write about. Collect ideas about the topic and brainstorm useful word choices. Help the children develop clear ideas about:

- the subject matter
- the point of view
- the audience
- the degree of formality of language
- a sense of appropriate word choices.

Through shared and guided writing the teacher can model the requisite ingredients of any piece of writing, and children can begin to have mastery over this very challenging form of communication.

Developing a sense of audience

The National Curriculum also specifies that children at Key Stage 1 should write for a range of different audiences and should have some awareness that when writers choose what they want to write about, the language options open to them are influenced by the needs of the intended audience. For example, some writing will require a degree of formality whilst other tasks may be more informal. It is appropriate to use formal language when addressing an unknown stranger, such as the curator of a museum, but such language would be inappropriate when writing to a friend, where the register should be chatty and informal.

Another factor associated with audience is the need to determine the level of prior knowledge about the subject which the audience may or may not have.

Successful writing depends upon:

- meeting the needs of your audience
- achieving an acceptable tone of formality
- calculating the level of the audience's prior knowledge.

Writing for a range of readers

The National Curriculum specifies that children should identify the purpose for which they write and should write for a range of readers, for example their teacher, their family, their peers, themselves. The following list gives a few suggestions for possible purposes and audiences.

- Write to the school cook thanking him or her for a favourite meal.
- Write to the teacher explaining what they most enjoyed doing during the day.
- Write to a friend planning how to spend playtime.
- Write to a classroom assistant and list why he or she is so appreciated.
- Write to invite a visitor to the class.
- Write to thank the visitor.
- Write invitations to the class assembly.

Writing in a range of genres

As children begin to acquire the basic skills of writing narrative ideas in an ordered fashion, these early concepts about writing should be extended to include opportunities to write in a variety of genres and to highlight the importance of writing to meet the needs of an intended audience. It used to be thought that it was only older children who could handle the variety of forms which we use when writing for particular purposes, but the National Curriculum has stressed the importance of young children being made aware of the range of genres of writing.

This includes teaching children both the form and content of specific writing tasks such as lists, captions, notes, messages, notices, invitations, instructions. Each of these examples has its own recognisable features and particular uses of language which we should make very evident to children as we work with them.

Genre can be defined as the form of writing which authors choose in order to achieve their purposes (Littlefair 1991). This means that there are different organisational and language choices to be made if a writer intends his or her writing to be effective. It is not that one kind of writing is better than another; it is just that each writing situation has its own needs, and sorting out the appropriate form and language is one of the challenges facing any writer. Whilst a detailed understanding of language uses and genre features is more the domain of Key Stage 2 (see Chapter 12), even little children should be introduced to the key characteristics of certain types of writing. In this way they can learn to distinguish writing tasks in the non-fiction genre and writing tasks in the fiction genre.

Non-fiction writing

Children usually have a wide experience of narrative from hearing stories read and from the reading scheme. Their experience of non-fiction may be less developed. We need to ensure that we offer a diversity of reading genres in the classroom.

- Bring to the classroom a collection of different types of writing, for example a recipe book, an information book, a business letter, a telephone directory, a catalogue. Share the examples of the different texts with the children. Ask them to close their eyes and see if they can recognise which text you are reading from based on what they hear of the content and language. (*The Jolly Postman* by Janet and Allan Ahlberg can be a very useful resource in these circumstances as the book itself includes a wide range of different text types in the form of various letters.)
- Study one example of writing, for example a party invitation. Share the details with the class then jointly construct an invitation to an event relevant to the school. Talk about the appropriate language for an invitation – informative and welcoming but brief. Ask children to use the class text as a model and to construct their own invitation to a special event. Children could work with a partner and create their invitation, then swap over and fill in each other's invitations.

Poetry

Essentially poetry is crafted writing, when considerable care is taken over every word choice, and this can be achieved by young children if they are given sufficient support. As with other writing forms the procedure for introducing a particular genre to children should be as follows:

- introducing the genre: familiarising children with features of the genre
- joint creation of a text with the teacher modelling the writing process
- children dictating ideas for the teacher to scribe
- children attempting to write their own poems
- plenary session: children sharing their efforts with the rest of the class.

First of all choose a poem that the children will enjoy and share it with them. If possible prepare your reading of the poem so that the delivery is polished and effective. Read the poem several times and, if there is a repeated phrase, encourage the children to join in. As you read the poem emphasise the rhythm and metre of the verse and, of course, ensure that any rhymes are easily iden-

tified. Ask the children to close their eyes as you read the poem and then ask them what they could 'see' as they heard the words. Invite response to the poem by asking open-ended questions. Use a big book or enlarge the text so that all the children can see the poem. Read the poem again, this time pointing at the words as you say them. Tell the children that you are going to create your own version of the poem based on the stimulus poem, by copying either its format or its theme. Encourage the children to suggest ideas for the poem. Discuss appropriate word choices, offer alternatives, etc. Share the jointly created text with the children. If appropriate, ask the children to attempt their own versions of part of the poem based on the original and the class version. Share the children's poems.

Supported writing

If children are to develop as confident writers we must provide a scaffold, which enables them to see the link between their developed skills of speaking and listening and their developing skills of writing. To achieve this it is beneficial if children begin the writing process with the teacher acting as scribe for their ideas. In this way the children control the creative aspect of writing while the teacher deals with the secretarial aspects. In these first stages of writing, when the teacher supports the children through scribing, highlighter writing and group writing, the focus is upon exploiting children's speaking and listening skills to build up their grammatical competence. As this grammatical knowledge develops, the focus shifts and becomes the management of narrative and story structure. Once their own skills of handwriting and spelling develop children are ready to take on more responsibility for the whole writing process – from creation through to production. In this way they progress from non-written to written composition.

1 Scribing

Scribing for a child is the process whereby an adult assumes secretarial responsibility for a writing task and writes down whatever a child dictates. The advantage of this approach is that it enables a child to compose at length without being hindered by the presentational aspects of writing – handwriting and spelling. The child sees the direct link between the words he or she has spoken and the written forms of those words as they appear on the page.

Scribing is an alternative to the child dictating a sentence to accompany a picture and the teacher writing the sentence and then the child copying the writing by writing underneath the teacher's writing. When children copy underneath an adult's writing they are reluctant to compose at length because they learn that this makes their subsequent task – copying the teacher's writing – very arduous and time-consuming. Children will suggest as short a sentence as possible to accompany their picture as this reduces the amount of copy-writing they have to do. Moreover, once children have attempted to copy underneath the teacher's writing they have clear visual evidence of the discrepancy between their own efforts to produce the letters and words in the correct orientation and the teacher's example. This can discourage young writers. Possibly, the greatest disadvantage of children copying writing is that the end product does not look like something to read. Consider the example in Figure 11.2.

When a child has written underneath a teacher's line of writing there are two lines of writing for each line of spoken text. If we were to ask the child to read back what they had written they would have to remember to ignore the teacher's version. All of this creates a gulf between reading and writing when what we should be striving for is a close relationship between the two so that children should always be encouraged to read what they have written and write about what they have read. Copy-writing can interfere with this important cycle of reciprocal activities.

By contrast, scribing enables the child and the teacher to 'paired read' the writing. The child can partially remember what has been written because he or she composed it, and the teacher can model reading skills by following the text and demonstrating the left-to-right movement of reading the English script, plus modelling the all-important 'swing back' at the end of each line to start again at the left-hand side of the line below.

Classroom organisation

Obviously, allowing a child to compose at length for the teacher to transcribe makes heavy demands upon teacher time. How can the classroom teacher organise this?

1 Expect to transcribe for each child once a term.
2 Scribe the ideas of one child, but work with a group of children as they observe how you commit that child's ideas to paper; in this way you all share in the reading of the transcribed text.
3 Invite classroom assistants and parents who help in the classroom to act as scribes.
4 Ask a child to record their 'story' on to tape and transcribe it for them later when you have time.

2 Highlighter writing

As an alternative to children copying underneath the teacher's writing, some teachers have found 'highlighter' writing very successful. A child who wants to write a caption or sentence to accompany a picture can dictate the sentence to the teacher, who writes the words using a highlighter pen or a yellow felt-tip pen with a broad nib. Then the child writes in pencil 'inside' the highlighter writing. The advantages of this technique are:

- There is no 'double' writing effect, unlike when children write underneath a teacher's writing.
- The end result looks as though the teacher has highlighted the child's writing, giving it a status.
- The writing invites to be read, thereby encouraging the important link between reading and writing.

3 Group writing

When the teacher is working with a group of children during the group tasks of the literacy hour, scribing for the group can help them gain a sense of story structure and the children benefit from the group interaction.

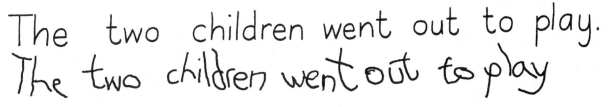

Figure 11.2 Example of child's copying underneath the teacher's writing

Unaided writing

Although children need many opportunities to see writing modelled, and need support and guidance for many of their writing tasks, it is also very important to give children plenty of scope to explore and experiment with writing. In these situations children should be encouraged to write without seeking assistance from the teacher but to use all their own developing skills to communicate in the written form. Inevitably this will result in many 'errors' and considerable discrepancy between what the child intends to write and the correct form of writing it, but, nevertheless, unaided writing is a valuable learning experience for both the teacher and the child.

The value of unaided writing

- It convinces the child that the priority is the message of the writing and not the surface features of spelling and handwriting.
- It allows the child to develop a 'voice' in their own writing unhampered by technicalities of spelling and handwriting.
- It provides the teacher with useful information about the rate of acquisition of all writing skills.
- If a child always copies an adult's writing the teacher will only learn how well that child can copy. If the teacher hands all responsibility over to the child the extent to which writing skills are being mastered can be seen, and this in turn indicates to the teacher what the next appropriate step in teaching might be for each individual child.

Managing writing in the classroom

The combination of unaided writing drawing on the experiences of aided writing can be exploited in writing opportunities within the literacy hour. The teacher introduces the writing task and models some its features during the whole-class shared reading and writing session. The writing can be managed in the following way:

- the use of speaking and listening to assist planning of the writing task (undertaken during whole-class work)
- the unaided production of the piece of writing (independent work)
- the development/feedback which results from the sharing/discussing process (plenary).

The teacher guides the class through the following processes:

- orally *planning* what they are going to write (whole class)
- getting on with the business of *writing* their 'story' (independent/group)
- *sharing* their writing with others (plenary)
- *discussing* how their writing might be improved in terms of audience interest or plot continuity (whole class)
- working with the teacher *reviewing* the writing and selecting particular aspects of writing that a child might be able to improve upon (group).

In the writing stage children should be encouraged to be independent and not to ask for help with their writing, and so they will need to be aware of the strategies they can employ if they are stuck. For example:

- The teacher can suggest that children draw a line to represent a word they are not sure how to spell, but they should be encouraged to attempt to write the first letter of the word if they can.
- Children can draw a picture to represent a word they cannot write.
- They can look around the classroom for help with words that might be on useful lists.

All of these procedures encourage children to work independently at this stage of the process.

In the plenary session, after children have finished what they want to put in writing, they are given the opportunity to share their writing with the rest of the class. This means they can 'read' what they intended the writing to convey (with embellishments if required). This means that even children who are at the very beginning stages of mastery over the forms of writing can still behave like writers and imbue meaning to their marks on the page. It is important at this stage that everybody in the workshop (including the teacher) responds to the content and intention of the writing without being distracted by failures in its presentation. The teacher can also share some of his or her writing with the class.

In the *discussion* stage, peers are invited to respond as an audience and to give the author guidance about aspects of the 'story' they found particularly successful; for example 'I liked the funny way you described ...', 'I thought the ending was scary'. The children can also be encouraged to respond to the teacher's writing, praising any particularly effective aspects.

In the *review* stage the teacher now looks at the written attempts and praises appropriately the evidence of the child's success. It is at this point that the teacher might also use the occasion to introduce some focused teaching. For example, working with a group of children the teacher may comment on one child's correct use/spelling of a word and invite the rest of the group to spell it, first with help and finally unaided. The teacher might also praise evidence of particularly good handwriting or evidence of correct letter formation, and invite everyone in the group to practise this particular letter and other letters in that handwriting family (see Chapter 14).

The priority with this kind of unaided writing is to give young writers the opportunity to work through a piece of writing beyond the secretarial skills of form and presentation, and to focus on the aspects of communication and meeting the needs of an audience.

Assessment and record-keeping

When assessing writing there is the advantage that there is tangible evidence to assess. Each piece of writing a child produces is proof of the progress the child is making on the road to becoming a writer. However, the teacher who tries to keep every mark every child makes on every piece of paper is going to run into organisational difficulties. To keep the lid on a vast quantity of written work the teacher needs to plan for assessment and to have considered the assessment potential of all writing tasks before they are undertaken.

Activities may provide evidence of a child's growing mastery of:

- letter shapes
- sound/letter correspondence
- the concept of a word
- left-to-right direction of print
- top-to-bottom direction of print
- handwriting
- written sight words
- story structure
- punctuation
- sense of audience
- word choices.

All of these aspects are components in successful writing. What matters is that the teacher does not assess every piece of writing a child completes against this very comprehensive and demanding standard. When setting up the writing task the teacher should prioritise the different components, for example mastery of story form, effective opening, descriptive language, punctuation, spelling.

It is all too easy to fall into the trap of assessing all aspects of a piece of writing at once, and this makes it very difficult for the young writer as it is impossible for them to juggle all features of writing with the same degree of efficiency.

Children cannot put everything right at the same time and they are entitled to know the criteria against which any piece of writing may be assessed. This also enables the teacher to introduce aspects of self-assessment even with very young children. After a writing task has been carefully introduced in terms of teacher expectation, it is quite natural to ask the children to review their writing in the light of those expectations.

When forming judgements about a piece of writing there are certain questions to take into account:

- What kind of writing is it? Does it achieve the author's goal?
- How was the writing initiated?
- How did the children work? (whole class/group/ partner/individual).
- How did I respond after the writing? (read the piece alone/read with child, etc.).
- What happened to the writing after the task? (revised/redrafted/typed on to computer/shared with others).

As teachers we need to review our ways of introducing and responding to writing tasks so that children have experiences of as wide a range of writing opportunities as possible.

It is useful to keep a range of samples of children's writing showing development of skills over time and across different writing environments. These conditions should be logged with the date on each piece of writing to be filed. It should be recorded on the sample what the 'prompt' was for the writing – whether the focus was imaginative writing, description, or a particular genre of non-fiction – and what had been discussed with the children regarding the assessment of spelling and handwriting.

SUMMARY

This chapter has outlined the importance of introducing young children to a variety of writing experiences. It has:

- outlined the importance of teaching children about writing as a form of communication

- suggested ways of achieving a balance between unaided writing and guided writing

- considered practical ways of encouraging children to write for a variety of audiences and in a variety of forms.

References

Ahlberg, J. and Ahlberg, A. (1986) *The Jolly Postman*, Heinemann Educational Books

Dewsbury, A. (1994) *First Steps: Developmental Continuum and Resource Books*, Heinemann Educational Books

Graves, D. H. (1983) *Writing: Teachers and Children at Work*, Heinemann Educational Books

Littlefair, A. (1991) *Reading All Types of Writing*, Open University Press

Further reading

Bissex, G. L. (1980) *GNYS AT WRK: A Child Learns to Read and Write*, Harvard University Press
   A celebration of children's early writing as they move towards independent writing.

Clay, M. M. (1975) *'What Did I Write?'* Heinemann
   An explanation of the processes of early writing.

Czerniewska, P. (1992) *Learning about Writing*, Blackwell
   A very clear overview of the writing process from early mark making to sophisticated written communication.

Hall, Nigel (ed.) (1989) *Writing with Reason: The Emergence of Authorship in Young Children*, Hodder and Stoughton
   A detailed coverage of the range and opportunities that children can be given as writing prompts and supports.

Temple, C. A., Nathan, R., Temple, F. and Burris, N. A. (revised 1993) *The Beginnings of Writing*, Allyn and Bacon
   A thorough description of the early acquisition of early writing skills.

12 Writing at Key Stage 2

OBJECTIVES

By the end of this chapter you should:

- understand how to implement the National Curriculum requirements for Writing at Key Stage 2

- understand the importance of modelling and structuring children's writing

- have a clear idea of practical ways to teach writing in Year 3 to Year 6.

Writing skills developed at Key Stage 1

Many children progress from Key Stage 1 having acquired basic writing skills. Indeed to have achieved National Curriculum Level 2 in the end of Key Stage 1 assessments their writing will show the following characteristics:

- It communicates meaning in both narrative and non-narrative forms.
- There is evidence of appropriate and interesting vocabulary.
- There is some awareness of the reader.
- Ideas are developed in a sequence of sentences, sometimes demarcated by capital letters and full stops.

So for many children the foundations for writing may be in place and now they are ready for the next stages of development in the acquisition of writing skills.

Writing skills required at Key Stage 2

The National Curriculum (as described in Chapter 3) divides its requirements for writing at Key Stage 2 into the same three sections that are evident in

all the other English programmes of study at Key Stage 2. These sections are Range, Key Skills, and Standard English and Language Study.

Range sets out the requirements for giving children the opportunity to write for varied purposes; to write for an extended range of audiences; and to write in different forms, such as argument, commentary, narrative, dialogue. These three hallmarks of effective writing – purpose, audience and form – will characterise how writing should be taught at this key stage.

The *Key Skills* specified in the curriculum are taught in the context of children's growing mastery of purpose, form and audience.

Purpose, form and audience in writing

The following diagram may help in understanding the interplay between purpose, form and audience.

Purpose
(Why am I writing it?)

Form
(What is the type of writing most appropriate to my purpose, in which to organise my ideas?)

Audience
(Who do I intend to read my writing?)

It is only when writers are in control of all these three elements of the writing process that successful writing can ensue. As teachers we need to create an extensive range of purposes, forms and audiences so that children understand the choices facing a writer and make those choices appropriately.

Young writers are most likely to undertake writing tasks using the language conventions close to spoken language. The early curriculum documents for

English recognised the difficulty posed by the gulf between appropriate language for spoken communication and appropriate language for written communication:

> As pupils write for a wider range of purposes, they should be taught to distinguish degrees of formality in writing for unfamiliar audiences. They should begin to make judgements about when a particular tone, style, format or vocabulary is appropriate.
>
> (DfE 1993)

As teachers we need to share with our pupils the variety of writing forms, both fiction (e.g. stories, poems, dialogues, drama scripts, diaries) and non-fiction (e.g. reports, instructions, explanations, notes and letters).

If writing is to be effective it must meet a purpose and address an audience. The juggling of these two factors will create choices about the appropriate language to use and the format for the writing. These will be resolved when the form of the writing is selected. Some combinations of purpose, audience and form are obvious: for example, a class register is most effective as a list (form) and it is used by the teacher (audience) to check on attendance (purpose). Other writing tasks may have less clearly defined roles for purpose, audience and form, but all will need to be considered and children need specific instruction in all these aspects of writing.

Writing for a purpose

Every writing task has a purpose – to explain, to report, to persuade, to argue, to amuse, to inform, etc. As adults we usually only write when the purpose is patently obvious. Indeed we would not engage in a writing task if we were not clear about its purpose. Writing is a time-consuming activity and we would not embark on a project without a clear idea about why we were undertaking it. However, in the classroom it can be difficult for a teacher to keep the purpose of any writing task at the forefront of all writing activities.

The vast majority of purposes for writing in the classroom will be curricular and 'invented' by the teacher. This 'fabrication' of purposes does not detract from the importance of sharing with children the intended purpose. For example, the teacher could say to the class: 'Let's imagine we

want to make a welcome brochure for children who are new to our school.' By defining a clear purpose for the writing task (and incidentally, describing the intended audience – new children; and the form the writing should take – a brochure) the teacher is enabling children to be in command of the task.

Selecting an appropriate form for the writing

When a purpose for writing arises (or is invented), writers have to make certain choices about language structures and vocabulary to ensure the purpose is achieved. For example, the purpose for writing might be a letter of complaint to a shop, but if the text structure of a recipe layout and the vocabulary choices of poetry (with a particular emphasis on extended metaphors and similes) are selected then the purpose might not be achieved.

It is obvious to any adult writer that using the format of a recipe and writing in flowery poetic language in a letter of complaint would be foolish.

Many children too would see the foolishness of writing a letter of complaint in the form of a recipe sprinkled with poetic language. However, there are other, less extreme examples where the subtlety of difference in language form is less obvious to children.

Much of this subtlety depends upon capturing the correct degree of formality in the language which will render a piece of writing effective or not.

Meeting the needs of an audience

The third ingredient in successful writing is meeting the needs of an intended audience. In all writing tasks purpose and audience are closely linked. If you do not know to whom you are writing (or are aware that it is an unknown audience) it will be very hard to achieve a particular writing purpose. The audience will dictate the vocabulary used in the writing. Going back to the earlier example of writing a brochure for children new to the school, if we were later to decide to write a brochure for the parents of those children, then immediately certain changes would be made both to the language choices and to the prioritising of the information. The form would remain the same – it is still a brochure – but the audience needs of children and adults differ, and effective writing should reflect that difference.

Writing in a range of genres

Prior to the introduction of the National Curriculum the focus of writing tasks for children in Years 3–6 was the development of story writing. The National Curriculum, with its clear emphasis on non-fiction reading and writing, has altered that. Teachers are now required to give children opportunities to master different types of writing.

If children are to achieve this they need to have an understanding of how particular texts are structured. That is why they should be taught to recognise:

- what type of text is required by the task
- what is the structure of that text type
- what language characteristics, in terms of vocabulary and grammatical construction, will best achieve the purpose of the task.

For example:

Task
To explain how a telephone works

Text type
Explanation

Text structure
- The text is chronological: that is, it follows a clear sequence of time and one part of the explanation hinges upon the next.
- The text opens with an introductory statement, e.g. 'The telephone was invented in 1875 by Alexander Bell.'
- Then the text follows a series of logically organised steps, e.g. 'When you speak into the handset of a telephone the vibrations made by your voice are turned into electric signals by a microphone.'

Language characteristics
- The text is written in the *present tense* ('you speak …').
- The text is punctuated with words to signify the order of events or the reasons for the events ('When …' or 'Because …').
- The text is usually accompanied by diagrams and illustrations.

As children move from Year 3 to Year 6 they should build up a repertoire of characteristics of text types so that it may not be necessary to revisit each text type from the starting point of studying examples. It may be sufficient just to recap upon the text characteristics before children embark on a writing task.

Each school's scheme of work should ensure comprehensive coverage of the range of test types. In this way all teachers can be aware at what stage a particular text type is introduced; where and how it is practised; how and when it is revisited and refined.

Such a systematic programme of introducing writing tasks is specified in the National Literacy Strategy document (DfEE 1998) so that for example:

- Note-making appears in Year 3, Term 1.
- Letters, notes and messages appear in Year 3, Term 3.
- Reports and newspaper articles appear in Year 4, Term 1.

Developing writing skills: non-narrative

Modelling the writing process

To help children to gain experience of a wide variety of writing tasks it is important that the teacher frequently models the writing process to the class/group. This can best be done in shared reading and writing during the literacy hour.

Stage 1

First of all the children should be shown examples of the particular text type. So, for example, if the children have been given the task of writing a set of instructions they should study a range of examples of this text type with the teacher. This might include instructions from boxed games; instructions from a manufacturer on how to make something; recipe books which explain how to prepare and cook particular foods.

Stage 2

The teacher should then discuss with the whole class, or a group:

- the reasons why these texts are organised in this way
- how the content is structured and presented
- what type of language characterises the writing, e.g. formal/informal, technical/familiar, and also the tone of the language

It is worth reminding children that these exemplars of instruction will have been devised with a perceived, yet unknown, audience in mind. That is, the authors will have anticipated that readers of their instructions will be people who desire to play the game or make the item. They will, therefore, be quite committed readers. At the same time, the authors will have no personal knowledge of the audience and the tone of the passage will be distant and formal.

Stage 3

Next the teacher should remind the children of the text features and invite them to suggest the reasons for particular characteristics. For example:

text feature	contents of game presented in a list
reason	quick reference for reader to check all items are present
text feature	instruction set out either with numbers 1, 2, 3, etc., or text markers, First, Next, When, etc.
reason	so that readers can follow instructions in clear chronological order

Stage 4

Finally, the teacher should choose a particular example of the text type, for example instructions to play hopscotch. He or she should discuss with the children the anticipated audience (any child using the playground?), and then they should jointly construct a text which conforms to the characteristics of the text type. This joint construction of the text can be written for the children on the board.

In order to create the joint text the teacher should ask the class/group questions such as:

- How should I begin?
- How should I set out the text?

As the children provide answers the teacher should pursue the questions further, asking for example:

- Why should I begin in the centre of the piece of paper? What advantages are there for the reader if I do so?
- Why do I need a statement of goals and a list of contents first?

In this way the teacher draws together the features of the form of the writing and the rationale behind those features.

This discussion of the creation of the text should extend to probing children about particular vocabulary choices, for example:

- Can you think of a more accurate verb to describe how the stone is placed in the appropriate hopscotch square?

Stage 5

Once the class text has been constructed this can become a model for the children to produce individual texts of a similar type, for example to write a set of instructions for playing rounders.

Because the children have been exposed to explicit teaching about characteristics of the text type, its typical structure and language characteristics, it becomes much easier to craft children's writing. The teacher can ask questions to help children review the effectiveness of their writing; for example:

- Are you happy that your chosen layout is clear for your audience?
- Have you kept to the strict chronological sequence?
- Have you discarded extra material that might confuse or distract the reader from the main purpose of the writing, i.e. to provide a clear set of instructions?
- Have you remembered the language characteristics of instructions, which often omit the pronoun 'you' and use instead the imperative form of the verb on its own, e.g. 'Throw the stone …'?

A particularly useful resource for helping children to structure their non-fiction writing are the Writing Frames devised by David Wray and Maureen Lewis. These provide the scaffolding for particular forms of writing, such as argument, discussion, procedural texts, etc. The scaffolding takes the form of text markers to support children's writing as they undertake a particular writing task.

A writing frame enables children to concentrate on the content they wish to convey without having to worry simultaneously about the form. It is hoped that in due course children will become so familiar with the form that they will no longer need the scaffold of the frame and will be able to handle both the content and the form.

Drafting and revising

The National Curriculum sets out requirements for teaching writing beyond range, purpose, form and audience. There is also a set of Key Skills that must be taught. These particularly refer to the process of writing, that is the creation of texts and a built-in procedure to evaluate that text and, where necessary, to make revisions to the text.

The National Curriculum emphasises the importance of 'crafting' writing, that is modifying writing in an attempt to make it more effective. Prior to the National Curriculum much of children's writing was 'one off'. That is, they only had one stab at the task and they were judged on that attempt. Professional writers often describe the length of time they spend perfecting small sections of text (sometimes as little as one sentence) until they are content with the effect of particular word choices. If children are to develop as writers they must be given the opportunity to craft their writing.

Teachers need to help children to:

- plan a writing task (taking account of purpose, form and audience)
- produce a first draft developed from the initial plan (this gives children the opportunity to test the effectiveness of their writing by trialling their first attempt with the teacher and peers)
- revise the draft (this will be done in the light of comments from 'readers' and will encourage the writer to make clear any aspects of the writing that readers found unclear)
- proof-read the revised draft (this involves checking the writing for spelling and punctuation errors)
- present the final version (this will involve writing out a fair copy or typing it on to the word processor).

Not all writing tasks need to move from plan to fair copy. It is important that the teacher decides which of the procedures are relevant for any particular piece of writing. It may be that several tasks never move beyond the planning stage. That might be where the maximum amount of learning surrounds that activity. Many writing tasks will move on to a first draft and will be amended in the light of suggestions from the teacher and peers regarding clarity and effectiveness but will not be developed into a spelling activity (proof-reading). Finally there will be activities which will follow through the whole procedure.

What is important is that the teacher makes a clear decision about the process. It is all too easy for writing time at Key Stage 2 to be dominated by checking for spelling errors and practising handwriting. The processes of writing should be shared with children so that they understand the terminology and are involved in some of the decisions about how far any one piece of writing should be followed through to 'publication'.

(The remaining aspects of Key Skills for Writing in the National Curriculum concern spelling and handwriting, which are discussed in Chapters 13 and 14 respectively.)

Response partners

One way to help young writers to meet the needs of an audience is to set up response partners or authors' circles. These involve pairs or small groups of children, usually of similar ability, who meet regularly and who provide a forum for the writer to bounce ideas off or to discuss clarity. These response groups only function successfully when they are carefully set up by the teacher and the arrangement is preceded by some sensitive discussion about supporting one another and the difference between constructive and negative criticism. You could devise a set of guidelines for response partners.

What should response partners do?

- Read the writing through once to understand the content.
- Read it again to concentrate upon how it is written.
- Consider whether the form suits the purpose.
- Consider whether the writing holds a reader's attention.
- Identify any words, phrases or sentences that were thought to be particularly effective.
- Discuss any section where they lost the thread of the narrative.
- Discuss with the writer any possible improvements.

Forums like these can help young writers to concentrate upon ensuring their writing engages with an audience. It also helps children to develop a critical language with which to discuss language, which will be very valuable.

Developing writing skills: narrative

With so much emphasis in the National Curriculum on giving children mastery over the writing skills involved in non-fiction writing it is sometimes easy to overlook the importance of developing children's story writing. This neglect may also be due in part to the fact that this is the form of writing young children adopt most readily. This is for three main reasons:

- It is closest to the language of speech as we weave little oral narratives to tell others our experiences.
- Many children have learned to read using a preponderance of fiction texts, and this constant exposure to the model of narrative has an effect upon children when they come to write.
- In narrative writing children usually have control over the content of what they write. They know about it because it is the subject of their own experience or their own imagination. The who, what, when, how, why and where of a subject is within their imaginative control. Just because young readers appear to have more mastery over the form of narrative writing than they may have over writing argument or writing a report this does not mean that there isn't a clear teaching role for us to help children progress in this mode of writing too.

The range of narrative writing

Just as non-fiction writing divides into clear text types, each with its own characteristics, so there are divisions within fiction into separate genres. These divisions have less to do with form (although some genres, e.g. playscripts and diaries, do have specific features of form) and are more to do with differences in content. In some terminology this is described as 'imaginative' writing, implying that the writer has control over the content in a way that is usually not found in non-fiction writing.

Examples of narrative writing

- Adventure stories
- Autobiographies/biographies
- Curriculum vitae
- Diaries
- Fairy tales/fables/myths/parables
- Playscripts
- Poems
- Postcards
- Invitations
- Journals
- Letters

(Obviously some of the above list could also fall into the category 'non-fiction': for example, a 'letter' could be informal and discursive or a formal letter of complaint. The fact that the genre divisions are not watertight is not a problem. What is important is to give children a variety of writing tasks both narrative and non-narrative so that they practise the form of writing required by a particular purpose.)

Scaffolding children's story writing

Once children have mastered the skill of writing a connected narrative it can be quite difficult to sort out exactly where their control of the story form is still weak. Two children may write stories which are similar in terms of length and spelling accuracy and yet the stories may be very different in terms of text organisation and language features. One writer may link all 'sentences' with 'and then … and then …' while the other is consciously striving for a more literary style using more sophisticated connectives and figurative language.

The best way to help children juggle all the components of story writing (and also to give both you and the children a language with which to dissect stories) is to present children with a list of story ingredients.

Story ingredients

- Characters
- Setting
- Action
- Complication
- Reflection – which may include figurative language
- Resolution

When children are listening to a story being read aloud, or when a group of children are reading and discussing a story, they should be encouraged to observe how that particular author has weighed out the story ingredients. The teacher should direct their discussion towards:

- the portrayal of the characters
- the significance of the setting
- the sequence of the plot actions
- the events of the story that are unexpected
- evidence of the author providing a commentary upon the action of the plot
- how the author draws together the threads of the story into a conclusion.

If children are familiar with interpreting how published stories are constructed then when they set about the task of creating their own imagined narratives the teacher can discuss components of their stories using the same language that he or she has used when dissecting the published stories. For example:

- Are you trying to sustain too many characters in this story (and are they therefore more like 'caricatures'?)?
- Would it be helpful to have further descriptions of the setting?
- Is there too much action, making it difficult for the reader to follow?
- Does anything unpredictable happen or could the reader have accurately predicted all the events right from the start?
- Would the reader's attention be better held if the story contained more reflection upon the plot instead of a solid diet of events?
- Does the writer pull together all the loose ends of the narrative to the satisfaction of the reader?

Once this language for talking about fiction reading and fiction writing is in place it is much easier for the teacher to suggest modifications to a narrative at the drafting stage.

Writing poetry

The National Curriculum requires children to write in response to poems and also to organise and structure their writing in a variety of ways using their experience of poetry.

Many children enjoy writing poetry but may feel inhibited if they believe rhyme to be a pre-requisite of successful poetry.

As with all other writing tasks children need regular exposure to the genre if they are to understand its writing requirements.

The poetry experience

If children are to develop as confident writers of poetry it is important that the library/book corner is well stocked with poetry books for children to choose for individual reading. It is also valuable to have sets of books so that groups of children can explore the oral language of poetry as well as sharing interpretations about possible meanings of poems.

Finally, poetry should be read and re-read by the teacher so that he or she can explore the structures and patterns of language and draw children's attention to them.

Poetry models

The modelling process can be particularly effective when applied to poetry. This involves the teacher choosing a poem, sharing it with the class and then making word deletions so that the children can explore different word choices within the structure of the poem.

Linking reading and writing

Children at Key Stage 2 should be encouraged to read from a wide range of literature, some of it by significant children's authors and some of it forming part of long-established children's fiction. Exposure to this wide range of texts during individual reading sessions, supplemented by experiences of different genres in group reading and whole-class reading, provides children with models of different forms of writing. It is part of our role as teachers to ensure that children come across this range of reading experiences and then draw upon this reading to become models for writing.

Using texts as models for children's writing

Texts can be used as exemplars for particular story features. For example:

- The teacher could focus upon different types of *story beginnings* – mysterious beginnings; puzzling beginnings; traditional beginnings. The teacher could share with the class a variety of story openers and then ask the children to write their own story beginning.
- The teacher could share with the children different types of *story endings* – open-ended endings; moral endings; stories which end with a question. The children could then try writing an ending to a story.

The use of texts in this way as the support or scaffold for children's fiction writing is equivalent to modelling as the support for non-fiction writing.

Using stories as writing prompts

Books can also give rise to a whole range of legitimate writing tasks which set out a clear purpose and audience for children's writing. After you have read a book to the class you could ask them to write to a character in the book. It is important to specify the form of the writing and its purpose.

For example:

- Write a letter of apology to Little Red Hen from the cat, the rat and the pig explaining how they will be more helpful next time.
- Write a postcard from Plop, the owl who was afraid of the dark, describing how he now enjoys night time.
- Write the diary entry for the Hodgeheg on the day leading up to his accident and the following two days.

Journal writing

Children also need the opportunity to explore writing as a means of communicating personal experience. Some teachers have enabled this kind of writing to go on in their classrooms by providing Journal Books. This protects the confidential nature of this writing.

The Journal Book can be a source of written communication between individual children and the teacher. Children receive no help when writing in their journals and the teacher does not read the message when the children are present. This preserves the differences between children telling the teacher something and children privately writing to the teacher.

The teacher needs to reply to each child in writing, and although this is an extra commitment for the teacher, many teachers have found that the value of the journal writing outweighs the burden of the extra work involved.

In journal writing the child is first and foremost a writer (not a learner) and the teacher is a correspondent (not an assessor). The teacher might ask questions to prompt the child to provide more information, or offer gentle advice. Teachers have reported that when the use of the journal is voluntary it is rare that the whole class opts to write at length. Usually the pattern varies, and a group of children use the journal for a period of time and then perhaps others decide they want to write, so the burden of 'responding' is not too onerous.

Time can be allocated for journal writing. Some teachers provide time at the beginning of the day as the class settles, or during 'quiet reading'. Other teachers have allowed children to write in their journals in break or lunch times.

Term 1

Teacher reads aloud	Group reading	Individual reading
Historical story	Myths and legends	Adventure/mystery stories
Teacher highlights textual characteristics of the form	Children attempt to write own myth for peers	

Term 2

Teacher reads aloud	Group reading	Individual reading
Science fiction	Groups read myths written by peers	Stories by the same author
	Children attempt to write own science fiction story for younger children	Teacher provides background to author and examples of different texts
	Children write author profile for other classes	

Term 3

Teacher reads aloud	Group reading	Individual reading
Stories from other cultures	Play script	Stories that 'raise issues'
	Teacher scaffolds children's writing of a play based on 'issues', e.g. bullying	

Figure 12.1 A framework for linking reading and writing

The journal writing is private and confidential and children should be reassured that the teacher will not share the content of the journal with others without obtaining their permission.

For some children journal writing can be their first opportunity to experience the power of writing as a form of communication.

Assessment of writing

Effective assessment informs teaching and promotes learning. There is always the danger that writing is assessed solely in terms of its surface features of spelling and handwriting or that teachers respond by making an evaluative comment such as 'What an exciting story!' If children are to progress as writers it is very important that assessment focuses upon the nature of the writing task so that children are given credit for achieving mastery over aspects of the writing process even though not all elements may be fully developed.

The marking criteria provided by the Qualifications and Curriculum Authority (QCA) in the mark schemes which accompany the Key Stage 2 test give clear guidance about how to assess children's writing, both narrative and non-narrative. The assessment is divided into two categories:

- Purpose and Organisation
- Grammar (subdivided into Punctuation and Style).

This grid is often called the POGS grid (Purpose/ Organisation/Grammar/Style).

The descriptions of the language features expected at each National Curriculum level help teachers both to credit children with aspects of the writing process that are successful and to indicate where specific parts of the writing could be improved. For example, tracking the development of story cohesion:

Well below Level 3: ... isolated statements
Below Level 3: ... one or two events in chronological
  sequence
Level 3: ... main features of story structure are used to
  organise events
Level 4: ... coherent and well paced ... events logically
  related
Level 5: ... well-structured ...

High Level 5: ... well-constructed ... development of a theme.

(Further examples of grids to aid assessment can be found in *The Writing Repertoire: Developing Writing at Key Stage 2* (NFER 1997).)

Once teachers can successfully isolate particular skills that may need honing these can become the feature of subsequent teaching. and in this way there is a cycle from teaching to assessment to teaching.

Teachers need to assess writing across the range of writing experiences to ensure that children are developing in all areas of writing and are not just becoming proficient at a particular form of writing.

Types of assessment

To be fully comprehensive assessment should take place in a range of ways:

- observing children writing
- discussing their finished piece of writing with them
- marking their work (perhaps according to the POGS (Purpose/Organisation/Grammar/Style) grid
- using response partners to gauge peer response
- self-evaluation: with guidance children can become adept at assessing the success of their own writing. The teacher can focus their response to the piece of writing by asking questions:
  Is your choice of audience obvious?
  Are there any bits where another reader might get muddled?
  Are there any bits that you would now like to extend/reduce?
  Children can become very skilled at evaluating their own writing but they are likely to model their evaluations on those they have experienced from their teacher. If they expect little more than a generic comment from the teacher in the form of assessment of a piece of writing then it is unreasonable to expect them to do anything more when evaluating their own writing. We should teach by good example!

All of these kinds of assessment are valid and should form part of the overview of the child as a writer.

The Indicators for Writing Development which form part of the Writing Developmental Continuum of the *First Steps* literacy programme provide clear guidance on characteristics of each phase of writing development and are very useful when assessing children's writing.

SUMMARY

This chapter has outlined the breadth of writing experiences that children should meet at Key Stage 2.

- It has stressed the importance of giving children a clear focus for each writing task in terms of purpose, audience and form.

- It has explored the particular writing requirements of both fiction and non-fiction and considered some practical ways in which these can be introduced in the classroom.

- Finally it has looked at effective assessment which informs teaching and identifies learning opportunities.

References

Anon. (1993) *The Little Red Hen*, Ladybird: Favourite Tales
Dewsbury, A. (1994) *First Steps: Developmental Continuum* and *Resource Books*, Heinemann Educational Books
DfE (1993) *English for Ages 5 to 16: Proposals of the Secretary of State for Education*, HMSO
DfEE (1998) *The National Literacy Strategy: Framework for Teaching*, DfEE
King-Smith, Dick (1989) *The Hodgeheg*, Puffin
Rees, F. (ed.) (1996) *The Writing Repertoire: Developing Writing at Key Stage 2*, NFER
Tomlinson, Jill (1968) *The Owl Who Was Afraid of the Dark*, Puffin
Wray, David and Lewis, Maureen (1996) *Writing Frames: Scaffolding Children's Writing*, Reading and Language Information Centre, University of Reading

Further reading

Beard, R. (1984) *Children's Writing in the Primary School*, Hodder and Stoughton
    A broad overview of the writing process. Although written before the introduction of the National Curriculum this book still is a useful read.
Rees, F. (ed.) (1996) *The Writing Repertoire: Developing Writing at Key Stage 2*, NFER
    A thorough explanation of the writing demands of Key Stage 2, followed by useful practical suggestions for meeting the requirements of range, audience and purpose.
Wray, David and Lewis, Maureen (1995) *Non-Fiction Writing*, Primary Professional Bookshelf series, Scholastic
Wray, David and Lewis, Maureen (1996) *Writing Frames: Scaffolding Children's Writing*, Reading and Language Information Centre, University of Reading
    Both these books provide very useful guidance for supporting a range of writing tasks. The many examples of children's work help to make *Non-Fiction Writing* very practical. *Writing Frames* includes photocopiable frames to structure children's writing.

13 Developing spelling at Key Stage 1 and Key Stage 2

OBJECTIVES

By the end of this chapter you should:

- understand the developmental stages of spelling

- be able to suggest ways of helping the child to move to the next developmental stage

- be able to begin to diagnose reading errors

- be able to suggest strategies to help weak spellers

- know about different approaches to marking spellings

- be able to talk to parents about ways they can support their child's spelling.

> Learning how to spell is an important part of learning to write. Correct spelling makes writing more readable and enables the writer to communicate more easily with his audience. However it is not the main purpose of writing. It is easy to focus on spelling errors first and the content of what was written second when reading children's writing ... Unfortunately if teachers concentrate on spelling, particularly with children who are just beginning to write, they risk inhibiting children's desire to write.
>
> Ann Browne (1996)

Spelling remains one of the more controversial subjects in the National Curriculum. When glaring spelling errors occur in any piece of work it is very difficult to try to look for the message and not be irritated by the intrusion of the poor spelling. Teachers and parents alike want children to write with enjoyment and fluency, and if children are expected to spell every word correctly, and criticised if this is not the case, then many children spend more time seeking help with the spelling of words than they spend on the content of their writing.

We need to ensure that children become confident spellers so that spelling does not become an ogre who prevents children from wanting to write.

Spelling was traditionally taught by offering the children a preselected list of words which they were expected to learn at home, and these were then tested on a selected day of the week. Marks for spellings were taken in by the teacher and sometimes results were displayed on the classroom wall in the belief that this would spur poor spellers to greater effort. Very little information was offered to the children or parents on how to learn these spellings, and frequently the selected words bore very little relationship to the words the children wanted to write.

The importance of achieving a good spelling standard is emphasised in the National Curriculum and the assessment at the end of Key Stage 1 and Key Stage 2. However, it is now generally accepted that children need to be encouraged to write the message first and then 'edit' their writing for clarity and spelling. This is not to ignore spelling but rather to place it in its context as a secretarial and not a creative skill.

The school spelling policy

The majority of schools have a clear spelling policy and scheme of work in place. It is essential that any teacher new to a school should carefully consult this document. The introduction of spelling, the emphasis on rhyme, analogies, and the order of teaching letter sounds should be clearly stated. The approach that the school has towards unaided writing or more formal writing, and the emphasis that is given to spelling within a child's writing, should be set out in this document. However, by the end of Key Stage 1 children are expected to:

- write each letter of the alphabet
- use their knowledge of sound–symbol relationships and phonological patterns
- recognise and use simple spelling patterns
- write common letter strings within familiar and common words
- spell commonly occurring words
- spell words with common prefixes and suffixes
- check the accuracy of their spelling
- use word books and dictionaries, identifying initial letters as the means of locating words.

At the end of Key Stage 2 children are expected to 'be accumulating a bank of words they can spell correctly, and should be taught to check spellings and meanings of words, using dictionaries where appropriate'. They should be taught to:

- spell complex, polysyllabic words that conform to a regular patterns, and to break long and complex words into more manageable units, by using their knowledge of meaning and word structure;
- memorise the visual patterns of words, including those that are irregular;
- recognise silent letters;
- use the apostrophe to spell shortened forms of words;
- use appropriate terminology, including vowel and consonant.

In order to achieve these goals teachers need to understand the developmental stages of spelling and be able to assess and diagnose each child's work in order to help them to move to the next developmental stage. (See Figure 13.1.)

Stage of development	Child's knowledge	Teacher's task
Preliminary	• understands that mark-making • represents a message scribbles • may 'write' from left to right • may produce some letter shapes	• show how print represents words in books • demonstrate by writing for child • draw attention to print in the environment • play rhyming games
Semi-phonetic	• makes more letter shapes • knows left–right direction • knows sounds are represented by letters • may leave space between words	• write sentences for child in highlighter pen • encourage word–print matching • encourage rhyme analogy • introduce 'invented' spellings
Phonetic	• writing can be decoded • knows most letter sounds • has a bank of basic words spelled correctly • begins to use analogies • has some understanding about • importance of vowels	• provide interesting writing tasks • teach initial letter sounds • keep record of words known • teach initial letter and vowel combinations • teach digraphs and blends
Transitional	• begins to look at words • releases phonic spelling • uses 'known' spellings liberally • likes to get spellings correct • uses 'Look, Say, Cover, Think, Write and Check' to learn spellings	• teach 'Look, Say, Cover, Think, Write and Check' routine • show use of analogies • play dictionary games • help child to select and learn own spellings • encourage interest in words
Conventional	• has large number of words correct • finds learning new words easy • realises if spelling is incorrect • has interest in new words • is a confident writer	• introduce thesaurus • continue dictionary skills • encourage use of wide range of exciting words • explain word roots

Figure 13.1 The developmental stages of spelling

The preliminary stage

Many children come to school with considerable knowledge about writing. They know that marks on paper have meaning and that adults can interpret these marks. At this stage children often draw lines or 'scribble', perhaps with some letter shapes included, and ask the adult 'What does this say?' They believe that they have written something meaningful and whatever the adult suggests is likely to be accepted. What the child is demonstrating by this remark is that they know that marks made on paper carry meanings.

However they have not yet understood that there is a correspondence between the marks/letters produced and the sounds in words.

Some children at this stage make marks which generally go from left to right; other children may include letter shapes within their writing and often intersperse this with numbers.

Figure 13.2 Example of writing of child in preliminary stage of development

What the teacher needs to do
When children are at this stage teachers need to teach them to understand that letters have specific forms and that they are used to represent definite words. They also need to begin to attend more to the sounds of words and try to identify those words which rhyme.

- Surround the children with print and talk about what is written.
- Draw attention to print and explain to the children what you are doing when you write. For example: 'I am writing today's day on the board. This says "Wednesday" .'
- Play rhyming games with the children. For example: 'Do these words rhyme?' (cat/mat cat/grass cat/cut). Teach them nursery rhymes and then deliberately make mistakes so that the children offer the correct rhyme. For example: 'Hickory, dickory dock / The mouse ran up the window'.

The semi-phonetic stage

After children have been in school for a short time, many start to try to write using more and more letter shapes. They begin to understand that 'letter sounds' are a way of representing the words they want to write. They often use letter names to convey whole syllables. For example, they use r for 'are', *AT* for 'eighty'.

At the same time they are learning how to form their letters correctly and they are acquiring some words that they can write from memory, for example 'I', 'am', 'the'. However, for words they do not know they often only use consonants, for example *jgn* for 'dragon'.

What the teacher needs to do
- Continue to surround the child with print and point out how this represents words.
- Offer opportunities for the child to experiment with writing
- Let the child point to the printed words when

This is me w   f the d

To u

This is me waiting for the door to open

Figure 13.3 Example of writing of child in semi-phonetic stage of development reading to encourage voice/word match.

- Write sentences for the child using their own language, for example 'I am playing in the garden'. Read the sentence to the child and point to the words as you read. Make a second strip of the same sentence and cut it into individual words. Ask the child to match and identify the words.
- Write a sentence for the child using highlighter pen. Let the child write over this sentence with a pencil. Try to encourage the correct formation of these letters.
- Continue to play rhyming games. Ask the child to identify the two words that rhyme out of a choice of three: for example dog/log/mat, floor/window/door, fat/fan/mat. Ensure that the child understands the concept of rhyme.
- Ask the children to clap syllables in words: for example win-dow, walk-ing, book-case.
- Ask the children to identify the words in a sentence by putting down a counter for each word.
- Teach initial letter sounds. There is no 'best' order for introducing letters, but many schools combine the letters they introduce to complement the letter-formation pattern they have chosen for handwriting. Other teachers may follow a commercial programme which has an order already specified.

Children need many enjoyable activities to help them consolidate letter sounds. For example, play card games:

- Provide cards with pictures on them and ask the child to put down any card that has a picture starting with the sound of the letter card you have placed on the table.
- Put objects down on a tray starting with different letter sounds. Show the child a letter card and ask them to pick up the object that starts with the sound of the letter card.

The phonetic stage

At this stage children have developed a system of writing that can be read by others even though many words may not be correctly spelt. They are able to separate individual letter sounds (phonemes) out of words but they are only just beginning to explore the rules by which letters represent phonemes. They begin to apply phonic knowledge from one word to another: for example rat-cat-hat, make-cake-take. They are acquiring many more 'sight words' which they incorporate into their writing. They are beginning to understand certain spelling forms, for example -*ing*, -*ed*. Most words now contain a vowel but some children need more specific help in order to identify which vowel sound is required in a word.

What the teacher needs to do

- Encourage the child to continue writing – provide a steady agenda of interesting writing tasks.
- Praise the child's efforts and show the child which letters are correct in any misspelt words.
- Keep a record of the words the child now has as a spelling vocabulary.
- Check for common words that are misspelled and encourage the child to learn these.
- Introduce the child to the 'Look, Say, Cover, Think, Write and Check' procedure (see page 125).
- Teach initial letter and vowel combinations. For example, show the children the letters *ba, be, bi, bo, bu,* and ask them what word is made when they add the letters t, n, d. When they are secure in blending initial letter and vowel to a final letter, change to splitting the first consonant from the vowel and consonant: for example *b- at, b-et, b-it, b-ut*. Children need to be able to hear the different vowel sounds within words.

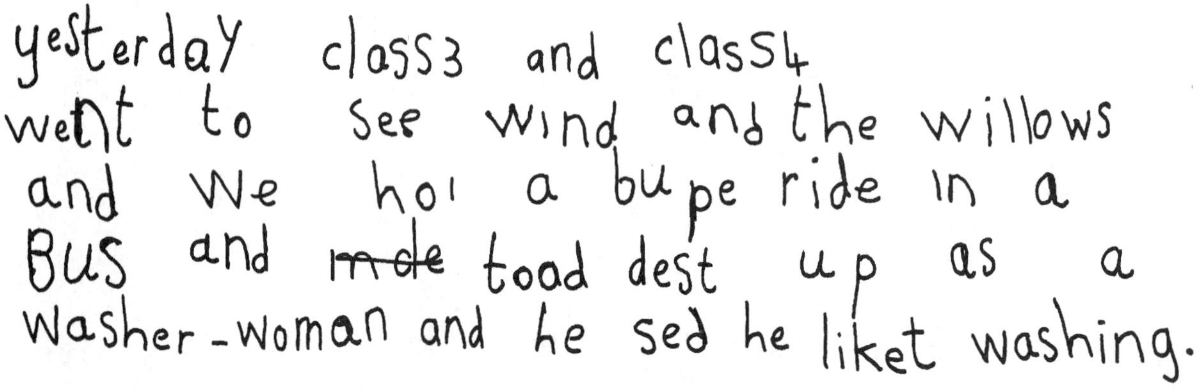

yesterday class3 and class4
went to see wind and the willows
and we hoı a bupe ride in a
Bus and mde toad dest up as a
washer-woman and he sed he liket washing.

Figure 13.4 Example of writing of child in phonetic stage of development

- Teach children to use analogy to help them to spell words. Explain to them that if they can spell *can* they are also able to spell *man, pan, fan, ran, van*. Use the words they are writing in unaided writing time to select the analogy pattern.

Note that this stage of development can often take two to three years of schooling and is likely to be the main approach used by children in Year 2 for the majority of their words.

The transitional stage

This stage covers most of the primary school years 3–6. Children now begin to release phonic spellings and pay more attention to the letters within words. They are able to break out phonemes from words and find letters to spell them. They start to use more conventional letter patterns to represent sounds although they may get them incorrect, for example the child who writes 'nitgh' for 'night'. They usually include a vowel in each word and are aware that it is the vowels that cause them problems. They use their 'known' words in great abundance and may limit their writing by trying to keep within this known vocabulary.

What the teacher needs to do
- Praise the children for trying to 'do their best' when

spelling an unknown word. If children believe that the teacher wants correct spelling above content then children in this stage tend to remain within their known vocabulary and it is difficult to persuade them to be more adventurous.
- Provide lots of opportunities for children to see the importance of analogies. It is possible to take a 'letter string' of the week and ask children to seek for words which contain this string. For example, *ake* could lead to the obvious 'make/take/lake' analogies but also be found in 'mistake' and 'baker'.
- Correct children's spelling by linking errors to analogies so that they practise the letter string from a word they wanted to write. For example, if they misspelt 'night' they could be given a list which included 'right' and also 'height', 'slight', etc.
- Encourage the children to try to learn spellings using the 'Look, Say, Cover, Think, Write and Check' approach. This was advocated by Margaret Peters to enable children to move away from relying too greatly upon phonic representation.

The 'Look, Say, Cover, Think, Write and Check' approach
In this approach the teacher writes the chosen word for the children in the handwriting style of the school. The children look carefully at the word with the intent to reproduce it. The teacher then covers the word and asks the children if they can 'see' in it their head. The children then try to write the word correctly from memory and finally check their attempt against the original.

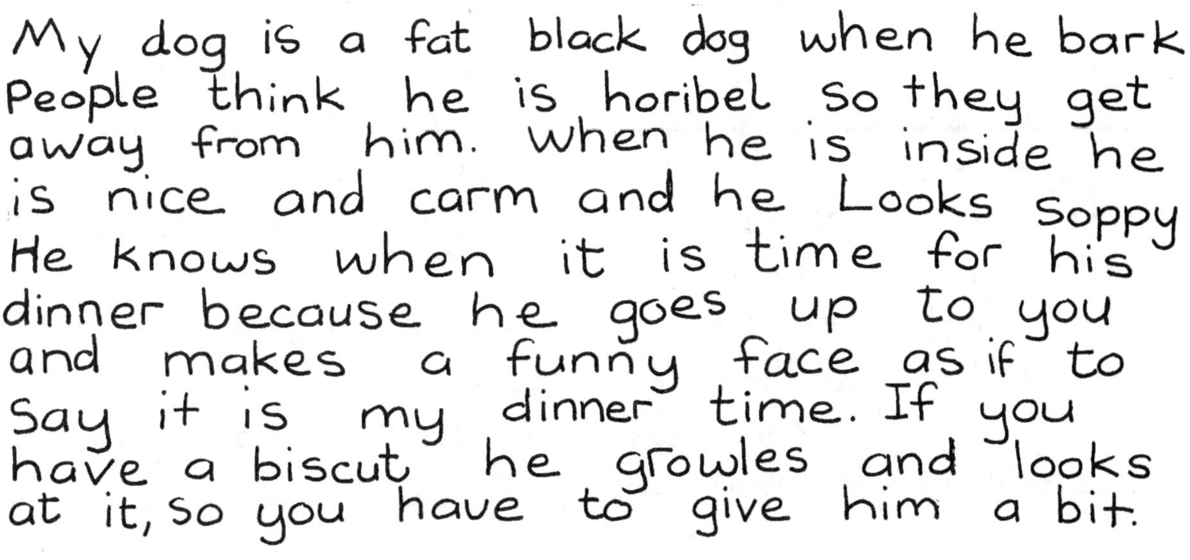

My dog is a fat black dog when he bark People think he is horibel so they get away from him. When he is inside he is nice and carm and he Looks soppy He knows when it is time for his dinner because he goes up to you and makes a funny face as if to say it is my dinner time. If you have a biscut he growles and looks at it, so you have to give him a bit.

Figure 13.5 Example of child writing within 'known' vocabulary

If this is to be really effective the children need to make a conscious effort to hold the spelling in their spelling repertoire. To encourage this, ask the children to look at the spelling of the word they requested on your desk and to retain it in their heads until they return to their table. If they just glance at the word you have written for them and then write the chosen word immediately their retention is likely to be very superficial and they 'forget' the spelling very quickly.

The conventional stage (the correct speller)

Children who reach this stage may still spell words incorrectly but they usually know when this has occurred although they may not know how to correct the spelling. They rely upon a visual approach to spelling and when in doubt they tend to write several alternative spellings for the word they want and recognise the correct one. These children have a good basic knowledge of our spelling system and its rules. They recognise features of words, for example prefixes and suffixes, and apply this knowledge when they are writing. They are able to distinguish homophones and generally use the correct form: for example meet/meat, night/knight, there/their. They become interested in words and acquire a rapidly increasing vocabulary which they then endeavour to write. They are not afraid of

making spelling mistakes and quickly learn the 'correct' spelling if this is pointed out to them.

What the teacher needs to do

- Praise the children for using adventurous and exciting language.
- Encourage the children to use a thesaurus for alternative words.
- Ask the children to 'collect' words which have some common pattern, e.g. suffix and prefix.
- Encourage the children to note words that they read but they may not fully understand. Let the children look these up in a dictionary and discuss their meaning and possible use within a sentence.

Diagnosing why children are making spelling errors

If we can understand what the child is trying to do when writing a word that is incorrectly spelt it is easier to help them correct this word. In the early years of schooling children are now encouraged to use 'invented' spelling when they are writing stories and to concentrate upon what they want to say rather than queue up at the teacher's desk to ask for a word. By looking carefully at what the child does when writing a 'new' word it is possible to diagnose the child's approach and to use this information to help with future spellings.

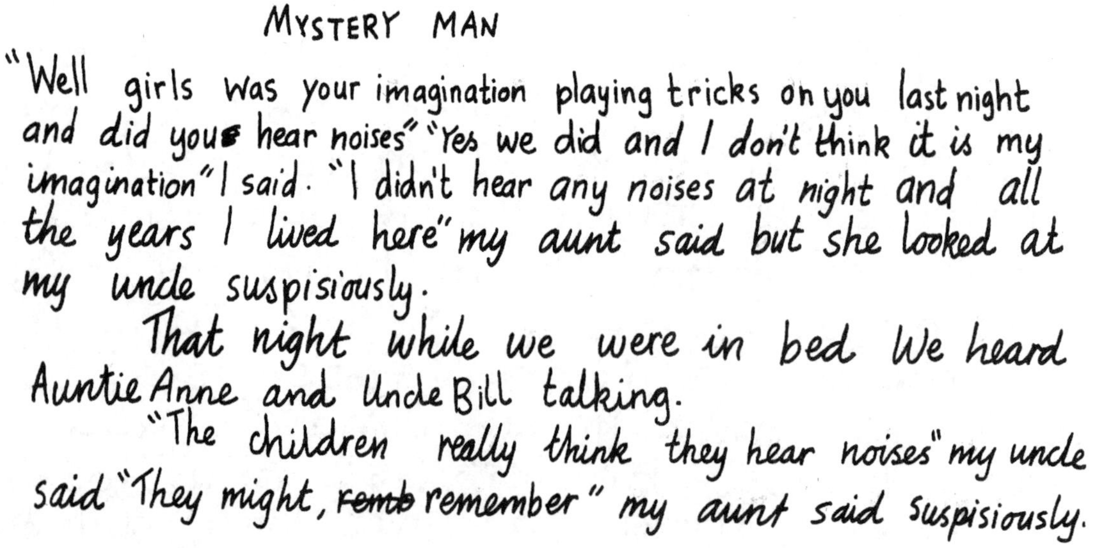

MYSTERY MAN

"Well girls was your imagination playing tricks on you last night and did yous hear noises" "Yes we did and I don't think it is my imagination" I said. "I didn't hear any noises at night and all the years I lived here" my aunt said but she looked at my uncle suspisiously.

That night while we were in bed We heard Auntie Anne and Uncle Bill talking.

"The children really think they hear noises" my uncle said "They might, ~~remb~~ remember" my aunt said suspisiously.

Figure 13.6 Example of writing of child in 'correct' stage of development

Some possible explanations for spelling errors

- The children write the letter *y* for words beginning with *w*. This is because they know that the letter y is called 'wye' and that *w* is called 'double yu'. So *y* sounds more like the beginning sound in 'went' and 'once'.
- They use letter names to represent letter strings, for example *r* for 'are', *u* for 'you'.
- They start words beginning with *tr* using *chr*. This is because the two sounds are very close and our recognition of the *tr* is more likely to come from knowing the spelling rather than from hearing a difference.
- They write *j* for *dr*. This is because the sound we produce for *dr* is closer to a *j* sound. Our recognition is driven by knowledge of the spelling rather than a clear hearing of the sound. So children may write *jragon* for 'dragon', *jrive* for 'drive', *jrink* for 'drink'.
- They write *hey* for 'he'. This is because they try to 'sound out' the sounds in a word by exaggerating them, and consequently they produce phonic features that are not usually sounded; for example *huw* for 'who', *miy* for 'my'.
- They represent two words as one because they hear them together; for example *mustof* for 'must have', *wonsa ponatim* for 'once upon a time', *havto* for 'have to'.
- Some children seem to reverse words they intend to write. For example, the child wants to write 'was' but produces 'saw'. This is because they put down the last letter of the word they want as it was the letter they 'held onto' within their head. Having put down the *s* they then switch to remembering the other letters and write *aw*.
- Older children have often learnt that it pays to be indeterminate, and they make small letter shapes that could be interpreted as *ie* or *ei*, placing the dot somewhere in the middle.

By looking carefully at the letters the child is putting into 'invented' spellings it is possible to see the reason behind their choice and to guide the child to use other more effective strategies next time.

Correcting children's spelling errors

The teacher's job is not to correct mistakes the pupil has already made but to help him not to make the mistake next time.

Mike Torbe (1977)

It should always be clear to the child how and why a teacher is marking work. If all that the child does is put away the work and never refer to it again, the time and effort a teacher has spent on marking is wasted.

After sharing work on the content of a piece of writing, the teacher may decide to help the children to get the secretarial skills correct.

1   If the writing is a first draft and something that the child is quite happy to spend editing, then helping to indicate incorrect spellings is often welcomed by them. Either ask the child to look over their own work and underline any words about which they are uncertain, or suggest they exchange work with their response partner and check each other's spellings. When they have finished doing this, write the correct word in the margin, or, if the work is on separate sheets of 'practice' paper, write the corrections on the reverse of the page. Tell the children then to write the corrections over their mistakes. They should use the 'Look, Say, Cover, Think, Write and Check' technique.

2   If the writing is not to be edited be careful not to select too many words for correction. Select a few of the most useful words for the child to learn and encourage them to make these a priority.

3   Sometimes telling the child they have got a certain number of mistakes and seeing if they can find them helps the child to scan their work and look more carefully at the words. Again select a reasonable number for the child to learn.

4   Asking the child to read their work aloud can help them to realise where punctuation has gone astray.

5   When correcting errors it is important that the teacher writes out the complete word and does not just insert missing letters. The child needs to get a good visual picture of the word. Writing above the incorrect word can help the child to see where their mistake lay. If the child has written in pencil they could correct the spellings and then erase the teacher's word.

6   Praise the child's attempt at a word and try to show where the 'sticky' bit is that has caused the problem. It is rare for a child to get the first letter wrong, and in many cases it is the middle of the word that causes the problem, for example double letters or two vowels.

7   With words that are constantly causing a problem, try the SOS approach that was devised by Lynette Bradley. She provided plastic letters for the child to use to make the word. Then she asked the child to finger-trace the word on to a tactile surface, for example a piece of carpet, saying the names of the letters as they formed them. Finally the child wrote the word three times on to a piece of paper. She

suggested that they should practise this word every day for a week.

Remember that marking children's errors is always less important than sharing the content of the work and helping the children to express themselves clearly.

Helping the weak speller in Key Stage 2

Many children on entering Year 3 are anxious about spelling, and as they progress up the school can easily be convinced that they will never gain mastery over spelling.

What the teacher needs to know

It is essential to know what words the child can spell with confidence. (A list of common words is provided in Figure 9.1 on page 87. This could form the basis for this assessment. Remember it can be very exhausting for a child to struggle with writing words for more than a short period of time. It is more effective to select a few words to check each time than to try to assess all 100 words in one sitting.)

It is important to assess what strategies the child is using to write unknown words. In many cases their phonic knowledge is patchy and they use some initial letter knowledge or some consonant cluster knowledge to start the words they need but rarely finish the word with letter-sound matching. It is this varied acquisition of words that tends to make their attempts appear bizarre. They will have some difficult words correct and some 'easy' words far from correct.

What the teacher needs to do

- In order to assess what the child can manage either ask them to write words from the list of 100 common words in Figure 9.1 or dictate simple sentences using high-frequency words, for example 'Are you in here?' 'I will go and find him.' If possible do not include difficult nouns.
- Assess the phonic knowledge that the child has firmly established. Start with checking the child's ability to recognise rhyme, then look at initial letter sounds and the names of the letters. Continue by checking whether the child knows the five main digraphs (*th, ch, sh, wh* and final *ck*). Check that the

child can identify a short medial vowel when linked to a consonant, for example *be, be, bi, bo, bu*. Finally check which consonant clusters the child can produce.
- Ask the child what they do when they are uncertain of a spelling.
- Look carefully at the spelling errors the child makes when asked to use invented spelling.
- Draw the child's attention to analogies. If they can write one word this knowledge can be used to help with the spellings of other words, for example 'king', 'ring', 'sing', 'spring', etc.
- Ask the child to learn to write words which they frequently misspell and use the kinaesthetic approach. Select the word for the child to learn and write it on to card. Show the child the word and ask them to say the names of the letters. Tell the child to trace the letters onto a tactile surface, for example a piece of carpet, saying the names of the letters as they do so. Repeat this three times and then ask the child to write the word without copying on to paper. This word should be practised daily for a week.
- When marking spelling, endeavour to show the child the letters that they have written correctly and to identify the 'problem' part of the word.
- Offer as many games and activities to support the learning of words as possible. A game with an element of luck removes the blame for not 'winning' away from the responsibility of the individual child.
- Praise the child for good attempts, and for correct work.
- Do not place impossible goals before worried learners. It is essential that the child perceives that they will learn to spell, and encouragement is more likely to achieve this than any criticism.
- Many parents worry that a school is not 'teaching' their child to spell because the school is allowing first drafts of creative writing to contain spelling errors. It is essential that parents know and understand what the school is doing in order to help their child become a confident and correct speller.

Parents and spelling

- Provide a written description of the spelling policy and explain the aims and methods used for teaching spelling.
- Explain to parents the phonic teaching that the school follows.
- Help parents to help their child learn spellings by explaining the 'Look, Say, Cover, Think, Write and Check' approach.
- Ask parents to alert you to any problems that their

child has with spelling. A worried parent often produces a worried child.

- Ensure that parents realise the importance of *not* criticising.
- Talk to parents about possible games that help with spelling, such as 'Scrabble', 'Boggle', 'I spy'.
- Remind parents that spelling ability is not an indication of intelligence nor is weak spelling a sign of laziness.

Spelling is important and children need to want to get their final writing correct and readable, but this is far more likely to be achieved if the teacher is sympathetic to problems and ensures that the children are given clear strategies and achievable goals, rather than criticism and tests.

Remember that as children become better spellers mistakes appear more surprising, and consequently it is often just as the child is becoming a confident writer that we start to say 'mind your spellings'!

SUMMARY

This chapter has discussed:

- the developmental stages of spelling
- what teachers can do to encourage correct spelling
- possible explanations of spelling errors
- ways of correcting a child's spelling
- the place and importance of parents.

Further reading

Dewsbury, Alison (1994) *First Steps. Spelling: Developmental Continuum* and *Spelling: Resource Book*, Heinemann Educational Books
These two substantial volumes provide a very thorough overview of the development of spelling and provide extensive ideas for implementing a spelling policy in the classroom. They are an excellent resource, providing activities and ideas for every spelling situation.

Gentry, R. (1987) *Spel Is a Four-Letter Word*, Scholastic
This is a very readable book. It describes the different stages of spelling development, and the sympathetic approach to spelling difficulties gives teachers greater insights into the anxieties of weak spellers.

Goswami, U. and Bryant, P. (1990) *Phonological Skills and Learning to Read*, Laurence Erlbaum Associates
This academic book describes the research of Goswami and Bryant into the phonological development of young children. They explore the importance of 'onset' and 'rime' and suggest ways in which this could be introduced into the classroom.

Mudd, Norma (1994) *Effective Spelling: A Practical Guide for Teachers*, Hodder and Stoughton
This readable book provides an overview of the teaching of spelling through the twentieth century and looks at ways of helping children to become confident and competent spellers.

14 Developing handwriting at Key Stages 1 and 2

OBJECTIVES

By the end of this chapter you should:

- understand the developmental stages of handwriting

- be aware of the problems that children experience with handwriting in Key Stages 1 and 2

- be able to assess and help children to progress through the stages of handwriting development.

Developing handwriting at Key Stage 1

Handwriting is a taught skill, nothing about it is natural. It is a motor skill. This means that the body learns, then automates the movement of the hand and arm which in turn produce the written trace. Once a movement is automated, it is very difficult to alter. For this reason it is very important to have an efficient method of teaching handwriting right from the beginning.

Rosemary Sassoon (1983)

If children are to become swift writers of information, ideas and stories they need to be able to 'write' quickly and accurately. Ensuring that handwriting and spelling are taught systematically, thoroughly and carefully will enable children to put down their ideas without being held up by the physical act of handwriting. The importance of this aspect of the National Curriculum is recognised in the inclusion of handwriting for assessment at the end of both Key Stage 1 (Year 2) and Key Stage 2 (Year 6):

[Pupils] should be taught the conventional ways of forming letters, both lower case and capitals. They should build on their knowledge of letter formation to join letters in words. They should develop an awareness of the importance of clear and neat presentation in order to communicate meaning effectively.

(Key Skills, KS1 Writing)

They should be taught to use different forms of handwriting for different purposes, *eg print for labelling maps or diagrams; a clear, neat hand for finished, presented work; a faster script for notes*.

(Key Skills, KS2 Writing)

The school handwriting policy

The majority of schools now have a clear handwriting policy and scheme of work firmly in place. It is essential that any teacher new to the school should consult this document. The school's style of writing and a suggestion as to when children are expected to assimilate handwriting knowledge should be clearly indicated. Each school has a choice with regard to the style of handwriting and the stage at which children are helped to join their letters. However, by the end of Key Stage 1 children are expected to:

- form all their letters correctly, both lower case and capitals
- produce letters of the same size with clear ascenders and descenders
- produce uniform spacing between the words
- join most letters in words
- be aware of the importance of clear and neat presentation.

In order to achieve these goals children need to be taught systematically and imaginatively as soon as they enter school.

Pre-school writing experiences

Most children come to school having made marks with a writing tool, usually upon paper! It is now recognised that even the earliest of mark-making will show some development. When a child is first

Figure 14.1 Example of early mark-making

given a crayon they are likely to hold it in a fist-like grip. The hand movements are large and often sweeping. The marks owe much to the random contact with the paper rather than deliberate strokes. As the child becomes more familiar with this activity the marks become more numerous and deliberate.

Children who have had encouragement at home to experiment with pencil and paper start to try to emulate the writing they see adults performing. They begin to do some or all of the following:

- change from holding the 'pencil' like a fist to often placing all their fingers round the stem of the pencil (sometimes called the tripod grasp)
- begin to make much smaller marks, which may go from left to right across the page
- sometimes leave spaces between these marks
- may make marks which have a specific shape to them: go up, down or side to side
- with increased control produce small circular marks or a combination of marks
- finally begin to produce some letter-like shapes, and children often state 'I'm writing'.

The role of the parents

Parents need to be told about this development and encouraged to see the importance of 'scribble'. They need to know how to help their child progress through these early stages. It is essential that they do not demean the efforts of the child to make 'writing-like marks' but instead respond with praise and encouragement so that the child comes to school with a positive attitude and enthusiasm for using pencils.

It is not easy to say exactly when children are ready to learn to write in a more formal and accurate way. The skill of pencil control does not depend upon intelligence but upon the development of fine motor control. Parents need to be told how to help their children with writing, and as many children are ready to make letter shapes before they come to school it is best if parents can be shown how to help their child form these letters correctly. Schools need to have written guidelines for parents on how to help their children with writing and letter formation. A clear sheet of instructions on letter formation should be available as well as information on how to support their child's writing.

Advice to pre-school parents/carers

The following suggestions could be sent home to guide parents or carers on ways to support their child's handwriting development.

- Encourage your child to hold thick crayons (or felt tips so long as the ink will only go on to paper and not clothes or walls) and make marks. Praise and comment on their achievement.
- Offer your child a variety of pencils or crayons and encourage them to choose different implements for writing.
- Talk to your child about writing, for example when you are making a shopping list, writing a letter, taking down a telephone message. Let your child 'pretend' to do the same. Praise your child for their efforts.

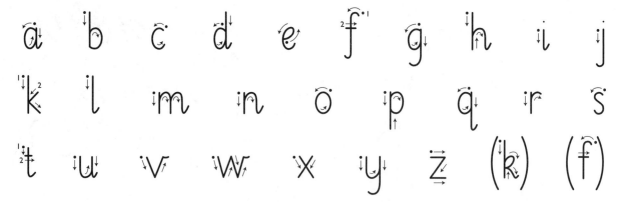

Figure 14.2 Lower-case letter formation

- Show your child how you write from left to right and how you represent the words that you say in print. Point out that you leave spaces between the words. Praise your child if they make a similar movement across the page and possibly leave spaces between the marks.
- Look at the 'scribble' and note the development from up-and-down marks to small circular movements. Do not try to force this development as this only makes your child anxious and less likely to think of writing as something that is enjoyable or fun.
- Encourage your child to colour in large outline drawings or their own drawing. Children appreciate it if you help by colouring in some of the page and they also watch how you move your crayon to keep within the lines. In this way you demonstrate what they should be trying to achieve and they begin to try to copy what you are doing.
- Try to ensure they are sitting comfortably, with their feet on the ground and their arm resting on the table.
- Give lots of praise and encouragement when your child 'writes' for you. If children come to school having enjoyed writing and understand the purpose of writing they move easily into the more formal tasks of writing that they encounter at school.

The developmental stages of handwriting

Children acquire writing skills at different rates, and although it is possible to relate this roughly to a child's chronological age it can be very inaccurate. It is far more productive to try to assess what a child can do and to build upon this knowledge

rather than to worry that a child has not reached a certain standard by a certain age.

The preliminary stage

This is likely to have begun before children arrive at school. In this stage children understand that writing represents a message or a story. They may know that writing goes from left to right and that it is made up of marks. Some children may use some letter shapes to represent their message and some may even be using phonic knowledge to help them to write their message. They may also be aware that some letters are larger than others.

Figure 14.3 Example of writing by child in the preliminary stage

What the teacher needs to do

When children are at this stage it is essential that they understand that words represent information. All children have to understand the purpose of writing and to want to write their own messages in a way that will be understood by their readers.

- When reading to the class talk to the children about words, letters and the importance of writing.
- Demonstrate to the children how you write down what they say. Talk to the children as you write and talk about letters and spacing.
- Introduce the children to letter patterns and set aside a time when they can do this without interruptions.
- Display important words on posters on the classroom wall and label drawings and paintings done by the children. Read these to the children and talk about the letters and words that are displayed.
- Begin to teach the children specific letter shapes. Draw the letter on the board and talk through the letter formation as you do this. Ask the children to 'draw' this letter in the air and to say aloud the same description as you gave. For example, 'Round, down, up, down and flick' could describe the letter 'a'.
- Provide the children with sheets of paper on which you have drawn the outline of the letter in highlighter pen. Tell the children to go over your example and to verbalise the way the letter is made as they go over the letter shape.
- Check the sitting position of the children and ensure they are comfortable. Some children are at tables that are too high for them and some children are too tall for the chairs. Remember if children are uncomfortable they soon wish to abandon the task.

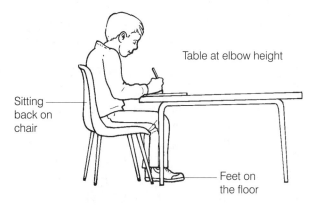

Figure 14.4 Child in correct seating position

- Encourage the children to hold the pencil correctly. There are several commercial 'pencil grips' on the market that help children to become accustomed to holding the pencil correctly.
- Check for left-handed children in the class and ensure that you give them specific help with letter formation. If possible show them how to form the letters using your left hand.
- Give the children plenty of practice in both letter patterns and letter shapes.

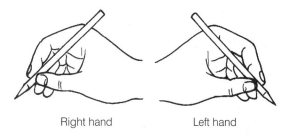

Figure 14.5 Correct pencil hold for right- and left-handers

First letter shapes

As children become more aware of letter shapes in the environment so they begin to try to use them more and more. It is very easy for children to reproduce a letter but *not* to use correct letter formation. For example, most children prefer to make a line going from the bottom of the letter to the top. In the busy classroom it is impossible to check that all children are forming their letters correctly all the time. However, if it does not interrupt the flow of a child's writing, reminding them how to form a letter by giving them a starting dot and encouraging correct letter formation as often as possible will produce results.

The school policy and scheme of work is likely to indicate which letters the teacher needs to teach first. This may be linked to a commercial product or be the result of staff discussion. There is no definite 'best' order but all letters do need to be taught until their formation is 'automatic' and some connection between letters which have a similar formation is generally accepted as more valuable. The letters shown in Figure 14.6 have been grouped together because they are formed in a similar way.

Note: The characters *e f k j s z* are not in a letter family and they have to be taught individually.

It is always worth explaining to children how the letter pattern will help them to form their letters and to show them how many letters are formed from a basic pattern. Children need to practise their letter formation until it is neat and automatic.

What the teacher needs to do

- Teach letter formation by modelling the formation to the class.
- Talk about the way the letter is formed.
- Let the children trace over the letter shape. Letters can be cut out of very fine sandpaper or sticky-backed baize. There are also commercial alphabet

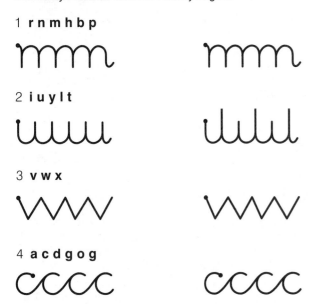

1 **r n m h b p**

2 **i u y l t**

3 **v w x**

4 **a c d g o g**

Figure 14.6 Examples of letter groups and associated letter patterns

friezes available which have raised letters so that the children receive a tactile feel of the letter shape when they trace over the letters with the index finger of their writing hand.

- Ask the children to form the letter in the air with the index finger of their writing hand.
- Provide a variety of activities which encourage the children to form the letters. For example: writing the letter in sand; drawing the letter with paint on large sheets of paper; providing practice sheets which have the outline of the letter clearly visible for the children to go over; providing 'best' pieces of paper for the children to decorate with the chosen letter from memory.
- Encourage the children to look carefully at the letters they have made and to select those that are the best. Children need to judge for themselves which letters look the best and then strive to form all their letters to this standard.
- Praise those letters that are correctly formed.
- Praise the progress that the children make over time. It is very helpful if children can begin to assess for themselves the progress they have made, and showing them the change from their first letter attempts to their later letter formation enables children and their parents to see what they have achieved.

Moving towards a joined hand

When children can form each letter correctly they should be encouraged to start to join letters. The school policy document and the scheme of work is likely to have guidelines on when this should be introduced to children and the order in which to introduce the joining of letters. Before the National Curriculum emphasised the importance of encouraging a joined hand in the early years, most schools left this to Year 3. Now it is expected that most children will be joining many words by Year 2.

In response to the National Curriculum some schools encourage joining from the start of school. However, many children do not have the fine motor control necessary for this and find it very difficult to achieve. Children are also beginning to learn to read, and the difference between their joined letters and the printed letters found in books can lead to confusion. It is more usual for children to start to join some letters in Year 1 and to continue this in Year 2.

Although some children may start to join some letters within words almost without instruction other children do need careful teaching of this action. The following letters have been grouped together because of the way that they move.

1 Letters which join from a low right-side exit point.
a c d e h k l m n p t u x z

These letters join more easily on to another in their group. The teacher needs to model how the join is achieved and use these letters to form short words or letter strings; for example: am, an, up, let, hut, dad, had, put, nut, zap.

2 Letters with a high left-side entry point but without ascenders on the left
a c d e g i j m n o r s u v w x z

Letters in group 1 can be linked to any letter in group 2. Children need to practise joining them either as short words, for example *is, it, am, an, no,* or as letter strings, for example *ant, ate, ac, de, tion.* Some letters are common to both groups and this helps to encourage continuous writing; for example *ate, din, aim, mud, men.*

3 Letters with left-side ascenders
b f h k l t

These letters join quite easily with letters in group 1. The most important thing for the children is to practise the height of the ascenders well as the join. Encourage the children to write common letter strings, for example *ch, th, bl,* or whole words: bad, hill, fan, chap.

More difficult for some children are letters which join from a horizontal line, for example *f, s, r, v, w.* It is easier if children first join these letters to those with a high left-side entry point, as this allows the horizontal entry; for example: *fo, wo, om, ru, va.* These can then be joined to those letters which have high left-side ascenders, for example *ob, fl, ol, ot.*

Depending on the school policy the letters *g, y, p, q, j* and *b* may be left 'free standing' or joined. Many policies leave *g, y, p, q, j* and sometimes *b* without joins. Other handwriting schemes may suggest a more cursive (looped) style, and then these letters form part of continuous writing, as shown in Figure 14.7.

Capital letters

The introduction of capital (upper case) letters should be clearly indicated in the school handwriting policy and scheme of work. Most schools concentrate on teaching the lower-case letters before teaching the capital letters. However, children do need to be able to form both letters correctly and to be able to match the lower case to its capital. Careful teaching of the formation of capital letters is as important as the teaching of the lower case. The capital letters in our alphabet are easier to form than the lower case and most of them are formed by strong straight lines. If children have conquered forming the 'c' pattern in the lower-case letters then the capitals that do need some curved strokes should not be a problem.

Developing handwriting at KS2

Once children are completely accurate in their letter formation and are able to join letters with ease they need to start to develop handwriting skills at different levels for different purposes.

- They need a fast hand for taking notes.
- They need a neat and slower hand for final presentation.

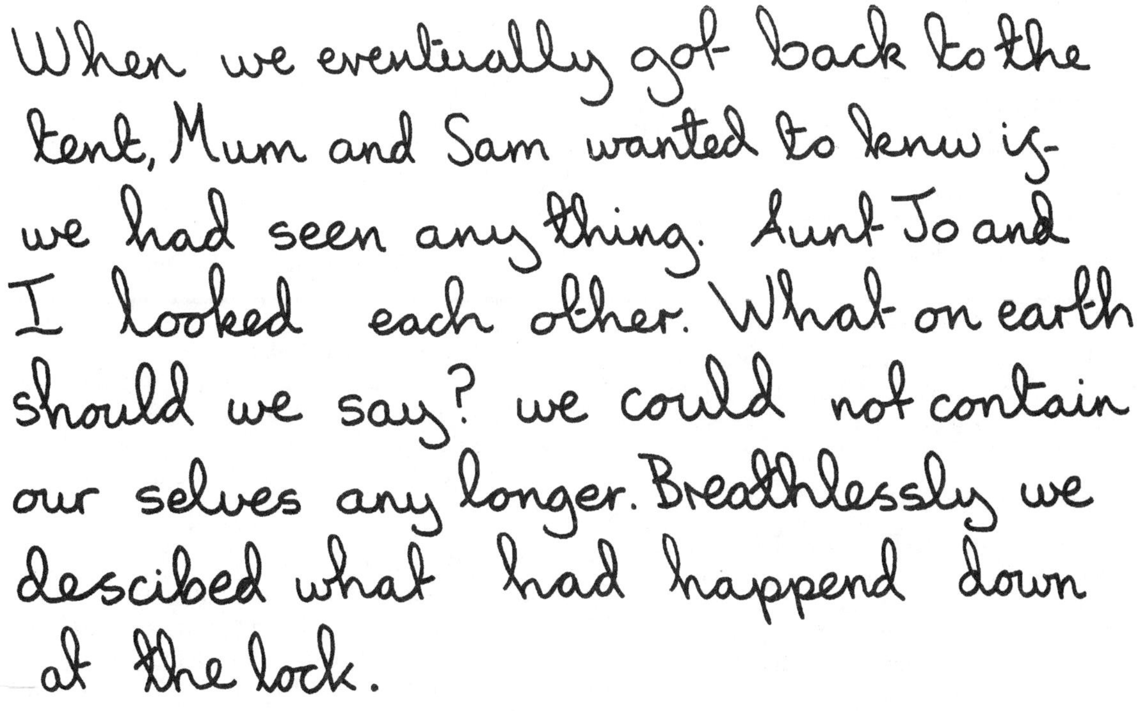

When we eventually got back to the
tent, Mum and Sam wanted to know if
we had seen anything. Aunt Jo and
I looked each other. What on earth
should we say? we could not contain
our selves any longer. Breathlessly we
descibed what had happend down
at the lock.

Figure 14.7 Example of looped handwriting style

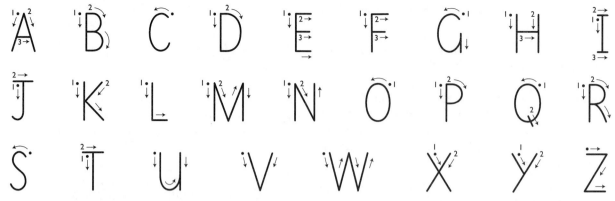

Figure 14.8 Example of upper-case letter formation

- They need to explore different ways of presenting work, for example using capital letters for labelling maps or diagrams.

What the teacher needs to do

- Offer the children different purposes for their writing which need different forms of presentation, for example writing advertisements, invitations, stories, experiments, recipes, letters, etc.
- Offer the children different pen-nib sizes and different writing implements so that they can explore the impact that different writing 'hands' make. For example, they might try the italic form or a looping cursive style for different presentations.
- Encourage the children to assess their own handwriting and select that which retains an individuality but at the same time is neat, swift and readable.
- Talk to the class about the difference between writing at speed when taking notes and the care that is needed for final presentations.

Common problems

Teachers need to intervene as soon as possible when they notice children having handwriting difficulties. The following are some of the most common problems encountered in Years 3–6.

The left-handed child

- Ensure you know which children are left handed and which children are uncertain when they enter school.
- Talk to the parents of any child about whom you have concerns. Ask them which hand they think the child uses most.
- Demonstrate how to form letters using your left hand.

- Help the child to use their left hand to draw the letters in the air.
- Give the left-handed child a thick, soft pencil to write with as this holds the paper more firmly and the thick barrel of the pencil helps to mitigate the very tight grip that these children generally use.
- Sit the left-handed child on the non-writing side of a neighbour so that they do not bump each other's elbows.
- Provide a high enough chair or raise the seat (some schools find the 'Yellow Pages' very useful for this) for the left-handed child to sit on so that their elbow is not 'locked' on to the table.
- Model how to hold the pencil or use a commercial preformed shape to help with the pencil grip.
- Encourage the child to place the paper slightly to the left side and on a slant. This allows that hand to remain below the writing and should not obstruct the writer's view of their writing.
- Explain to the child the need to lift the hand between words in order to see that a space is left between the words. It is not helpful to tell the left-handed child to leave a finger space between words as this causes them to twist their wrists together and the result is disastrous!
- Draw a coloured margin down the left side of the page and remind the left-handed writer to start writing from that side. Many left-handed children seem to want to start to write from right to left.

Starting letters

Some children find it very difficult to gauge the entry point of most letters, and so some schools have adopted a policy of 'every letter starts on the line'. This does give the children a clear starting point but it also perverts some letter shapes, so that children learning to read are faced with the standard printed f or s when reading but are asked to write the more complex 'f' and '$\mathcal{S}$'. These letter shapes bear little resemblance to the printed form, and careful consideration needs to be given to the effect this has on children learning to read if the whole school adopts this policy to help a few children with writing.

A lack of space between words.

If children are copying below a model of writing the spacing between the words is often lost as the child's writing tends to be larger and more erratically formed. Children need to be given a model to trace over until they can form the letters without having to copy the shapes. Using a highlighter pen to provide this model is very effective.

If children have difficulty leaving spaces when they are doing unaided writing the teacher needs to show them the importance of spaces and praise the words that do have spaces between them. Encourage the children to look where they will start a new word before they start to write the next word. Finger spacing is often very interruptive and does not seem to lead many children to getting a feel for the right amount of space they should leave.

In order to emphasise the need for spacing it is possible to write a sentence that the child offers on to a strip of paper and then to cut each word into single units. Ask the child to place down the sentence in order, and when they have done this separate the words and explain that you are leaving the gaps between the words.

The incorrect pencil grip

Show the children the correct grip and provide commercial pencil grips so that their fingers get used to the hold. Try to encourage children to put these grips on to any pencil they are using for continuous writing.

An uncomfortable sitting position

Some children seem to lean half-way across their table when writing, others sit on the very edge of their chairs and some sit with their noses about two centimetres away from the table. Both feet should be on the floor when children are writing, and the non-writing hand should be used to hold the paper steady. Check that the chair is the right size for the table and that the child does have enough room to write.

Not writing along lines

When children first learn to form their letters, it is very difficult to insist that they also write on a line or between lines. Until children have conquered the correct letter formation it is not really advisable to also insist on lines. When children can produce uniform, correctly orientated letters of a reasonable size the introduction of lines is helpful. Some schools find that providing two lines for ensuring a uniform height for lower-case simple letters does help in 'handwriting practice'. The ascenders and descenders are left to the child's discretion. Other schools like to provide two further lines to ensure that height differential is also supported with lines.

In conclusion it should be stressed that all children need to strive for a clear and neat presentation. However, it should be remembered that not all children progress at the same time and that overemphasis upon handwriting style may prevent the child from offering the best language in a piece of writing or even turn them away from enjoying writing. Handwriting is important but it is a secretarial skill and should be the servant of the message that the writer wishes to convey.

SUMMARY

This chapter has looked at the development of handwriting. It has considered:

- the left-to-right direction of our writing system
- the correct formation of the letters
- the importance of the height differential of the ascenders and descenders.
- the need to keep a consistent size and slant to the letters
- the need to leave a regular space between words.

Further reading

Alston, J. (1989) *Writing Left-Handed*, The Left-Handed Company
  A very practical and useful book that describes the problems of left-handed children and ways they can be helped to develop a fluent and neat handwriting style.
Alston, J. and Taylor, J. (1987) *Handwriting Theory, Research and Practice*, Croom Helm
  This book reviews the theory and research on handwriting. It looks at children who have handwriting problems and gives practical suggestions for helping them. It suggests principles and recommendations for a school policy.
Sassoon, R. (1990) *Handwriting: The Way to Teach It*, Stanley Thornes
  A very clearly written book which outlines the ways to teach children handwriting. The author also looks at those children who have made a poor start and developed 'bad habits' and suggests ways of helping and encouraging these children.

15 The use and development of language across the curriculum

OBJECTIVES

By the end of this chapter you should:

- have developed your understanding of the use of language in thinking and learning across the curriculum

- have raised your awareness of the potential of other subjects for developing English skills

- have gained knowledge of how to prepare medium- and short-term plans which include the use and development of language in other subjects.

All lessons include, and largely depend on, oral and written communication. The teacher's role in explaining, questioning, describing, organising and evaluating in the classroom is mostly conducted through talk, and sometimes writing. Pupils are often answering, discussing and working out ideas through talk, and they commonly write in order to record, summarise, note, show evidence of understanding and develop ideas and arguments. To be successful learners, pupils need to read in order to gain access to information and ideas from a range of texts and sources and to evaluate them.

SCAA, *Use of Language: A Common Approach* (1997)

Language and learning are inseparable. Children learn through language, and as they use language to learn they learn more about language. In this chapter we will explore both aspects: the crucial role of language in thinking and learning in other subjects and the potential of other subjects for developing spoken and written language.

The role of language in thinking and learning

Over the past 40 years we have learnt a lot about children's thinking and learning. Piaget (1954) increased our understanding of the remarkable power of children's minds. He established that children develop knowledge through a process of active learning, exploration, experimentation and discovery.

Vygotsky (1978) argued that children solve problems with the help of their speech as well as their eyes and hands and emphasised that language both organises and directs the thinking process.

For Bruner (1986) language was the all-important 'mental tool' which supported thought and understanding. According to Bruner, for children to learn to use that tool efficiently they needed two factors: social participation and instruction. Like Vygotsky (1962) he saw the role of adults as crucial, likening it to a form of 'scaffolding' whereby adults create a framework for children to move from one level of understanding to another. Examples of many of these thinking and learning processes will be given shortly, but first let us look at why we should use other subjects to develop children's abilities as speakers, readers and writers.

Using and developing spoken and written language in other subjects

In our everyday lives, language is central to everything we do. We use talk to establish relationships, to share information, to get things done or to talk over events of the day. Our audiences vary from the large to the small and from the formal to the informal; they may include people we know and trust or complete strangers.

Every day we read and make sense of many kinds of 'texts' for many different purposes, for example bus/train tickets, letters, memos, receipts, cheques. We also write different types of texts for different purposes and audiences ranging from the personal note or shopping list to the formal letter or report.

Children can do the same and develop as real users of language when they use language for different purposes in other subjects. In history, religious education, geography, art and music they can discuss, evaluate and make sense of how meaning is conveyed in a whole range of 'texts'. In other subjects they can also write different texts of their own, including notes, charts, grids, diagrams, lists.

Not only does this develop important knowledge about texts, their different forms and characteristics, it also helps children see more clearly the purpose of written language – for instance why it is useful to write a survey for maths or make notes for a geography field trip or a history project.

This kind of approach is based on a functional view of language (Halliday 1985), which argues that meaning is the very reason for the existence and development of language. A functional approach is concerned with how people use real language for real purposes. When we weave language and literacy into all areas of learning we are reinforcing the centrality of meaning by highlighting the relevance of spoken and written language in all our daily lives. Above all, through a meaning-based approach we are helping children feel that what is taught is worth learning.

The National Curriculum

The importance of language in learning is highlighted in all subjects of the National Curriculum. When we look closely at the programmes of study for each subject we find many common language, thinking and learning processes, such as exploring, comparing, problem-solving, interpreting, classifying, predicting, relating, planning, describing, investigating, questioning and recording.

There is also explicit support in the National Curriculum for using and developing language in other subjects. All now have a common requirement which stresses the importance of developing competence in speaking and listening, reading and writing.

In order to support teachers in achieving this, SCAA (now the QCA) developed support materials in conjunction with representatives of the subject associations, including the National Association for Teaching English and the National Association for English Advisers. SCAA's core booklet, *Use of Language: A Common Approach* (1997b), provides a clear rationale for using language in every area of the curriculum. It aims to enhance existing good practice and to help those schools who need to develop a more coherent approach to using language effectively across the curriculum. It also provides very interesting examples of classroom practice, showing how teachers can develop children's abilities in using and developing language for learning. Subject leaflets are available for English and for each of the other National Curriculum subjects. These highlight the opportunities for language in each subject and give guidance on planning and teaching appropriate activities.

The National Literacy Strategy

In 1988 the DfEE produced the document *The National Literacy Strategy: Framework for Teaching*. This sets out teaching objectives for Reception to Year 6 in an attempt to enable all children to become fully literate. It also gives guidance on the literacy hour in which this teaching takes place.

The document states that links with the rest of the curriculum are fundamental to effective literacy teaching, and 'where appropriate' literacy teaching should be linked to work in other curricular areas. It gives as examples: searching and retrieving from information texts used in science; writing instructions in technology; studying myths, autobiographies or stories in history.

Module 6, 'Reading and Writing for Information', in the National Literacy Strategy's *Literacy Training Pack*, reiterates how other curriculum areas provide a more meaningful, purposeful context for children's learning than a series of decontextualised skills exercises. So in the literacy hour children can work on texts related to other subjects providing the focus stays on the explicit teaching of reading and writing and the literacy objectives set out in the framework. Of course, the curriculum aspects of a text can be developed at other times. Children might be taught how to make effective notes in the literacy hour, and in a subsequent history session the notes could be used to make a map or model of a Roman town (Module 6, page 4).

Now let us take a closer look at children using language for thinking and learning in other subjects. We will also see how these subjects provide important opportunities for children to develop specific skills in speaking and listening, reading and writing.

Using talk to learn

In everyday life we all use talk for very important social reasons, to:

- interact
- communicate
- question
- reason
- persuade
- build relationships
- make contact with and relate to others
- share ideas
- get things done
- express our thoughts and feelings.

We also use different kinds of talk in order to think and learn and to:

- reveal, reshape, represent our thinking
- work out what we mean
- make sense of new situations and experiences
- achieve different purposes, e.g. argue, plan, describe, inform, instruct, explain, question, predict, narrate, imagine, interpret, classify
- analyse and solve problems.
- reflect on experiences
- relate what we know to new ideas and experiences.

In order to develop these social and cognitive skills it is vital that children work together on meaningful tasks in all areas of the curriculum. Grouping should be as flexible and as varied as possible, to include pairs; groups based on friendship, gender or the same language; ability groups with or without the teacher present; children of other ages. As children work with others on different tasks, talk should be an integral part of their learning, a means of communication and a tool for learning.

In the example in Figure 15.1 we can see how one child, Raina, is able to use many of these thinking and learning processes as she works in science with her teacher. Her learning is active, exploratory and experimental, as advocated by Piaget, but the teacher as 'scaffolder' plays a vital role in promoting effective talk for learning.

Teacher How's the experiment going then?
Raina Well . . . it's OK but, well, . . . I can't work out why this one isn't working very well.
Teacher You're not entirely happy with this one?
Raina No, cos . . . it's not right . . . it's falling too much.
Teacher Tell me about it.
Raina Right, well, . . . it looks OK, doesn't it? . . . I mean . . . you know, it looks like it'd work . . . float down and that . . . but when you throw it up . . . erooom plop . . .
Teacher Shall we try it . . . oh yes . . . plop . . . I see what you mean.
Raina Something needs changing.
Teacher Yes, you're right . . . have you any thoughts?
Riana I thought maybe . . . to change the apple . . . use a bit smaller one.
Teacher That's a good idea, yes . . . to lighten the load a bit.
Raina Yeah. Lighten the load, that's first.
Teacher Yes.
Raina Mmm . . . and then if that doesn't do it . . . doesn't work.
Teacher We'd need to look elsewhere then. I think . . . mmm . . . to make changes somewhere else perhaps.
Raina Well, all these . . . I might have too many strings . . . you know . . . if I had a few less strings.
Teacher To make it lighter, yes . . .
Raina And, yeah, and cos they're pulling it all in too tight . . . too much.
Teacher Oh, I see . . . right . . . it needs to catch enough air doesn't it, to stop it plopping?
Raina Yeah to stop it doing a plop dive . . . that's the main thing that is . . . catching . . . spreading out flat to catch the air . . . I think that's the main problem, the strings are pulling the paper down too much . . . like too tight.
Teacher Mmm . . . I'm wondering what we can do about it.
Raina Change the apple for a littler one . . . take some strings off . . . and then shall I test it?
Teacher Yes, give me a shout and I'll come with you.

Figure 15.1 Using talk to learn in science: investigating parachutes at Key Stage 1
Source: Corden 1992, pp.177–8

Comment

The teacher begins by encouraging Raina to reveal her thinking. Raina is able to clarify the nature of the problem and identify that 'something needs changing'. The teacher's well-timed comment 'have you any thoughts?' encourages Raina to use tentative talk to explore, question, describe, think out aloud and consider possible solutions to the problem. The teacher encourage Raina when she is on the right lines and guides her to consider factors other than the weight of the apple: 'We'd need to look elsewhere then, I think … mmm'.

Different tasks often demand different language, especially where technical or subject-specific language is required. In this case the teacher skilfully introduces appropriate scientific language like 'lighten the load' and 'make it lighter' and 'catch enough air', which Raina then uses as she reasons and talks herself into making sense of the experience. Raina finally reaches her own conclusions and summarises for the teacher and herself what she needs to do next.

Developing speaking and listening skills in other subjects

In this brief science activity Raina used language very effectively to learn more about the properties of materials and some of the physical processes involved in forces and motion. But science also provided Raina with a real, purposeful, meaningful context in which to develop her language skills.

In relation to the Key Stage 1 programme of study for Speaking and Listening Raina had opportunities to talk for a range of purposes, including exploring, developing and clarifying ideas; predicting outcomes and discussing possibilities (1a). She described events, observations and experiences (1a) and asked and answered thoughtful questions that clarified her understanding (2b). Clearly she used talk to develop thinking and extend her ideas (2b).

The following list shows some further opportunities for developing speaking and listening in other areas of the curriculum.

Design and technology
● Presenting design ideas and outcomes to the class

Maths
● Talking in order to solve problems
● Discussing the results and presentation of a survey

Science
● Asking questions, e.g. How? Why?
● Using specific vocabulary when talking about living things, materials, processes, etc.

PE
Talking to a partner: agreeing how to play a game

History
● Listening to and asking questions about the past
● Listening to and discussing stories
● Role play about a dramatic event in the past

Geography
● Using a newspaper report to discuss a natural event in a distant place
● Book talk around information texts on other places/cultures

IT
● Asking questions and problem-solving in programs
● Discussing use of IT in the world

Art
● Expressing ideas and opinions about works of art using specific vocabulary
● Reflecting upon their own art work and discussing future projects

(See SCAA's subject leaflets (1997a) for more details.)

Using and developing reading across the curriculum

Using reading to learn

In most classrooms children have opportunities to use reading to learn about other subjects. One trainee teacher planned activities for a Year 2 class for a period of two to three weeks. The general theme was 'Ourselves and our world', and the objectives were:

● to increase children's awareness of the purpose and pleasure of reading
● to use a variety of meaningful texts relevant to different areas of the curriculum
● to build children's awareness of literacy as a useful and enjoyable activity that serves a wide range of real functions.

To achieve her objectives the trainee planned authentic literacy activities across the curriculum for different ability groups as follows:

Assembly
● Reading out work done in geography

Maths
● Reading written caption cards to introduce and explore terms like 'more than' and 'less than', 'equal to', 'the same as'
● Making block graphs based on 'Our favourite chocolate bars'. Children read wrappers, select bar and transfer wrapper to graph
● Number sets: creating and labelling sets of objects

up to ten. Reading numerals and number words.
- Playing games in groups: reading titles, captions and instructions. Matching title on class tick list to record the game that has been played

PE
- Playing 'islands' as a warm-up activity. Reading the labels on each island (hoop), for example 'no more than 4', 'no less than 5'.
- Team games: creating score chart for children to complete

Geography
- Using local newspapers and property pages to discover the range of buildings in the local area
- Using reference books to make comparisons with other countries
- Using specialised vocabulary, e.g. roof, wall, door, window, stone

RE
- Creating a chart to list ideas about 'What makes me happy and healthy'

Science
- Germinating cress seeds, recording methods by labelling and sequencing pictures in zigzag books. Creating tick lists.

History
- Comparing illustrated diary entries of a grandmother with those of ourselves. Creating a diary for a typical week..

Art
- Painting houses: children reading instructions to organise work.

These activities offered children so many rich and exciting opportunities to read and learn about themselves and their world. In addition children developed important cross-curricular skills, such as:

- gaining access to information and ideas from a range of texts and sources and evaluating them
- using research skills
- re-presenting the information gained
- categorising information
- questioning and reflecting on different texts.

In line with the guidance in the Framework for Teaching children also had frequent opportunities to develop their understanding of a range of non-fiction texts.

In addition to helping children learn a great deal about geography, maths, history and other subjects, reading different texts can make a real contribution to the development of specific reading skills, as we now see in the next section.

Developing reading skills in other subjects

Genre and register
It is usual for teachers to discuss the structure of stories in term of beginnings, middles and endings. It is still relatively rare, however, for teachers to discuss the structure of non-fiction texts. Genre theorists have argued for the need to introduce primary school children to a wider range of genres. By genre they mean the overall structure and form of different texts; for example, instructions are very different from invitations or reports.

Genre theorists also urge teachers to discuss explicitly the layout, vocabulary and grammar (register) of different texts. (A good introduction to genre theory can be found in Littlefair 1992.)

In general most theorists tend to agree on these six main non-fiction genres:

- recount
- report
- procedure
- explanation
- argument
- discussion.

If we look back at our Year 2 class we see that over a period of two to three weeks the children had frequent opportunities to explore different genres and learn the register or language of different subjects. Subjects challenge children because they make particular demands upon their use of spoken and written language and because the register varies.

For example, history books contain many facts and make much use of generalisations. In geography, language is used to group, classify, analyse and explain. In maths, children find lists, disjointed sentences, numbers and mathematical symbols. In science they will come across much technical language and sentences packed with meaning. Much of this non-fiction writing is formal in tenor, that is, it is distanced, logical, objective, abstract and complex. At a different time in the week the trainee and her class teacher looked for opportunities to make these features of register explicit to the children. In addition, they frequently modelled a range of reading styles so that children could learn to choose and use the one most appropriate for the text, such as:

- skimming: reading quickly for a general idea of the meaning
- scanning: looking quickly to find a small part of the text
- reading intensively: reading slowly and thoughtfully, considering all the points.

These and other key skills can now be introduced and then revisited during word and sentence-level work in the literacy hour. Analysis of any non-fiction text would naturally include discussion of the structure of a text as well as sentence structure, verb tense, connectives, etc.

In relation to the Reading programme of study for Key Stage 1, children in this class were encouraged to develop as enthusiastic, independent and reflective readers by reading and evaluating a wide range of challenging and demanding texts (1a), including IT-based reference materials and newspapers (1b). These texts provided them with subject matter which broadened perspectives and extended thinking. They also contained a variety of structural and organisational features (1c).

Using and developing writing across the curriculum

Using writing to learn

Like speaking, writing has an important function in supporting thinking and learning. Here are examples of some of the processes at work as children use writing to learn in different areas of the curriculum

In Figure 15.2 Christine worked unaided and made appropriate observations using her senses. She supplemented the observations using a hand lens. The brainstorming process had been modelled first by her teacher. The notes were then shared with a partner through talk. After drafting Christine was asked to put spots under incorrect spelling before moving on to write the text unaided. This text successfully recorded her observations; revealed and represented her thinking ('looks like lickwid';

made comparisons 'as big as my ear'); and planned for future work.

In the next example (Figure 15.3) the children worked in groups and made their own lists of different ways of cooking potatoes. This information was shared with other groups. Each group then listed their favourite ways of cooking potatoes, which the teacher collected and recorded on the board. The class made a graph and talked about what was needed for others to understand the information. Lyndsey recorded her graph on the paper provided and then made up some questions to go with it. In these ways writing helped the children to organise their thinking; record information; classify and interpret their findings; question others; and plan for future work.

Developing writing skills in other subjects

Christine and Lyndsey both had opportunities to develop knowledge of different genres of writing, having been shown by their teacher how to select the most appropriate genre for the subject matter and their purpose.

In relation to the Key Stage 2 programme of study for Writing, the children were able to write for varied purposes and to use writing for thinking and learning (1a). Writing was also a means of developing, organising and communicating their ideas (1a). Interesting discussions developed around the characteristics of different kinds of writing and their different layout and presentation (1c).

These examples cover just science and maths, so the following list suggests a few additional opportunities for developing writing in other curriculum areas.

Geography
- Recording the movements of people in and around school
- Writing about a local issue involving change to the environment

IT
- Making notes whilst working on a computer model
- Using IT equipment and software to produce texts, graphs, pictures and sound

History
- Writing a description of events, e.g. the Great Plague

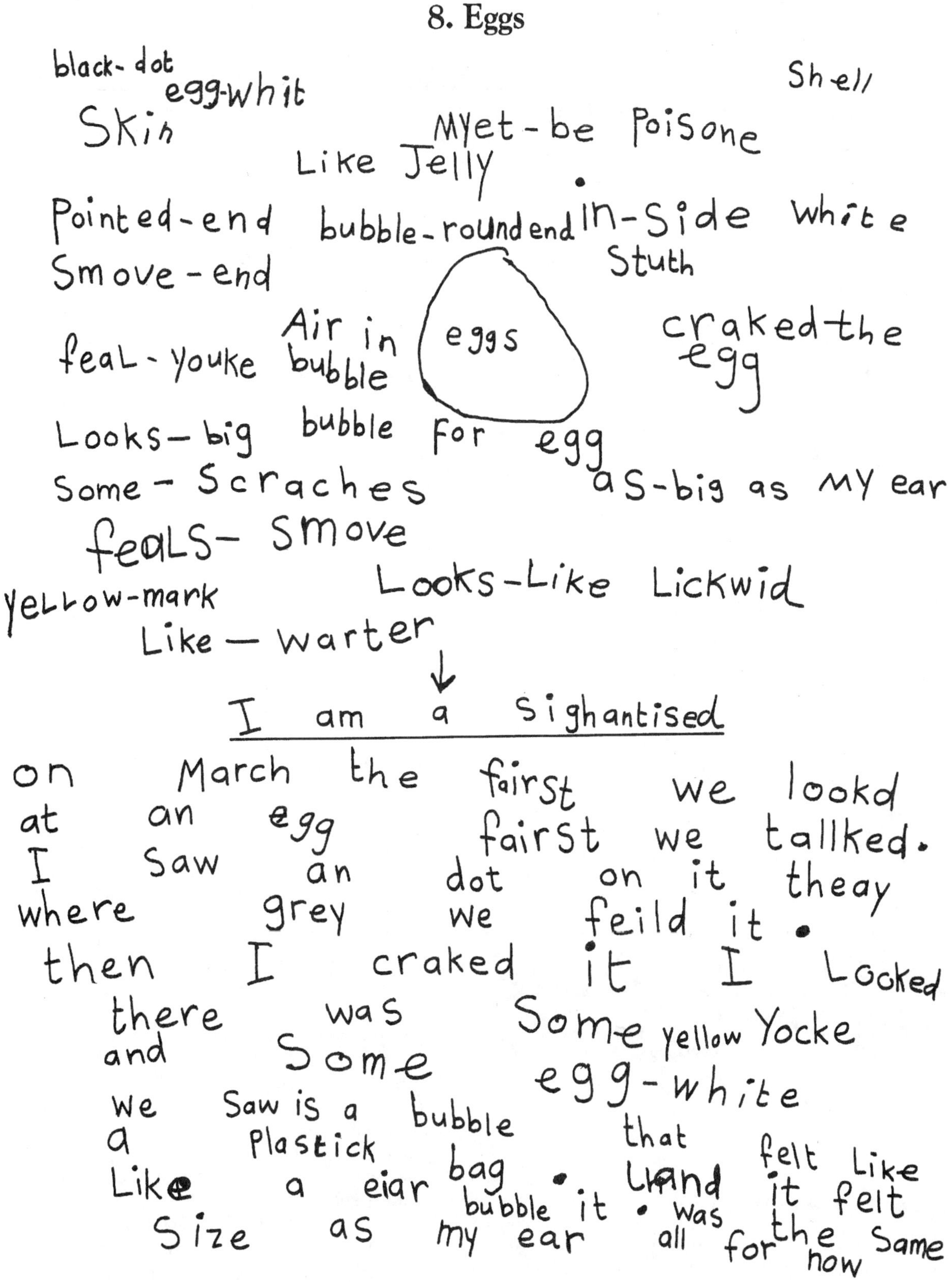

8. Eggs

black-dot
egg-whit   Shell
Skin   MYet-be Poisone
      Like Jelly   .
Pointed-end bubble-round end IN-Side white
Smove-end   Stuth
feaL-youke Air in (eggs)   craked the
            bubble   egg
Looks-big bubble for egg
Some - Scraches   aS-big as MY ear
  feaLS- Smove
yeLLow-mark   Looks-Like Lickwid
   Like — warter
            ↓
   I am a Sighantised

on   March   the   fairst   we   lookd
at   an   egg   fairst we   tallked.
I   Saw   an   dot   on   it   theay
where   grey   we   feild it .
 then   I   craked   it   I   Looked
   there   was   Some yellow Yocke
  and   Some   egg-white
 We Saw is a bubble   that
a   Plastick bag   . Uand felt Like
Like   a eiar bubble it . was it felt
  Size   as my ear   all for the Same
                            now

Figure 15.2 Writing in science: a brainstorm on eggs

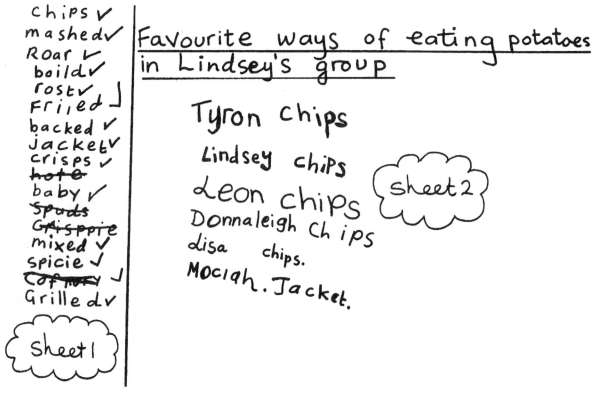

Figure 15.3 Writing in maths: ways of cooking potatoes

Music
- Drafting and redrafting compositions using different notation

Art
- Gathering and recording ideas, observations in a sketchbook

Planning for using and developing language across the curriculum

What follows now is guidance on developing a long-term plan which highlights the use and development of language across the curriculum.

A plan for each subject

This should include a rationale for developing children's use of language and enhancing their work in the particular subject. It might incorporate some of the principles explored at the beginning of this chapter. Ideally the statement should make reference to the following:

- The Common Requirements on the use of language
- How the subject can promote general language and thinking processes and make a contribution to the whole-school approach to language development, e.g. exploring, comparing, problem solving, interpreting, classifying, predicting, relating, planning, describing, investigating, questioning, recording.
- How the subject offers children opportunities to develop major aspects of speaking and listening, reading and writing. For example, in history:
  speaking and listening: talking about documents and sources
  reading: understanding sequence, story, narrative and structure; exploring different texts, about sources such as pictures and films, and the genre and register in which they are written
- How the children's understanding of the subject is to be enhanced by language. For example, in geography the use of language and literacy in:

– expressing views on features of the environment
– using a range of reading skills to access information in secondary sources like books, CD-ROM encyclopaedias, newspapers, etc.
– recording in different ways how weather conditions vary around the world.

Identifying links between language skills and the subject

For example:

- talk 'for a range of purposes', including describing, predicting, explaining, reporting (1a) in design and technology as children present ideas to the rest of the class, or in maths as children talk about how to solve a problem
- reading 'texts drawn from a variety of cultures' (1d) in history and music
- writing 'in a variety of ways' (2b) in history as children write a description of the London Plague and then an explanation of its causes.

Subject-specific vocabulary

Children need to learn the specialist vocabulary of the subject as well as the uses of words in other contexts. These lists can be drawn from the respective programmes of study, taking into account children's individual needs and prior experience and learning. Here are just a few possible examples of starter lists of subject-specific vocabulary:

Maths
- Bigger than, next to, before, odd/even, digits, remainders, sides, edges, surfaces, cubes, hexagons (other shapes), symmetry, rotate, standard, unit, scale ...

Design and technology
- Design, shape, assemble, textiles, axles, joints, load, function, stable, flexible, component, circuit ...

Music
- Sound, pitch, tempo, pattern, rhythm, symbol, composition, timbre, percussion, melody, chord ...

Resources

As we saw earlier, much of the information children need to investigate their topics is found in a range of texts, such as:

- textbooks
- reports, guidebooks, leaflets, letters

- personal accounts
- encyclopaedias and reference books
- information on CD-ROM
- fiction, including myths, legends and poems
- media – TV, magazines, video, slides, newspapers
- the Internet.

The National Literacy Strategy has made it clear that such texts can be chosen for the literacy hour provided the focus of teaching is on the literacy objectives from the Framework for Teaching. So plans should try to identify a wide range of possible sources of information using similar lists and the Range sections in both the programmes of study for English and the Framework.

Planning for progression

Some statement will be needed on children's previous experience and how new work will extend what children already know. In speaking and listening children might move from discussion in pairs or small groups to speaking to a larger audience. In writing they may begin using words and short sentences, progressing to longer sustained pieces of writing.

In reading they might first simply retrieve information but later move on to evaluating its reliability and usefulness. (See SCAA 1997a and relevant sections in the Framework for Teaching for more details.)

SUMMARY

This chapter has focused upon the crucial role of language in thinking and learning and the potential of other areas of the curriculum for developing a wide range of speaking, listening, reading and writing skills.

You should now have:

- more awareness of how children learn and think through language

- greater understanding of the potential of other subjects for developing skills in both spoken and written language

- knowledge of how to plan work which includes the use and development of language across the curriculum.

References

Bruner, J. (1986) *Actual Minds, Possible Worlds*, Harvard University Press

Corden, R. (1992) 'The Role of the Teacher', in K. Norman (ed.) *Thinking Voices: The Work of the National Oracy Project*, Hodder and Stoughton

DfEE (1998) *The National Literacy Strategy: Framework for Teaching*, DfEE

DfEE and SCAA (1996) *Desirable Outcomes for Children's Learning on Entering Compulsory Education*, DfEE

Halliday, K. (1985) *Learning How to Mean: Explorations in the Development of Language*, Edward Arnold

Littlefair, A. (1992) *Genres in the Classroom*, UKRA

Piaget, J. (1954) *The Language and Thought of the Child*, Routledge and Kegan Paul

SCAA (1997a) *English and the Use of Language Requirement in Other Subjects*, DfEE

SCAA (1997b) *Use of Language: A Common Approach*, HMSO

Vygotsky, L. S. (1962) *Thought and Language*, MIT Press

Vygotsky, L. S. (1978) *Mind in Society: The Development of Higher Psychological Processes*, Harvard University Press

Further reading

Littlefair, A. (1991) *Reading All Types of Writing*, Open University Press.
A most accessible book which outlines the thinking behind the importance of children using and developing their knowledge of how genre and register work.

NLS (1998) *Literacy Training Pack, Module 6*: 'Reading and Writing for Information', DfEE
This training package aims to develop teachers' own understanding and knowledge of how information texts can be used in their teaching of reading and writing across the curriculum. It includes some excellent activity resource sheets for Key Stage 2, although they can be adapted for other age ranges.

National Writing Project (1989/90) *Writing for Learning and Audiences for Writing*, Thomas Nelson
Readable booklets full of practical suggestions and real examples from classrooms on many aspects of using and developing language in all areas of the curriculum.

Reid, D. and Bentley, D. (eds) (1996) *Reading On: Developing Reading at Key Stage 2*, Scholastic (see especially Chapter 2, 'Developing the Reading of Non-Fiction')
This chapter, like others in the book, deals with how to develop children's reading skills once they are competent readers. It provides many practical examples of how children can develop skills in reading and writing information texts in different areas of the curriculum.

16 English as an additional language

OBJECTIVES

By the end of this chapter, you should be able to:

- understand the challenges faced by children learning English as an additional language (EAL)

- appreciate the benefits of bilingualism and the role of heritage languages

- appreciate ways to effectively support EAL children's understanding and language development in school

- ensure that EAL children have access to the curriculum.

Key principles in EAL

Before considering practical ways to help children learn English as an additional language, it is important to establish some key principles about language acquisition and development.

- Most of the human race speaks two or more languages.
- There is evidence to suggest that bilingual children enjoy cognitive benefits from being bilingual. Baker (1995) reports that bilinguals are often '… ahead of monolinguals on divergent thinking tests'.
- Use of the mother tongue in the home and the classroom does not hinder progress in a second language. Children who are encouraged to express themselves in their home language as well as in English tend to make better progress in school.
- Most children will take up to two years to learn Basic Interpersonal Communication Skills (BICS: see Cummins 1988). Academic English, of the level required by work at secondary school level, known as 'Cognitive Academic Language Proficiency' (CALP: see Cummins 1984), can take anything from five to seven years.
- Teachers can do a great deal to enhance and accelerate learning English, by adapting their teaching styles, planning, support strategies and resources.
- Children who are complete beginners, such as very young children starting school or recent arrivals or refugees, need extra-sensitive support.
- Where teachers have a good understanding of their own language and are willing to make efforts to learn about features of children's home languages, the whole class, including the monolingual children, can benefit from increased attention to and informed discussion of language differences and similarities.
- Each EAL child is an individual case. There are huge differences between a rising five whose family and community all speak the same language and a nine-year-old arriving in a monolingual neighbourhood, yet both may have beginners' needs.

ESL, ESOL, EAL?

There are many terms relating to children who belong to more than one language community.

In literature about the teaching of English, the term ESL (English as a second language) was most commonly used but it does not adequately acknowledge the fact that English may be a third or even fourth language for some children. Consequently, the terms ESOL (English for speakers of other languages) and EAL (English as an additional language) are now widely used, with the latter being preferred because it feels more inclusive than ESOL.

What is bilingualism?

Many schoolchildren come to school as emergent bilinguals. They are gaining fluency in their first language (L1), mother tongue or home language and are ready to improve upon the English they have already picked up through the media and environment. A child's mother tongue is also called a community or heritage language. Because the contexts for language use can be so complex,

Mills and Mills (1993) suggest teachers use the term 'preferred language'.

Where each parent speaks a different language at home, for example Farsi and French, a child may arrive with two languages already quite fluent and English will be their third language system.

There are many good reasons for helping children to maintain their home language(s), while becoming successful users of English. Losing the home language can involve losing valuable cultural dimensions and links with older generations.

Some language groups, therefore, organise Saturday or evening classes, sometimes called Heritage Language Schools, where children can sustain development in their mother tongue or, for religious reasons, develop another language, such as Arabic or Hebrew.

Where children are competent users of two languages, they can be said to be bilingual. However, true bilingualism takes some time to develop. A bilingual may not be fully literate, competent or fluent in both languages. Being a bilingual means that two languages are 'lived' in and used to function in two different language communities.

Bilingualism can be perceived differently, however, depending on social attitudes to the languages involved. Where high-status languages like French or Italian are involved, bilingualism is often held in high esteem. Being bilingual in Gujerati and Bengali, however, does not always carry the same status.

Other languages: appreciating diversity

Schools which have pupils who speak more than one language usually benefit when diversity is seen as an asset: 'Such an approach increases monolingual children's knowledge about language; it also raises the status of bilingual children. It can contribute to combating racism' (Edwards 1995).

Tolerance for other people's language, culture and identity is a crucial social value because Britain enjoys a culturally and linguistically rich heritage. According to recent figures, there are, in this country, at least half a million schoolchildren who speak another language before learning English at school (Blackledge 1994).

There are several ways teachers can increase their understanding of home languages spoken by children:

- By encouraging the children to teach the rest of the class words and phrases, for example by building up alphabetical English/ other languages mobiles or wall friezes.
- By enlisting parents or bilingual support teachers to help label displays in the languages spoken by children in the class.
- By researching the child's home language through the local education authority, support service, library or CILT (see Glossary). Increasing awareness of the way a language works may help teachers to appreciate more clearly the problems faced by a child attempting to learn English.
- By consulting the linguistic knowledge and experience of the local authority's Section 11 team, teachers can develop teaching strategies to match the needs of the child or children involved.

Before working with EAL children, it is important that we challenge our own personal stereotypes about bilingualism and specific linguistic or ethnic groups. Low teacher expectations of EAL children or children with any dialect other than standard English can lead to a self-fulfilling prophecy and low achievement. Many EAL children have high levels of ability in maths and in their mother tongue, but a low level of English can mask these talents in the early stages.

Baker (1995) notes that 'some teachers have a prejudice against bilingual children, find bilingual children difficult to teach, find bilingualism a strange and worrying phenomenon, and do not know how to approach parents who have a keen interest in their children becoming bilingual and biliterate'.

The following ideas can help to make a child feel that their home language is valued while raising the general level of language awareness within the class:

- A display of artefacts, storybooks, etc., from the EAL child's home and culture, can create a special space for the child which can be supported by books and photographs about the home country or language.
- The EAL child can teach the class to say a few phrases or to count in their L1, for example to take the register. Building up word banks and picture dictionaries to share with the class helps the EAL child feel that their language is welcome and can also develop the English speakers' appreciation of language diversity.

- Dual-language texts can be borrowed from the local library or teachers' centre, displayed in the class library and shared by all the children in class.

Bilingual education

Bilingual education is a complex concept and takes many forms. Frequently, these suggest that language is a 'liquid' commodity, contained within an educational 'swimming pool'. Terms used, for example, include submersion, immersion, mainstream.

The various forms of bilingual education are summarised below:

Transitional teaching: In the 1960s and 1970s, EAL children were often placed initially in language centres, where they were taught basic English before being assimilated into mainstream classrooms. It was argued that these centres were potentially racist. The Swann Report (DES 1985) urged that children were entered into the mainstream from the start and supported by Section 11 and bilingual support teachers. However, inadequate funding has meant that the current level of support in schools may be insufficient.

Submersion programmes: These usually forbid children to use their home language in the school environment. This is a 'sink or swim' approach which many children, for obvious reasons, find traumatic. However well meaning teachers are, submersion can give negative messages to the child about their home language, culture and therefore identity.

Immersion: A full immersion programme involves children learning all their subjects in the target language. It differs from a submersion programme, in that the home language is respected and permitted, for example in the playground and classroom. Immersion probably best describes the experience of refugee children arriving in Britain, though they may still encounter a submersion model.

Partial immersion: These programmes involve education in two languages. In Canada, English-speaking students can participate in total or partial immersion programmes, with all or a fraction of their subjects taught in French. Similar programmes enable French-speaking children to become bilingual with English.

Dual language: Where two languages are given equal time and status, children are said to follow a dual-language programme of education. Children learning to be Welsh/English bilingual enjoy this kind of education and receive official support, in the National Curriculum, for their bilingualism. As the Order for English states: 'The development of English and Welsh should be seen as mutually supportive'. It advocates activities that 'encourage pupils to transfer their skills in, and knowledge and understanding of, one language to the other' and 'develop pupils' understanding of the social contexts in which the languages are used'.

Mainstreaming: This is a term used to mean that EAL children will learn within the mainstream classroom and teaching will not involve withdrawal of any kind. It is related to the immersion model described above. In mainstreaming, the focus is the child who is supported by a language teacher (e.g. Section 11) in the classroom.

Partnership teaching: This is an important development of mainstreaming (Bourne 1994). This kind of teaching focuses less on individual children and more on developing a whole-school curriculum, with class teachers being supported and trained by Section 11 teachers. Designed to improve all children's access to the curriculum, partnership involves teams, pairs and groups of teachers working closely together within and outside the classroom.

Working with bilingual teachers

Working with other adults in the classroom demands skill and sensitivity. 'An alignment between mainstream and special English teachers is no simple matter to achieve' (Levine 1990).

Constraints of time, intercultural factors and lack of communication can mean bilingual children do not always receive effective support.

It is important to recognise that many bilingual teachers have been class teachers themselves and will be sympathetic to the inevitable demands of the classroom It is vital that class teachers, in return, never underestimate the educational professionalism of their bilingual colleagues. Many of these teachers may be graduates or qualified teachers in their countries of origin but the DfEE will not acknowledge their parity with the Postgraduate Certificate of Education (PGCE), BA (Qualified Teacher Status), Licensed Teacher Status or the BEd.

It is also essential that bilingual colleagues are not imposed upon unduly. The principles which apply to working with any colleague are outlined in more detail in Chapter 20.

Home–school partnerships

Many schools realise not only the value of good teacher partnerships but also the importance of good home–school partnerships. All parents, including those who speak languages other than English, should feel welcome and informed. School policy documents can be translated into the languages of the school community, and language classes for parents, based at the school, are sometimes organised by local authorities.

Some LEAs have initiated writing projects, designed to enhance the English of both parents and children. Edwards (1995) referred to a writing project where parents made translations of English storybooks. The sentences were stuck above

Bourne (1994) states that:

> Because there is no simple methodology and no one single set of teaching skills, it is probably best to think of language support work as a form of 'action research' where observation, discussion with pupils and parents, experimentation with new approaches and careful evaluation can lead to an improved, shared understanding of classroom processes.

When trying to involve parents in their children's learning, it is useful to consider possible cultural differences between their perceptions and the school's. Teachers need to be aware that:

- Parents will have experiences of their own schooling and these will not always be positive ones.
- In some cultures, parents are not expected or encouraged to participate in the process of their child's education at school.
- Some parents may have had little formal schooling in their own countries or may be illiterate in the standard form of their language (Hall 1995).

Nevertheless, by building up practical and sensitive partnerships with EAL families, teachers can make their teaching in school more effective. Both parents and teachers need to try to understand the challenges faced by the developing bilingual child coming to learn English.

Learning a second language

Interestingly, most learners of English follow a similar developmental path. They make similar errors and demonstrate some or all of the language-learning features or behaviours described below:

- *Silent period:* Some children are reluctant to produce any English at all in the initial stages. They may need time to simply listen and assimilate language in different contexts until they feel confident or secure.
- *Interlanguage:* L1 and L2 are used simultaneously in the same sentence: a useful stage of development.
- *Over-hypothesis:* The child over-hypothesises about the rules of English and applies the rules of grammar too strictly or consistently; for example 'He wented out'.
- *Errors:* These may be the result of over-hypothesis, mispronunciation or mismatching language with context. Just as miscues are valuable in understanding a young reader's learning needs, an EAL child's errors can be used as signposts to the next stages of learning English.
- *Mispronunciation:* Some languages do not have sounds found in English, and children may need extra help with the unfamiliar. For example, Japanese learners find *l* a difficult sound. To help them form the sound, using a mirror and demonstrating where the tongue is placed in relation to lips and teeth can be helpful.
- *Intonation:* Some languages are flat-sounding, even monotonal. Teachers need to stress intonation patterns and exaggerate these in order to help children speak expressively.
- *Fear of failure:* The way a teacher responds to a child's errors and the responses encouraged in the rest of the class will largely determine a child's confidence to make mistakes.
- *Intermediate plateau:* EAL children who have made rapid progress in conversational English sometimes seem to reach a plateau of development and progress slows down.

The stages of development

Because children tend to follow a similar developmental continuum, irrespective of their first language, many authorities have devised indicators of progress to help teachers identify which developmental stage a child has reached; for example:

Stage 1: new to English. The child may join in activities but may not speak. Sometimes imitates others but with partial understanding. Begins to name things and use phrases, though these may not be grammatically correct, e.g. 'Me no want …'. May write in L1. Is beginning to learn the alphabetic system and form letters, understand left–right directionality and appreciate simple rhymes and stories.

Stage 2: becoming familiar with English. The child can switch between languages to sustain a flow of ideas though this may be confusing for the listener. Small distinctions, e.g. difference between he and she, are being sorted out. Verb tenses are being used though there may be over-generalisation, e.g. 'I gave her a pen, given't I?' Vocabulary is growing. The child can understand more than he or she can say. There is growing confidence orally and in reading and the child is making a good attempt to label and write in English.

Stage 3: becoming confident as a user of English. The child has a growing command of syntax and a wide vocabulary. Can use structures in the appropriate situation and there is increasing accuracy in the use of verbs, prepositions, adverbs. Can read unfamiliar words with support, and understands oral language easily. Follows and gives instructions. Pronunciation and intonation are improving.

Stage 4: very fluent in English. The child can communicate effectively in most social and learning contexts. Is confident in collaboration with English-speaking peers. Writes confidently in English with a growing competence over different genres. Moves easily between L1 and English ('code-switching') and can translate or interpret for others.

Teaching EAL

The strategies which support young EAL learners are of benefit to all children, especially those who need more explicit guidance from the teacher. Effective EAL classrooms are places where language is used purposefully and meaningfully and for authentic communication. Teachers can help children by consciously drawing out the language features and patterns that are being used. It is also helpful to integrate language taught within the content of the wider curriculum and to provide a genuine context for its use.

When teachers design tasks for an EAL child they need to consider carefully how challenging they are, in terms of both language and cognition (see Figure 16.1).

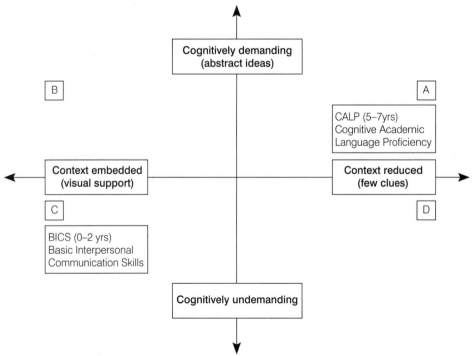

Figure 16.1 Planning for differentiation: using the Cummins framework
Source: Adapted from Hall, D. (1995) *Assessing the Needs of Bilingual Pupils: Living in Two Languages*. London: David Fulton Publishers

A task in quadrant A would be cognitively demanding and provide little visual or contextual support. Such a challenging and abstract task would clearly be beyond an EAL learner in the early stages of English learning. A beginner would need a task which was clearly embedded in contextual terms, though the level of cognitive challenge would depend on an individual's level of ability and development, for example in quadrants C and B.

Helping newcomers to settle

There are so many factors involved in learning a language that it is very difficult to predict which strategies will work best for an individual child. Making sure the child feels secure, welcome, accepted and included is a good place to start. Thereafter, the teacher's approach to developing the child's English will depend on careful observation, appreciation of the child's learning needs, sensitive intervention and appropriate resource provision.

Establishing predictable routines and teaching the formulaic phrases that accompany them can be very helpful. For example: 'Now who's here today. Arun, are you here today?' 'Yes Miss.' Once a routine has been internalised, another phrase, for example 'Where's Arun?' 'I'm here Miss', can be taught.

Not all of what we say to young EAL learners in the early stages of their learning of English will be comprehensible, but by deliberately 'fine tuning' the input (Krashen 1995) we can support understanding. Parents of children learning their first language or mother tongue realise this instinctively and use what is known as 'motherese' to help their offspring understand and negotiate meanings.

EAL in the classroom

One of the most useful teaching strategies is the ability to repeat, recycle and rephrase language in a way which is not tedious to the EAL child or the rest of the class. For example, new vocabulary learned in a science lesson could be reintroduced through a chant. It could be reinforced through a story or captions under a display and then reinforced in a group experiment.

Groupings

Varying the groupings for EAL children is impor-
tant so that they learn to adapt their new language to different contexts and audiences.

Group work provides planned opportunities for children to interact with mother-tongue speakers and to watch them devise solutions to problems. Grouping the EAL child with the special needs group could lead the rest of the class to adopt a negative impression of the EAL child. The group which is most articulate can often supply good language models for the EAL child to follow. It is always helpful to brief a group about ways they can help the EAL children understand and participate.

Paired work is often the least threatening context in which to work. Pairing the EAL child with a popular member of class can help with socialisation. A child with literacy difficulties can give occasional lessons in English to an EAL child. This pairing can be mutually beneficial and can greatly raise the self-esteem of the English-speaking child, who may rarely be given the chance to be an 'expert' in English.

Individual work: Blackledge (1994) talks about 'enhanced' individual work, or work which is supported by timely teacher intervention and suitable resources for reference. Work like this allows children to work at their own pace, and to develop good study skills.

Strategies and resources
The following resources and strategies are useful for all children who need supportive and intensive language work.

Using the blackboard or flip chart
Drawing pictures to reinforce meaning and adding labels as a new topic is introduced will support understanding for any child who finds processing aural information difficult. It is a good idea to define a 'Keywords' box in one corner of the blackboard. These words can be entered into a word bank, used as spellings, discussed and referred to over the course of the day.

Using props, visuals and mime
Using props or visuals to reinforce vocabulary, whenever telling a story or presenting a new topic, will reinforce meaning even more memorably than using blackboard sketches. Acting out words and using gestures and expressions is very helpful.

Using big books
These provide children with models of written English and can be shared by several children at once, making learning to read in English a social

activity. Other children can teach the EAL child new words and explain new structures.

Shared writing and making big books
Asking EAL children to dictate to an adult or peer-group scribe is an excellent way of demonstrating to them the formation of letters, spacing and punctuation. In a group working on a big book, the EAL child could contribute some simple phrases, for example making speech bubbles, repeating a simple phrase, such as 'No, he's not here!'

Making dual-language texts
Initially, this may need the involvement of parents, older children or bilingual teachers. Children can make a book of pictures, for example a story or a record of a class outing, then label the pictures in their mother tongue and in English. If displayed in the class library, the book can be read by everyone in class.

Group reading with multiple copies
In order to build up confidence, the EAL child can start off by listening to a group read aloud from a set of multiple copies (fiction or non-fiction). Later, the child can join a second group and start to read the occasional word or phrase, with support from the group.

Listening centres and activities
EAL children will benefit greatly from listening to taped stories where there are clear prompts as to when they should turn the page and strong visual support for the text. This is an activity they find unthreatening, and it can provide useful models for intonation and a clear context for language use. Videos of stories (e.g. the Watchword Video Library) are excellent for introducing new structures and vocabulary.

Sequencing activities
Using pictures for the child to put into sequence and either number or label provides a context for language and can help to develop an awareness of English word order.

Chants and songs
Language patterns, rhythms, chants, songs and rhymes are instinctively used by children learning L1 and are invaluable to support the learning of an additional language. Any new vocabulary being taught can be turned into a simple chant with a strong rhythm, for example:

Socks and shoes,
Socks and shoes,
Socks, socks, socks and shoes!

Jacket and tie,
Jacket and tie,
Jacket, jacket, jacket and tie!

Telling stories
Perhaps most valuable of all in language learning is the role of narrative. EAL children already bring to the learning of English their knowledge of story rules and structures. Telling a story instead of reading it tends to allow teachers to enjoy greater eye contact, so they can check understanding, and greater freedom to mime and use props (e.g. Storysacks).

Adapting a story
These are helpful steps to follow in order to adapt a story to make it accessible to EAL children:

- Make visuals and collect props.
- Identify keywords and characters, using props or visuals such as a beanstalk, giant, castle, hen, cow, beans, sky, fall, chop, climb.
- Simplify the language and look for refrains or repeated phrases, e.g. 'Fee, Fi, Fo, Fun, Look out boy, here I come!'
- Introduce and practise keywords and phrases with the children.
- Set the context, e.g. with a sketch or poster, and introduce the story.
- Tell the story, using visuals, props, expression, gesture, mime.
- Involve the children in the refrains; for example 'We can't go over it, we can't go under it, we can't go around it, we've got to go through it! – We're going on a bear hunt'.
- Devise cross-curricular follow-up activities.
- Involve the children in a retelling or acting out of the story, e.g. using card puppets on sticks.

Monitoring progress

Careful monitoring of a child's language competence in English is crucial if they are to make steady progress. Very few children arrive with zero English because many will have picked up English incidentally through television and environmental print. It is important to know where the child is starting from, in terms of communicative skills, confidence, fluency and vocabulary.

It is important to record social skills and behaviours as well as language development, for the two are so closely related. Figure 16.2 shows one assessment proforma which may be helpful.

Name:	G/B	D.O.B.	Other languages		
Achievements: I can . . .			Term 1	Term 2	Term 3
Ask questions					
Play with other children					
Take part in circle time					
Tell stories					
Share personal anecdotes					
Retell stories					
Make suggestions					
Take part in role play					
Describe objects					
Ask other children for help					
Contribute in whole-class work					
Describe people					
Ask adults for help					
Contribute in small groups					
Reflect on stories					
Relate own contribution to previous speaker					
Express physical feeling					
Express preferences/dislikes					
Describe story character					
Explain choices					
Self-correct					
Express wishes					
Express emotions					
Compare stories					
Convey messages					
Make comparisons – comparative					
Make comparisons – superlative					
Share resources					
Comment on other contributions					
Read aloud confidently					
Give instructions					
Reflect on differences/similarities between languages					
Ask for directions					
Lend and borrow objects					
Express opinions					
Give a report					
Enjoy chants/rhymes					
Give directions					
Explain procedure, e.g. how to make something					
Use effective language in playground					
Use effective language in classroom					
Play games (board games)					
Use evidence to support opinions					
Interview someone else					

Figure 16.2 An EAL assessment sheet

Wherever possible, it is valuable to involve the children themselves in their own assessment and record-keeping and to share progress with families and all the colleagues who are likely to teach the EAL learners.

- provide practical guidance and teaching and assessment strategies to enhance these children's experiences of learning English in school
- suggest ways of working more closely with parents and English support teachers to make the learning of EAL more effective.

SUMMARY

This chapter has tried to:

- present the positive aspects of language diversity and bilingual education
- raise awareness of the challenges facing children in British primary schools who are learning English as an additional language

Underpinning all work with EAL children is the teacher's approach towards the child's needs. The Bullock Report (DES 1975) stressed that it is important that schools should never ask a child to abandon their culture and identity: 'No child should be expected to cast off the language and culture of the home as he crosses the school threshold …'.

References

Baker, C. (1995) *A Parents and Teachers' Guide to Bilingualism*, Multilingual Matters
Blackledge, A. (ed.) (1994) *Teaching Bilingual Children*, Trentham Books
Bourne, J. (1994) *Partnership Teaching*, HMSO
Cummins, J. (1988) *Bilingualism in Education: Aspects of Theory, Research and Practice*, Longman
DES (1975) *A Language for Life* (The Bullock Report), HMSO
DES (1985) *Education for All* (The Swann Report), HMSO
Edwards, V. (1995) *Speaking and Listening in Multilingual Classrooms, Reading in Multilingual Classrooms and Writing in Multilingual Classrooms*, Reading and Language Information Centre, University of Reading
Hall, D. (1995) *Assessing the Needs of Bilingual Pupils*, David Fulton
Krashen, S. (1995) *Principles and Practice in Second Language Acquisition*, Harvard University Press
Levine, J. (ed.) (1990) *Bilingual Learners and the Mainstream Curriculum*, Falmer Press
Mills, R. W. and Mills, J. (1993) *Bilingualism in the Primary School*, Routledge

Further reading

Baker, C. (1995) *A Parents and Teachers' Guide to Bilingualism*, Multilingual Matters
The author is a parent of Welsh/English bilingual children and is one of this country's experts on bilingual education. This book takes the form of a Question–Answer dialogue. The chapters on education and literacy are particularly helpful to teachers.
Edwards, V. (1996) *The Other Languages*, Reading and Language Information Centre, University of Reading
In this slim volume, several of the languages spoken by ESOL children in this country are described. Linguistic and cultural features are discussed, making this a very useful reference for teachers who wish to try and understand the backgrounds and challenges faced by children learning English in school.
Gray, K. (1997) *Jet Primary Teachers Resource Book 1*, Delta
A photocopiable resource which is arranged in familiar primary topics. Originally aimed at the EFL market, this book has many useful language-practice activities to support EAL in the classroom.

Hester, H. (1989) *Stories in the Multilingual Classroom*, Harcourt Brace Jovanovitch
A timeless collection of stories and ideas for follow-up activities, well illustrated with examples of good classroom practice.
Holderness, J. and Hughes, A. (1997) *100+ Ideas for Children: Topic-Based Activities*, Heinemann
Practical and differentiated photocopiable activities, with listening activities, songs and chants on cassette.
Mills, R. W. and Mills, J. (1993) *Bilingualism in the Primary School*, Routledge
This book provides valuable insights into the experience of children learning to be bilingual and trying to learn English. It offers practical guidance on assessment and teaching strategies to support an EAL child and make learning English fun.

17 Drama and English

OBJECTIVES

By the end of this chapter you should be able to:

- discuss how drama can be used to teach the English curriculum

- give examples of how drama can be used to teach language across the curriculum

- select appropriate modes of drama for different types of learning

- plan drama activities in full knowledge of the organisational and assessment issues which also need to be considered.

What is drama?

Drama is a process by which children can learn through language and action. It is a way of working which offers opportunities to explore stories, situations, issues, dilemmas and characters, both real and imagined, and it provides centres of experience for language use and development. Drama is not about training children to act, or learning play scripts off by heart, but is a broad term which covers many very different ways of working in schools. At one end of the spectrum there is spontaneous role play where the child is experimenting with language and actions which may never be repeated in the same way. At the opposite end we might have the same child performing a practised role in front of an audience of parents. The former has its roots firmly embedded in learning through play, the latter is grounded in theatre arts.

The major difference between these two examples is that the play situation is purely for the child as she assimilates concepts and learns to respond to others as they respond to her. Ideas are open ended and there is a large measure of exploratory and experiential learning involved. In contrast, the performance is, by its very nature, for the audience – it is practised and developed as a product which can be repeated in the same form more than once. In this situation, the child is developing and applying specific skills for a particular purpose.

As with any two polarised examples from each end of a spectrum, there are also many variations in between. For example, children role-playing a police interview in pairs might then follow this up with a report-writing activity. On the other hand, a group who have constructed a series of scenes about Victorian children based on their research from reference books might show their piece to the class as the culmination of their work. In this way we can see that there are many levels of 'audience', and just as many ways of working with children in situations which we might called 'drama activities'.

Drama and language

Drama enables children to participate in language situations within the safe environment of the school. In other words, by entering a world of pretend, they can gain access to a range of 'real world' and 'fantasy world' situations. They can travel though time to other ages, through distance to other lands, through books to other stories and through space to other planets! Such a resource is a valuable asset to any teacher who wishes to inspire children in ways which will motivate and deepen their understanding and learning of language.

In the primary school, drama can provide:

- high levels of motivation, which means children stay on-task
- interactive learning opportunities
- the natural and appropriate integration of language skills
- opportunities to build concepts of language through active participation
- the acquisition of knowledge about language through actual use

- the provision of a wide variety of meaningful contexts within which to explore skills, concepts and knowledge in other subjects across the curriculum
- effective learning experiences which are memorable.

Drama, language and the National Curriculum

The programme of study for Speaking and Listening includes a whole paragraph dedicated to drama at each key stage, and drama scripts and plays are referred to in the programmes of study for Reading and Writing. However, in addition to these explicit requirements, it is also important to consider how many of the other requirements within the English Order might be delivered effectively through the drama medium. Figure 17.1 lists some examples of how this might be achieved.

Modes of working with drama

Drama modes offer a wide range of teaching techniques which you can select according to the purpose of the activity. Each technique can involve you and your children in very different ways. For example, sometimes you may be the only one in role and the children are asking you questions, whereas on another occasion the children may be working in pairs, writing in role. It is essential that you are informed by more detailed descriptions of these methods and many others in your further reading if you are to develop a thorough working knowledge of all that is available to you. However, for the purposes of this chapter, Figure 17.2 summarises the most common forms with an example for each key stage.

The organisation and management of drama

Just as there are different types of drama activity, there are also different ways of organisation and management. For instance, drama need not always be a whole-class activity, it need not necessarily last for longer than ten minutes, and it doesn't always take place in a large space.

Groupings

It can often give teachers much more scope for using drama as a teaching tool if they recognise the flexibility of different types of working groups for different purposes. Here are some examples.

	National Curriculum reference	Use of drama for delivery
Key Stage 1		
Speaking and Listening	exploring, developing and clarifying ideas	answering questions from class as a character from the class story (teacher and/or pupils in role)
Reading	read with fluency, accuracy, understanding and enjoyment	simple play scripts in the role-play corner
Writing	write for a range of readers	writing letter to the monster from the moon, encountered in a previous drama session
Key Stage 1		
Speaking and Listening	enacting stories and poems	sequence of tableau scenes inspired by poetry of war
Reading	respond imaginatively to plot, characters, ideas	improvised scene of plot beyond the text, character motivation, etc.
Writing	use writing as a means of developing, organising and communicating ideas	prepare a speech for a debate on a public issue to actually perform in role

Figure 17.1 Examples of teaching English through drama

Mode	Key Stage 1 example	Key Stage 2 example
Role play	Cafe role-play corner	Reporter interviewing a rebel footballer
Guided imagery	Teacher talks class through the exploration of a magic forest.	Teacher talks class through an imagined excavation of a pyramid.
Mime	Groups mime professions for class to guess.	Trios plan a mimed story sequence.
Tableau	Build a class picture of a market scene.	Groups create sequence of three linking tableaux to tell story of a Viking journey.
Hot seating	Story time: teacher in role as a character from yesterday's story. Children ask questions.	Groups research historical facts about a famous character. Individuals go to different groups for questioning.
Improvisation	Whole class journey to the moon (teacher in role).	Groups go into spontaneous (unplanned) scene of headteacher dealing with bullies.
Reconstructed improvisation	Develop moon journey into series of repeated scenes.	Develop bully scene into a documentary-type series of scenes.
Script-writing	Simple scripting following play with puppets	Record improvised scene for another group to then read.
Script-reading	Speech bubble cards in the role-play corner	Reading and creating movement to perform.

Figure 17.2 Examples of different drama modes in operation

Pairs
Spontaneous improvisation of a customer visiting a store manager to complain about a product bought last week (KS1)
Time: 5 minutes

Trios
Same as above with an observer who reports back on how each party handled the situation (KS1)
Time: 10 minutes

Fours
Planning a TV news report on the controversial building of a new motorway (KS2)
Time: 30 minutes

Whole class
Individual volunteers mime a Victorian occupation or character for rest of class to guess as a recap on yesterday's history lesson before introducing today's development of the theme (KS2)
Time: 8 minutes

Space
Another way to open up the possibilities for drama as a teaching tool is to consider a variety of spaces in which drama can take place. The hall is useful for large-scale activities, for example the reconstruction of a Tudor market scene with the teacher improvising in role along with the children. However, in some schools, hall space is limited because of the number of classes and the timetabling of PE. It is quite possible to use your classroom for certain types of drama. For example:

In pairs at tables
Spontaneous role play between a TV reporter and Goldilocks. This question and answer session would be a follow-up to hearing and discussing the story (KS1).
Time: 6 minutes

In groups of six round a table
Spontaneous role play of a parents' meeting to discuss whether school uniform should be abolished (KS2)
Time: 10 minutes

Home corner
Structured play following up a story read to the class, by placing new 'props' and dressing up clothes relating to the story into the home corner for use by the children (KS1)
Time: 20 minutes

Role-play corner

Set up part of the classroom for role play in connection with specific language tasks (e.g. travel agency at KS1, a court room at KS2), or work in another curriculum area (e.g. old-fashioned kitchen at KS1, a World War II air raid shelter at KS2). Children choose character cards from one box and problem cards from another to guide their time. Goal: to explore ideas then shape them into a piece to show to rest of class. Possibility for follow-up script-writing as a piece for Topic Book. (Topic Books need not contain writing from only one genre!)
Time: 20 minutes (role play)

Carpet time

Recapping on a chapter read by teacher yesterday by hot seating (see Glossary). The teacher or a child pretends to be one of the characters (or a group can represent several characters) and the class ask questions about what happened/what characters felt, etc., in yesterday's section. (KS1/2)
Time: 10 minutes

Tables rearranged

In rows to recreate a Victorian schoolroom, or into a boardroom situation for a village parish council meeting about planning a project for the Millennium (KS2)
Time: 30–40 minutes

Tables and chairs stacked

Clear a space for larger group activities, for example rehearsing the Christmas production! (KS1/2)
Time: 45 minutes absolute maximum!

Time

You will notice from the previous examples, as with those given for group sizes, that the timings can also vary enormously. Do not avoid doing drama because you think you can't spare the time! It is worth remembering the following points to reassure yourself that there can always be time for drama:

- A five-minute drama input at the beginning of a session can provide a stimulating and alternative approach to recapping previous work, reminding, reinforcing, explaining or introducing a topic.
- A five-minute drama summary at the end of a session can provide a different way of presenting work or asking/answering questions.
- Drama can provide a resource for other work, for example giving the children a reason for writing or reading.
- Drama is an invaluable teaching tool which can be used right across the curriculum, so your drama session might also be your geography session.
- Drama is an effective way for children to learn a range of language skills, so your drama session might also be your English session.

Drama and oracy

Drama offers a most useful framework within which you can provide contexts for speaking and listening. Even Year 6 children still like to play and pretend, but the usefulness of that play depends totally on the quality of the provision and the expectations of the teacher. When planning drama for the development of oracy skills, you will need to consider:

- *different situations*, e.g. shop, meeting, police station
- *different characters and roles*, e.g. a parent, a burglar, a news reader
- *different types of talk*, e.g. explaining, describing, reporting
- *different purposes for the talk*, e.g. to persuade, to give instructions
- *different outcomes for the talk*, e.g. to reach a decision, to perform to parents
- *different focuses for listening*, e.g. for enjoyment, for information, for analysis.

To understand how the detailed issues of oracy can connect with drama modes, you need to read this chapter in close conjunction with Chapters 7 and 8.

Drama and reading

The National Curriculum emphasises the importance of providing a wide range of reading opportunities for primary pupils. Drama can support you in providing such a range by offering contexts and purposes for reading many different kinds of texts. This in turn can enable children to develop active reading skills, for instance searching the text for meaning and hidden meaning, following instructions, developing opinions and shaping responses. With careful planning, drama can make considerable demands on children's reading because of the interactive nature of the process. The three obvious places where the reading might fit into the drama are:

- before the drama (e.g. folk tale which will be played out in the role-play corner)
- during the drama (e.g. travel agent reading brochure in role)
- after the drama (e.g. reading letters from 'evacuees' and writing back).

Word-building skills

Even some of the most basic reading activities can be enhanced through drama. For example:

Key Stage 1: Set up an easel or flip chart which faces you. Write a word (e.g. 'cut') for a chosen child to read. The child then mimes the word to the rest of the class for guessing. The words can be selected according to the individual needs of the child.

Key Stage 2: Older children who are behind with their reading still need lots of games and motivating activities through which they can practise the basic skills. The mime game could be played with a small group. You could even write a sentence or film title for children who are more advanced with their reading but who need practice in word-attack skills.

Exploring literature

If children are going to read for meaning, and read beyond the meaning, we should be offering situations which actually require active interrogation and exploration of texts. For example:

Key Stage 1: Change your home corner into a story corner. Provide drama sacks, each one containing a picture book with which the children are familiar, plus related props, masks, hats, dressing up clothes, etc. The children can re-enact the story and invent alternative versions.

Key Stage 2: Select a chapter to be read by a group, then choose one person to be a character from the chapter who sits in the hot seat to answer questions by the rest. Ideally, if the chapter has four characters, four members of the group could take turns to answer questions as a different character, introducing a range of perspectives.

Shakespeare

Shakespeare's stories can provide excellent starting points for story at Key Stage 1, and this work can be developed into more depth at Key Stage 2. A familiarity with the stories and exploration of some of Shakespeare's themes (from the comedy of confusion to jealousy and murder) can help many children overcome the barriers of fear about Shakespeare when they are later faced with this at secondary school. Don't feel you need to use the pure texts. There are some excellent abridged versions of these rich tales.

Key Stage 1: Extracts from *A Midsummer Night's Dream* can be played out with lollipop-stick puppets after the children have heard the story from you (told in your own words or from an illustrated version). Focus particularly on the humour and magic. Let the children use actual names from the play, e.g. Puck, Bottom, Titania, Master Cobweb, etc.

Key Stage 2: Tell the story of *Macbeth* using an illustrated version. Explore and discuss the moods and create collage pictures with mood words from the play included in the design, e.g. 'Fair is foul and foul is fair: Hover through the fog and filthy air' (I.1.11–12).

Play scripts

Play scripts can provide a highly enjoyable source of reading for children. Not only do they require reading for meaning and with expression, but also the stage directions in more advanced scripts can provide excellent opportunities for following instructions. For example:

Key Stage 1: Most reading schemes now provide plays as part of the range of texts offered. These can be used for group reading round a table, or can also be used in the role-play corner as a group activity to be shown later to the rest of the class.

Key Stage 2: Reading-scheme plays are invaluable for struggling readers at Key Stage 2, but more detailed texts are also excellent for challenging more able readers if the school is able to buy sets of these. For example, there are dramatised versions of novels available now from some publishers.

Non-fiction books

If we are to avoid the non-constructive 'copying of chunks' from information book to the child's own workbook, we need to be inventive about how we require children to read non-fiction. In other words, we need to create situations where children have a purpose to their reading which will motivate them and lead to satisfactory outcomes. For example:

Key Stage 1: Provide a hospital role-play corner which includes books about human life, parts of the body, etc. Ensure that the doctors and nurses need to refer to these in order to fill in their reports! Magazines might also be provided for waiting patients.

Key Stage 2: Ask the children, in groups of four, to research an aspect of Victorian home life and present a short documentary-type scene to the rest of the class which is based on actual facts. This might take the form of a narrator, with characters from the past coming to life at appropriate moments to illustrate the points being made. The factual evidence should be written down in list form, correctly referenced, to present as proof of their research at the end.

Other information texts

There are numerous texts which can be obtained from outside school and are absolutely free of charge! Many of these can be used in the classroom to provide interesting reading resources. For example:

Key Stage 1: Food posters and packets can be used in a shop role-play corner, not only to create an authentic environment, but also to use actively, for example writing receipts and making special-offer posters.

Key Stage 2: Newspaper cuttings given to the children in groups of six can provide a good basis for presenting a television news report. This might include interviews, narrative, reporting and action scenes.

Drama and writing

Drama can often provide frameworks for writing by offering a purpose, a role or an audience. This can be particularly supportive to children who lack confidence as writers.

Authorship and role play

When children in a nursery class enact the role of adult writing a shopping list, receptionist writing an appointment card or teacher marking the register, much valuable learning is taking place. These children are constructing their understandings of what it is to be writers and the functions which print serves in our society. It can be quite disconcerting, therefore, to observe such children suddenly demonstrate resistance, discomfort or even fear when they are put into a more formal situation and asked to write.

Drama can take the fear out of learning to write by giving the task a 'real' purpose and setting it into a situation which is motivating and rewarding. The drama enables the teacher to add structure to the play situation and thus integrate specific learning objectives into the activity. With older children, the drama situation can really help to bring their writing to life by setting it within contexts which will capture their interest. Writing in role is a useful tool which can motivate all children.

Developing story-writing using puppets

Experience is at the heart of all story-writing. Imagination uses experience as its raw material, regardless of how that is then shaped, changed or extended. Drama can provide experiences on which children can draw in their story-writing. By playing out their ideas first, the children have a means by which they can extend their imagination to the boundaries of their activity, and also organise and reorganise their ideas into meaningful and creative frameworks. Puppets can provide a very manageable vehicle for such play. It is worth remembering that puppets can be made in a wide range of ways, from simple decorated paper bags which fit over the hand, to more complex papier mâché sculptures operated by canes. Whatever the process of manufacture (and this might form part of your technology work, with content from history or RE), the important point to be made here is that children often feel safer with puppets when developing storylines because the puppet is one step removed from their real selves.

Genre writing and drama

When writing in different genres, drama can offer convincing reasons to write and consequently increase motivation. Figure 17.3 suggests some ways in which writing might take place before, during and after a drama activity.

Providing audiences for writing

The National Curriculum requires children to write for a range of audiences. Drama is one good way of structuring writing activities with this in mind: for example, at Key Stage 1 writing menus and bills in the cafe corner, and at Key Stage 2 writing a letter as a parent to ask the school to introduce

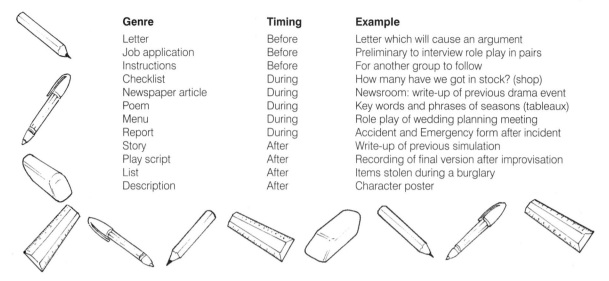

Genre	Timing	Example
Letter	Before	Letter which will cause an argument
Job application	Before	Preliminary to interview role play in pairs
Instructions	Before	For another group to follow
Checklist	During	How many have we got in stock? (shop)
Newspaper article	During	Newsroom: write-up of previous drama event
Poem	During	Key words and phrases of seasons (tableaux)
Menu	During	Role play of wedding planning meeting
Report	During	Accident and Emergency form after incident
Story	After	Write-up of previous simulation
Play script	After	Recording of final version after improvisation
List	After	Items stolen during a burglary
Description	After	Character poster

Figure 17.3 Relationships between drama and writing activities

homework! By providing imaginary contexts for writing and audiences which can be role-played, drama can help the children to feel motivated to write and also to empathise more realistically with their readers.

Editing in role

Even the most basic act of pretending can be employed effectively in the classroom – this is drama in its most natural form. For example, a group to whom you are teaching paragraphing skills are likely to be more motivated if you provide them with a situation in which they are tourist information officers and have to sort out the text you give them into sections for a brochure. Likewise, infant children love pretending to be teacher when checking each other's work! In contrast, if the secretarial skills of writing are placed into decontextualised and tedious tasks children can become bored and stray off task. By disguising these activities, even the most repetitive skills can be practised with a high level of concentration. A Victorian classroom where handwriting practice is conducted in silence can be amazingly exciting to children!

Drama and the literacy hour

The literacy hour should be planned in ways which enable children to develop their reading and writing skills in ways which have a meaningful context. Drama can be used to create interactive situations which provide opportunities to read, write, discuss, analyse, compare, dramatise, evaluate and much more. Examples are given below, for each key stage, of how drama might be used as a tool to teach key skills during the literacy hour session.

Text level
- After reading a story to the whole class, you go into role and answer questions as one of the characters, to enable the children to explore the text further.
- Provide the children with a short scene with stage directions (it is useful to write your own so that you can include a good range of stage directions and also differentiate for levels of ability). Ask the children to read it to allocate parts, practise the reading in character and follow the stage directions. They should have 20–25 minutes' group work and will then perform to the whole class. This enables the children to read for meaning, practise reading with fluency and expression and follow instructions.

Sentence level
- Provide the children with a continuous text which consists of a very short set of sentences spoken by different characters. Mix up the order of the sentences. Ask the children to sort out the text into individual sentences. They should then punctuate each sentence with a capital letter and full stop. Finally, ask them to sort the sentences into correct order to read aloud as a play script. Perform during the plenary and show each written sentence to the rest of the class.
- Ask the children to write sentence instructions for the role-play corner in role, e.g. notes from different members of the family in the home corner – 'Your tea is in the oven.'

165

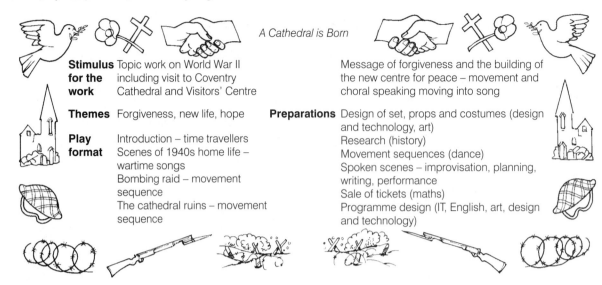

Figure 17.4 Curriculum work in performance

Stimulus for the work Topic work on World War II including visit to Coventry Cathedral and Visitors' Centre

Themes Forgiveness, new life, hope

Play format Introduction – time travellers
Scenes of 1940s home life – wartime songs
Bombing raid – movement sequence
The cathedral ruins – movement sequence

A Cathedral is Born

Message of forgiveness and the building of the new centre for peace – movement and choral speaking moving into song

Preparations Design of set, props and costumes (design and technology, art)
Research (history)
Movement sequences (dance)
Spoken scenes – improvisation, planning, writing, performance
Sale of tickets (maths)
Programme design (IT, English, art, design and technology)

Word level

- Introduce vocabulary cards with topic-related words written on each (for example, you might take new adjectives from a text which you have just read to the children). Ask the children to role-play in pairs a conversation during which they should use the vocabulary on their cards. The other children then guess which words were on the cards and describe their meaning.

- Practising handwriting in role can bring a somewhat tedious and repetitive task to life. For example if the children are pretending to be waiters and waitresses making menus for their cafe, they will enjoy the writing all the more because they can see the reason for its needing to be clear and attractive.

The place of performance

Class assemblies and Christmas plays have always been popular with children and parents. There is no doubt that children can benefit from such opportunities to speak to a different audience and the exploration of different ways of communicating their achievements. The expression and communication of ideas through this medium has already been highlighted as a valuable part of the curriculum.

However, to ensure that the maximum amount of learning takes place in the preparation (as well as the performance) of such events, it is important to consider the following:

1 What can the children learn during the preparation of such work?

2 What can children learn during the actual performance, and in the evaluations afterwards?
3 Which aspects of the National Curriculum can be integrated into the preparations and performance?
4 What can I afford to leave out of the working week in order to make the space for the preparations?
5 How can I justify this and plan it into my schemes of work?

The preparations should be designed to be equally important as the performance itself in terms of the children's learning. By regarding the performance as valid evidence of learning it is perfectly possible to justify such work in your planning objectives. Figure 17.4 illustrates a performance which was prepared with a class of Year 4 children to show parents at Christmas time. In this particular school, every class prepared their own performance, which took place in the classroom for the parents at night.

Assessment and planning

Assessment and planning are inextricably linked, and where drama is concerned this can prove to be quite complex. For example, in a role-play debate about town planning are you assessing the children's geography skills, their oracy skills or their drama skills?

The secret of success is to be clear about your aims. You will enjoy providing drama for your children if you feel confident that there are clear learning objectives. At different times, these objectives might relate to one or more of the following:

- English
- drama
- other areas of learning across the curriculum.

Whether you assess them on their drama skills as a separate area will depend very much on the policy of the school. However, it is certainly possible to assess certain aspects of English during drama activities, in particular speaking and listening. Indeed the children are often so fully absorbed that it is relatively easy to step back and observe – watching their responses and listening to their talk.

The examples below illustrate how you might assess the children against level descriptions during various types of drama activities.

Speaking and Listening
Level 1
'They listen to others and usually respond appropriately.'

Observe individuals (usually three at any one time) while they are watching another group showing their drama. Are they listening? Do they ask appropriate questions at the end? Can they make constructive comment? Can they be clear about one aspect which they particularly liked?

Level 4
'In discussion, they listen carefully, making contributions and asking questions that are responsive to others' ideas and views.'

Observe individuals during a role-played meeting. Are they asking appropriate questions? Are they considering others' ideas and views even if they disagree with them?

Reading
Level 2
'Pupils' reading of simple texts shows understanding and is generally accurate.'

Observe during play in the role-play corner where you have placed instruction cards to structure the play (e.g. a recipe card where they have to count and find things). Are they following the instructions accurately?

Level 5
'Pupils show understanding of a range of texts, selecting essential points and using inference and deduction where appropriate.'

Set up a mock TV debate about a news item with various viewpoints to be represented (e.g. in groups of three). Provide each child with a photocopy of the same news item from a newspaper. During the debate, observe them to see if they are reading beyond the text and drawing conclusions from their deductions.

Writing
Level 1
'Pupils' writing communicates through simple words and phrases.'

Role-play letter-writing to an imaginary character encountered during a drama session via a magic letter box.

Level 3
'The main features of different forms of writing are used appropriately, beginning to be adapted for different readers.'

In groups of three, role-play an incident such as rescuing an animal in distress. Write collaboratively three different versions of the event: one as a formal letter from the RSPCA to the children, one as an official RSPCA report of the incident, and the third as a short item in the local newspaper. Have they used appropriate language? Have they set out each piece in the correct way?

SUMMARY

This chapter has provided an introductory guide to the teaching of drama as required by the National Curriculum Order for English. It has also demonstrated how drama can be developed usefully, beyond the statutory requirements, to teach all aspects of English (including using drama in the literacy hour), and other areas of the curriculum. The chapter has demonstrated that:

- Drama provides effective and enjoyable contexts within which children can learn, practise and consolidate language skills in reading, writing and oracy.

- There are many different ways of organising and teaching drama.

- Performance drama is an important part of children's language and communication learning experience, and vital to the arts curriculum.

Further reading

Clipson-Boyles, S. B.(1996) 'Teaching Reading through Drama', in D. Reid and D. Bentley (eds) *Reading On! Developing Reading at Key Stage 2*, Scholastic
Practical ideas on how specific reading skills can be taught through drama.

Clipson-Boyles, S. B. (1998) *Drama in Primary English Teaching*, David Fulton
A comprehensive guide on how to plan, manage and deliver the National Curriculum requirements for drama using a wide range of approaches. This book includes a planning and assessment guide to drama from Year 1 through to Year 6 to assist with developing a whole-school drama scheme. It also provides activities for use in the literacy hour.

Crinson, J. and Leak, L. (eds) (1993) *Move Back the Desks*, NATE
A very useful practical guide to drama ideas, underpinned by a recognition of the potential for language learning.

Rankin, I. (1995) *Drama 5–14*, Hodder and Stoughton
Useful lesson plans for drama across the primary age range.

18 Media education and English

Media education and English

OBJECTIVES

By the end of this chapter you should be able to:

- discuss why media education has a place in the primary curriculum

- consider the potential which media education offers to teaching English

- identify the learning potential across the range of different media

- start planning media activities into your English scheme of work

- assess children's English skills during media activities.

Why teach media education?

As a primary teacher it is important for you to recognise that the media play a significant role in children's lives. Children cannot escape exposure to the technology revolution which generates so much information and so many ideas, nor should they. But the sheer volume of choice means that critical awareness is needed if they are to develop the skills to make informed choices and gain maximum benefit from their interactions with the media. There are five main reasons why media education should be taught in the primary school:

- to develop an understanding of the functions of the media
- to become aware of the differences between media
- to increase children's critical responses to the media
- to develop children's communication skills within different media
- to capitalise on children's usual interest in the media in order to teach English skills.

Traditionally, media studies in secondary and post-16 education covers broadcasting, film and pub-

lishing, but here we will also consider other communication technologies which can be employed as part of teaching English in the primary classroom, with the exception of computers, which are dealt with separately in Chapter 19.

Media education and English

The purpose of teaching English in the primary school is to 'develop pupils' abilities to communicate effectively in speech and writing and to listen with understanding. It should also enable them to be enthusiastic, responsive and knowledgeable readers' (National Curriculum Order for English (1995), p. 2, para. 1). Such communication is central to society, and the media encompass this in their everyday functions. In other words, the raison d'être of the media is communication, and to this end a rich tapestry of literacies are employed which reflect and shape society.

The teaching of English is concerned primarily with communication via the written and spoken word, and so it is easy to see that to exclude media education from the primary English curriculum would be to prevent children from accessing a significant language resource which is representative of a high proportion of society's communication. Just as we use books, pencils and paper in the classroom, so should we include other media.

Media education is not explicitly described in the National Curriculum Order for English at Key Stages 1 and 2, but it is implied. For example:

Radio, television, film
'Pupils should be encouraged to participate in drama activities, improvisation and performances of varying kinds ...' (p. 4, para. 1d).

'Pupils should be given opportunities to listen and respond to a range of people. They should be taught to identify and comment on key features of what they see and hear in a variety of media' (p. 11, para. 1c).

Newspapers

'The range of non-fiction should include … newspapers …' (p. 13, para.1b).

Media education is approached in different ways by different schools. Most often it is planned into the curriculum as a series of discrete English topics. In this way the children are able to learn, develop and practise English skills within meaningful media contexts whilst at the same time building up a knowledge and critical awareness of the media which are such an important part of our lives. In addition to providing excellent contexts for English teaching, this also lays good foundations for the more explicit requirements of media studies in English at Key Stages 3 and 4.

There is an enormous amount of scope for developing integrated language approaches to this work. For example, work on newspapers might include:

- discussion and debate
- reading for meaning, interpretation and response
- writing from 'real life' models.

Even an activity such as highlighting certain spelling patterns in a newspaper article involves overlap between reading and writing. That is the nature of the media, and is another reason why models of good practice can be developed through media education in very natural and appropriate ways. However, if the true potential of media education is to be maximised, whole-school planning for progression is vital.

Whole-school progression

Media education can be plotted on to a whole-school planning map in many different ways, and one of the strengths of team planning is that the curriculum delivery can be designed to meet the particular needs of the school. Some schools plan media 'themes' for the whole school (e.g. advertising) for their English teaching during a particular term in the year; others take a different form of media with each year group (e.g. Year 1 comics; Year 2 radio; Year 3 magazines; Year 4 newspapers; Year 5 television; Year 6 film).

Arguably, the optimum approach is to revisit different media each year in order to continually broaden existing knowledge and increase the depth of understanding. Although this demands

extensive planning, it is quite feasible for it to become an integrated part of English teaching rather than a bolt-on added extra. Figure 18.1 shows a skeletal progression grid which lists an exemplar Key Concept (KC) and Key Skill (KS) for each of the key media at every yearly stage to demonstrate how this type of approach might work.

Quite clearly, the grid would need to be developed into a much more comprehensive and detailed plan by individual schools, but this illustration is intended to assist the process by providing a starting point, perhaps in a school where media education can become an important part of the English teaching throughout both key stages.

Media education and the literacy hour

Media education has an important and useful part to play in the literacy hour. This can be divided broadly into two main functions: firstly direct use of media texts, and secondly use of the media as a vehicle to discuss, read and write other texts.

Media texts

The range of genres to be covered within the literacy hour include many direct references to media texts, for example adverts, newspapers, descriptions, notices, messages, and so on. Work on such texts can be enhanced by using media contexts for the activities. This gives relevance and meaning to the task and can also succeed in motivating children because of the familiar association. Many of the examples described in this chapter can be used usefully during the literacy hour.

The media as a vehicle for reading and writing other texts

During the literacy hour, children are required to learn and practise literacy skills at word, sentence and text levels. If true understanding is to develop, and high levels of interest to be maintained, this learning should take place within the context of relevant and meaningful activities. The media provide such contexts for all the reasons provided elsewhere in this chapter. So, for instance, Key Stage 1 children writing a description of a lost cat

	Magazines and newspapers	Radio	Television	Film
Year 1	KC: variety of fonts KS: using letters to construct words	KC: historical place of radio KS: listening and responding	KC: choice and preferences KS: justifying preferences	KC: links between books and films KS: express responses to film
Year 2	KC: variety of magazines KS: using contents page	KC: stations and tuning KS: reading stories fluently for tape	KC: real and pretend KS: stories for favourite characters	KC: differences: books and films KS: compare character representations
Year 3	KC: sections of a newspaper KS: page layout	KC: studo recording KS: creating own effects	KC: news item hierarchies KS: reporting an event	KC: effects of music KS: describe mood and atmosphere
Year 4	KC: understanding magazine genres KS: genre writing	KC: different programmes and audiences KS: writing range of scripts	KC: processes of programme-making KS: planning and 'making' a programme	KC: effects of different camera shots KS: plan shots for piece of text
Year 5	KC: differences between national and local newspapers KS: reading for meaning	KC: commercial radio and adverts KS: marketing a product	KC: purpose of advertising KS: analyse advert structures	KC: narrative structure KS: compare narrative structures of film and book
Year 6	KC: implied meaning and bias KS: comparing reports in different papers	KC: dialect and accent KS: using different talk for different purposes	KC: programme genres KS: analyse dialects in soap operas	KC: processes of film-making KS: critical reviews and comparisions

Figure 18.1 The progression of Key Concepts and Key Skills in media education

would be particularly focused if the end goal was to record this as a radio news item. Likewise, Key Stage 2 children conducting biographical research could write up and perform the fruits of their labour as a documentary to be filmed on video. In both cases, it would be important to present the children with real examples of these types of presentation, and to discuss these, before expecting them to work in this way.

The power of advertising

If you try to make a list of all the places where advertisements appear you will see that they lie within many contexts – television, local radio, magazines, bill boards, public notice boards, junk mail, and so on. These can provide excellent starting points for English activities and can also make appropriate links to cross-curricular themes, for instance industry and commerce or gender issues. Areas of study which might be covered include:

- types of text
- punctuation
- communication through pictures
- messages and hidden messages
- metaphor and simile
- rhyme
- persuasion
- comparison
- different types of talk.

One real advantage of working with advertisements is the sheer abundance of material which needn't cost you a penny! Used magazines and newspapers, recordings from local commercial radio stations and videos of television adverts can all provide a rich range of resources for discussion, observation, modelling, cutting and pasting!

Why are the three illustrations chosen? What effect do they have on the reader? How did the designer decide which text to enlarge and why? All these questions help children to look more critically and provide a model for them to emulate in their own work.

171

In the frame with photographs!

Many nursery teachers use photography widely to stimulate discussion and writing. Photographs can provide information which is directly relevant to children, such as buildings in their environment, people they know or scenes from a school trip. The excitement of actually using a camera, sending off the film and opening the packet of pictures when it arrives adds a truly motivating dimension to children's work. And of course if you can afford to use a Polaroid camera, perhaps for a special project, you have the instant results which keep children's enthusiasm at a peak. Here are just some of the ways in which photographs might be used:

- photographs from magazines as a stimulus for writing
- photographs from magazines to be examined through questions
- photographs from newspapers as a stimulus for articles
- designing storybooks with ready-printed or own photographs
- making information books about a topic which the children photograph themselves (e.g. Our School, The Supermarket, Foods, Plants, etc.)
- family albums
- making non-fiction books from ready-printed or planned photographs
- setting up scenes with toys to photograph which would then form the basis for stories.

As with all books made by children, the learning is not just in the planning and writing, but also in the reading afterwards. Books made by children are often the most well-thumbed texts in the reading corner!

From fiction to film ... and back again!

Cinema attendance has been in sharp continuous decline since the 1950s, although a slow increase has taken place since the introduction of multiplex cinemas in 1985. Despite this, the film industry is thriving, which is undoubtedly due to the introduction of video in the late 1970s to early 1980s.

Children's films form a significant part of this industry and you will find that most of your pupils are already well informed about the latest releases, along with a multitude of old favourites. Many quality children's films are available on video, and a large number of these have been developed from books, for example Anne Fine's *Madame Doubtfire* (Penguin, 1995), Roald Dahl's *Matilda* (Penguin, 1989) and Frances Hodgson Burnett's *The Secret Garden* (Puffin Classics, reissued 1994).

There is much to be gained educationally from the use of video in the primary classroom. However, this does not mean sitting the children in front of a screen to watch for an uninterrupted hour and a half! Rather, it means the skilful selection of parts of films as a stimulus for discussion, writing and reading. Indeed, the discussion in which children can engage, for example about the portrayal of character in a film, relates very closely to the book talk which so helps them to integrate ideas into their constructions of and responses to texts.

At primary level, this aspect of media education can be divided very simply into two broad categories: story studies and film studies. The first uses the medium in order to extend and develop the children's understanding of specific fictional texts and provides purposes for extended reading, writing and discussion about literature. The second provides activities which are more directly linked to topics and issues on film techniques and the film industry in general. Clearly there can be overlap between the two, and your area of focus will depend very much on the reasons why you are doing the work in the first place. However, the exploration of film studies with primary-age children can reap fruitful rewards in terms of developing English skills, not least because it is usually an area of great fascination for children. Figure 18.2 lists some examples of starting points for learning in each category.

At Key Stage 1, the observation of film clips can promote critical analysis at a level which is fun for the children whilst at the same time can lead to some useful comparative analysis.

For example, an activity could be based on a comparison of the films *101 Dalmatians* (the original, cartoon, Disney 1961, re-released 1996) and *101 Dalmatians – Live Action* (the real-life version starring Glenn Close, Disney 1997). After a preparatory discussion, the children are required to represent the two versions of Cruella De Vil quickly in drawing, and label adjectives to describe each. The activity can be differentiated at a higher level by writing the adjectives which describe each, then sorting them into the boxes to show where they are

Key Stage 1		Key Stage 2	
Story studies	comparing responses to book and film descriptions of short extracts character descriptions historical comparisions	*Story studies*	character portrayal settings representation from book to film explicit themes implicit themes story structure (compare) script-writing story-boards (with directions and effects) writing own interpretations using own experiences
Film studies	scene counting reading credits descriptions of music how cartoons are made film popularity surveys designing and marketing posters	*Film studies*	camera techniques (e.g. pan, zoom, fade, close-up shots, dissolve, etc.) scene length sound effects and music planning making marketing film genres comparisions of media (book and film)

Figure 18.2 Film studies and story studies

the same and where they are different. Children who are at the appropriate reading ability level could go on to look at the book (an abridged version of Dodie Smith's story is available published by Ladybird, 1991) to investigate how adjectives are used there and how they compare with their own.

This activity is not merely a drawing activity, but also enables the children to observe critically, compare and contrast, explore the use of adjectives, differentiate between the application of those adjectives and scan a text in order to search for adjectives.

At Key Stage 2, the breadth and depth of the potential activities derived from film are even greater, as would be expected. Story can be explored and film studies can be more technical, critical and interpretative. Figure 18.3 illustrates some key questions relating to *The Secret Garden* which might be asked of Year 5 children through close observation of selected film clips in conjunction with close reading of the text.

Tapping into television

Television is frequently criticised and blamed for many of society's problems. Low reading stan-

dards, lack of family activities and increased violent behaviour are only some of today's problems which are attributed to, amongst other things, television. However, the fact remains that the majority of children you teach will have regular exposure to television. Television is a major aspect of everyday life, and to assume that we can change that is unrealistic. However, there are other things which we can do, such as helping children to:

- become more critical and selective in their viewing
- develop a better awareness of genres and their different functions
- read implicit messages
- learn and use communication skills from the medium
- use information from the medium
- produce information for the medium.

Television is a medium with which children feel familiar and confident, and so it provides an excellent resource for learning. Below are some starting points to help you begin considering how you might use television in your English teaching.

Reading

Key Stage 1

Recognising words in familiar texts. Make a compi-

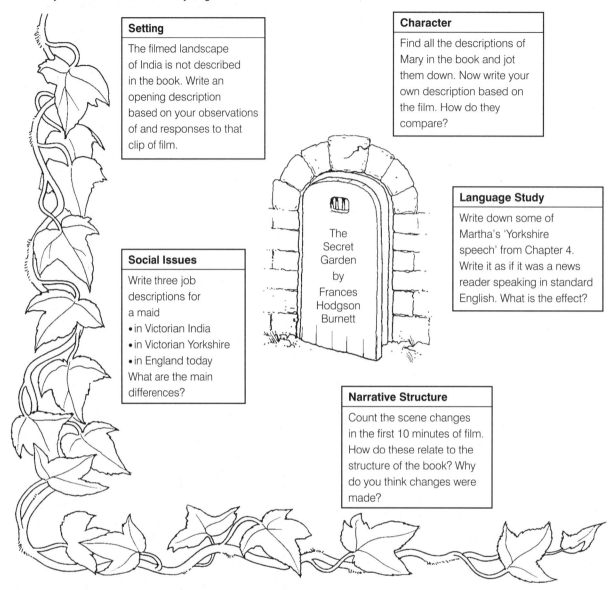

Setting

The filmed landscape of India is not described in the book. Write an opening description based on your observations of and responses to that clip of film.

Character

Find all the descriptions of Mary in the book and jot them down. Now write your own description based on the film. How do they compare?

Language Study

Write down some of Martha's 'Yorkshire speech' from Chapter 4. Write it as if it was a news reader speaking in standard English. What is the effect?

Social Issues

Write three job descriptions for a maid
• in Victorian India
• in Victorian Yorkshire
• in England today
What are the main differences?

The Secret Garden by Frances Hodgson Burnett

Narrative Structure

Count the scene changes in the first 10 minutes of film. How do these relate to the structure of the book? Why do you think changes were made?

Figure 18.3 Activities relating to *The Secret Garden* (Puffin Classic, 1994, first published 1911)

lation of the title frames of favourite programmes. Point and read the texts and use as a starting point for phonic work.

Key Stage 2

Using strategies appropriately to establish meaning. Use a TV guide to select all the programmes during one week which might appeal to someone who wants to learn more about cooking (scanning, skimming, reading for meaning, reading with understanding).

Writing

Key Stage 1

Writing in response to a variety of stimuli. Watch and discuss a programme, then write a letter to one of the characters.

Key Stage 2

Making judgements about when a particular tone, style, format or choice of vocabulary is appropriate. After watching a short extract of a book review programme, choose a book to review which would involve making notes about key points, writing into a readable format, then performing it (as if on a review chat show) to the class. A further extension of this would be to examine the difference between a review which is read on a book programme and one which is written for a newspaper.

Speaking and Listening

Key Stage 1

Considering how talk is influenced by the purpose and intended audience. Watch a short extract of *Teletubbies* having briefed the children that you want them to listen to the way the characters are talking. Use it as a starting point for a discussion on the nature of this 'toddler talk' and why the programme has been so popular. Compare it with an extract from *Tom and Jerry*. Discuss speed, volume, accent, effect, etc.

Key Stage 2

Investigating how language varies according to context and purpose and between standard and dialect forms. Use three short extracts from *East-Enders*, *Coronation Street* and *Brookside*. Discuss the reasons for regional variation and the rich tapestry of sounds and expressions. Focus on particular pronunciations and expressions in the clips and compare with standard forms. A possible extension could be to transpose into scripts and explore different ways of saying the same thing.

Revelling in radio

The BBC Schools' Broadcast Service offered a rich and extensive range of programmes for pupils long before televisions were used in schools. Today, the service continues to provide high-quality broadcasts which provide excellent opportunities for listening right across the curriculum. Indeed, without the visual images provided by television, radio can offer excellent contexts for developing the skills of concentration, imagination and response, as demanded by the National Curriculum: 'Pupils should be encouraged to listen with growing attention and concentration, to respond appropriately and effectively to what they have heard …' (p. 4, para. 2b).

Programmes are available in most curriculum areas, and, if taped, can be built up into a useful bank of resources. For example *Wordplay*, a poetry programme, often features poets reading their own work, and *Listening and Reading* offers stories which can be used over and over again by small groups of children independently. The BBC also supports teachers well through the Teacher's Handbook which accompanies each series. These give additional activity ideas, follow-up reading and associated resource references.

The listening opportunities offered by radio are also enhanced by the fact that this medium provides good models of talk. It can bring into your classroom a wide range of adults with a variety of speech patterns for discussion and modelling. This is an invaluable resource for language study. Other radio programmes outside the schools' broadcasts, including local radio, offer a vast range of genres and the different types of talk which accompany these.

In the press

Newspapers can provide starting points for learning on an extremely broad range of levels. It is usual to find that children enjoy using newspapers in their work because it feels like a very 'grown up' thing to do! The additional bonus is that used newspapers do not cost you anything!

Figure 18.4 Sentence-building using newspapers

Discussion, reading and writing activities can all take place as part of this work. Key Stage 1 children are usually better working with local news-papers as these tend to contain a higher number of human-interest stories (runaway dogs, prize winners and local issues) than the nationals. Older children can also use these productively (for instance the local sports pages can often prove to be an effective catalyst for boys who are struggling with reading), but they should also be moving on to the more complex issues such as different coverage (bias, fact, implied meaning, etc.) of the same story which can be compared by looking at a range of national papers published on the same day.

Activities using newspapers can include:

- word-building using large cut-out letters from headlines
- sentence-building using cut-out words from headlines
- matching headlines to story and/or photograph
- writing alternative stories
- writing an extension of a news story (what probably happened next)
- translating a written report into a TV news bulletin
- comparing different categories of adverts
- composing adverts (from ten-word classified to full-page promotions)
- making a class or school newspaper
- inviting visitors such as reporters, editors, printers to talk and answer children's questions
- the publishing process (emphasis on drafting, editing and proof-reading).

Comics and magazines

The range of genres offered by magazines falls into two broad categories. First, the type of magazine, for example home magazines, special interests, supermarket publications, DIY promotionals, general interest, and so on. Second, within a magazine there is usually a selection of different formats or models which children can use as stimuli for their own writing, for example contents lists, person profiles, reports of events, descriptions, interviews, short stories, comparative reporting, before and after pieces, recipes, advertisements (and these can vary, from the small lineage at the back to large full-page colour spectaculars), promotional offers, problem/troubleshooting pages, letters to the editor, etc. Magazines offer interesting reading opportunities for a variety of purposes, and children love to look at 'real-world texts'. Magazines also have the following advantages:

- They can usually be obtained free of charge.
- They can be cut up.

- They can be written on or highlighted.
- They provide different models of writing.
- You can make sets for group reading.

Comics also offer many starting points for English work. Speech bubbles are a classic way of teaching about speech punctuation, and the comic-strip format offers a useful framework for children when organising the sequence of a story. Some comics also offer models of other writing, such as letter pages, interviews with pop stars, puzzle pages, book reviews, etc. These can be a good way of motivating children into the discussion, modelling and use of different writing forms because they provide a child-centred starting point with which the children feel familiar and safe.

Top of the pops

Children have many interests which teachers can build upon in order to develop language skills. Looking at popular songs can provide not only high levels of motivation but also activities which enable children to develop skills relevant to English. These might include:

- debating about which of two songs is better
- writing and performing DJ introductions to songs
- role-playing interviews with singers
- writing new lyrics to popular tunes
- changing some words in existing lyrics
- changing the rhymes in lyrics.

Email in the classroom

Electronic mail is a rapidly growing means of communication. One day, all classrooms will be connected, not only by email, but also to the Internet, but in the meantime, most are not. Nevertheless, children need to know and understand this resource, just as they know about the telephone, and it is usually possible to show small groups at a time the system in the school office.

Back in the classroom, it is possible to set up a 'play email' situation in the writing corner by creating a file for each child on the computer. To send a message, the child finds the name of the person to whom they wish to write and adds a message to the end of the list. A tighter management procedure can sometimes be necessary to prevent abuse of the system; for example, each child is given a 'writing buddy' and they share a file which nobody

Bees buzz the town

Balloon chase

Edward takes charge for a day

Pupils scoop green award

Caring staff

Summer sport

THE FACE of Dennis the Menace will be flying high over Banbury in a charity balloon race this weekend. Balloons featuring the cartoon character will be launched from Banbury's Tesco store on Saturday (July 12) to raise money for Mencap charity. Balloons will be on sale for £1 and released at 3pm. Prizes will go to the owners of balloons which travel the furthest.

FIVE home care assistants in Banbury have been awarded national qualifications as a mark of their caring skills. Edna Humphries, Lyn Grant, Annette Jelfs, Wendy Newton, and Marlene Lines, employed by Oxfordshire Social Services, have achieved level two of the National Vocational Qualification for their home care work.

BORED children can liven up this years summer holiday by attending a sports course or day trip with Cherwell District Council. A touring sports van will be offering games sessions, while tennis courses will be available in Steeple Aston and Banbury's Horton View ground. Sports camps will be resident at Banbury and Drayton schools, and trips to adventure centres are also available.

BEEKEEPERS in full protective clothing were needed to remove a swarm of 20,000 bees from Banbury's High St. on Monday.
Mike Harris and Roy Burden were called out after a black cloud of bees descended on two flower baskets outside S.H. Jones wine merchants – sending shoppers running for cover.
The swarm was not seen as a serious danger to passers-by because the bees were too full of pollen to release a sting, but Cherwell District Council officers were keen to remove them as soon as possible.
Mr Harris said "This is our fourth callout this year but bees haven't been too much of a problem so far possibly due to the cold and wet weather."
The bees may have been disturbed from a blocked-up chimney or simply outgrew their hive, forcing the Queen bee to lead her swarm to an alternative residence.
The pavement was shut off for around half an hour while the bees were brushed off the posts and into cardboard boxes, before they were taken away to hives at Banbury's Crouch Farm.

GREEN pupils at Banbury's Queensway School have won top prize in an Oxfordshire school's environmental awareness competition.
The pupils walked away with a cheque for £1,000 and a pond-shaped trophy after they came first in the Rover Challenge.
The whole school took part in the competition. Infants focused on the school environment and recycling, the lower junioirs looked at the food chain and mini beasts and the upper juniors on world environments.

PUPIL power came to Croughton School this week when three of its pupils became headteachers and took charge of affairs.
Edward Stapleton, aged ten, Kate Webb aged eleven, and Dafydd Edwards, aged eleven, put in a bid of £22 to take charge of the school following an auction of promises on Sunday.
And first to take on headteacher Eve Wilson's role was Edward, who took charge of the school on Tuesday by taking assembly and answering the phone.
He even made sure the pupils had their PE kits in order and even got one pupil to write 50 lines after he failed to bring his in.
Kate carried out similar tasks yesterday (Wednesday) while Dafydd will be carrying out his duties tomorrow (Friday) which will include a meeting with the chair of governors.
The auction of promises raised over £1,000 for the school and a fun day held in the schoolgrounds also raised a further £1,000.

Figure 18.5 Matching headlines to news

else can access. In this way they can send messages to each other, and no child is forgotten.

Of course, it is very important to discuss with the children issues of privacy and confidentiality, and to explain that with real email, one cannot access someone else's file! Nevertheless, this message-sending can be great fun and a real motivation, particularly for reluctant writers.

Faxes, phones and overhead projectors

As with email, it can be great fun for children to send a fax from the school office, and even better if you can arrange for them to receive one back! In a writing corner, fax cover sheets can be filled in either by hand or on the computer and an in-tray created for 'incoming faxes'. To remind children exactly what they are doing you might even make a model fax machine to assist the play.

Telephones have long been used in role-play corners and continue to be a great favourite with children. Old answerphones can also be an asset because children can actually record messages on to these without being connected to a telephone line. With older children, role-playing a telephone call can provide a useful mechanism for oracy games or a stimulus for writing activities, for example making a complaint, reporting a burglary, requesting information.

An overhead projector can be useful to children as well as to teachers! Not only does it give status to their work by allowing them to use a 'grown up' piece of equipment, it can also extend the way they think about presenting their work. Bullet points, models, diagrams, flow charts, etc., all lend themselves to this type of approach and can help give children confidence when they are presenting work to the rest of the class. These visual aids also help the rest of the class to listen!

Assessing English skills during media activities

Because of the broad range of English skills which can be developed through media studies there are good assessment opportunities to be found whilst children are working. The following list provides examples of key skills which might be assessed within a media context. The list is not definitive, but merely a starting point for you to develop an assessment plan which fits the needs and organisation of your own school.

Key Stage 1

Speaking and Listening
How is talk influenced by the purpose and by the intended audience?

Assessment activity question: Can they compare a toddlers' programme with a programme for six-year-olds and discuss the differences in talk in relation to the two audiences?

Reading
Identify letter patterns in the final sounds of words.

Assessment activity question: Can they cut, read and sort words from newspaper headlines into pattern groups (e.g. -*ing*, -*ed*, *y*, etc.)?

Writing
Organise and present writing in a range of forms.

Assessment activity questions: Can they identify and describe three different types of writing in a comic? Can they successfully use the features of one of these in their own writing?

Key Stage 2

Speaking and Listening
Identify and comment on key features of what they see and hear in a variety of media.

Assessment activity questions: Can they discuss the format of a news programme, including introductory headlines, development of headlines, prioritising of stories, local, national and international balance, use of interviews and graphics? Can they write a script from four items which you present to them using at least three of the features listed above?

Reading
Use inference and deduction.

Assessment activity question: Having read a report from a newspaper, can they extend their interpretations to suggest motivation, bias, and at least two contrasting perspectives from the people involved?

Writing

Make judgements about when a particular tone, style, format or choice of vocabulary is appropriate.

Assessment activity question: In preparing two magazine advertisements, one for a stair lift for the elderly, the other for the latest run-faster trainers, can they use features which are appropriate to the relevant audience?

SUMMARY

The media are an important central feature of communication in our society and this should be reflected in the primary curriculum. Media education can help children to understand and be more critically aware of the media they encounter whilst at the same time providing a relevant context for teaching English. This chapter has provided an introduction to media education and English by focusing on:

- how you can use television, film, radio, newspapers, magazines, advertising and photography to teach language skills

- the important place of communication technologies such as email, phones and faxes

- the place of the media in the literacy hour

- English assessment opportunities within media education.

Further reading

Bazalgette, C. (1991) *Media Education*, Hodder and Stoughton
    Not specifically a primary text, but provides a good grounding in the principles and practice behind media education.
Clipson-Boyles, S. B. (1996) 'A Multi-Media Approach to Teaching Reading', in D. Reid and D. Bentley
    (eds) *Reading On! Developing Reading at Key Stage 2*, Scholastic
    Useful and practical ideas on how to use the media in the development of reading at Key Stage 2.
Craggs, C. (1992) *Media Education in the Primary School*, Routledge
    Provides some good starting points for work in English.
Webster, C. (1992) 'The Language of Media', in *The Essential Guide to Language*, Folens
    Activity ideas within the context of the wider frameworks of language teaching in the primary school.
    The Film Education Council provides excellent resource packs for teachers, most of which are free.
    You can join their mailing list by writing to them at:
Film Education, 41–42 Berners Street, London W1P 3AA.

19 Information technology and English

OBJECTIVES

By the end of this chapter you should:

- appreciate the need to specifically teach towards IT capability

- understand that IT, as both a subject and a means through which learning takes place, is in a unique position to support the development of language skills

- understand that skills-practice tasks are necessary to teach program knowledge and to allow children to apply skills and knowledge to an activity that can be directly related to another area of the curriculum

- appreciate that IT skills in writing can be specifically taught alongside the writing of various genres in English.

Information technology in the primary curriculum

Information technology is cross-curricular in the primary curriculum. It should be delivered through all subject areas. In order for this to happen IT must be taught. Children must be given insights and explanations at suitable points to enable them to grow in knowledge and understanding and so raise their levels of capability. It is not good enough to sit children in front of a computer and assume that they will, through experimentation, develop the necessary skills. Explicit teaching of IT skills is a must. It is as essential to use a range of strategies in the teaching of IT as it is with all other subjects, and this must be followed with purposeful teacher intervention. Motivation will rarely be a problem as information technology is a highly motivational tool for children. Whilst some few children may be reluctant to 'have go' in case they

make a mistake, such children will, if given suitable insight into what is required of them and the opportunity to develop the skills necessary to complete the task, take very little time to begin to enjoy IT.

Teachers must, therefore, 'let children into the secret' as to what is the required outcome of the set task. Thus when setting up the activity, the teacher must explain to the children the process they will be going through in order to complete the task. A short focused task to teach necessary program knowledge and develop the skills required to complete an open task is essential. Such tasks could be known as skills-practice tasks.

The sequence of teaching would then be:

1 explicit teaching to the class
2 short focused tasks in pairs or groups with teacher intervention (skills-practice tasks)
3 evaluation and possible further explicit teaching to clarify/correct misconceptions or difficulties experienced
4 outline of open task to be undertaken in pairs or groups with teacher intervention
5 plenary with evaluation and future targets.

Advice on pupil groupings

Children can be grouped in a variety of ways to work at the computer. It is important not to always use mixed-ability pairings. Some children's potential will be realised more if they work with others of the same ability. The task you ask children to complete together must be collaborative, where they are working together to a common outcome. There is always a time when children will develop more if they have the opportunity to work alone.

Skills-practice tasks: a closer look

These tasks should follow explicit teaching that could have been to the whole class or a small group.

Tasks can be either focused to teach a skill and/or a program function, or open to apply previously gained skills. Such tasks can be completed by the whole class or by a focused group over a week, depending on the purpose of the tasks.

When children are working at the computer, usually in pairs, there is a need to intervene in the learning that is taking place at the computer. Teachers must ensure that the opportunity for children to make progress during the lesson is not lost.

The open task
An open task allows children to apply previous skills and knowledge to an activity that can be related directly to another curriculum area. The successful completion of the open-ended task will indicate children's understanding of the use of IT.

When developing the use of the open-ended task with children it is important to appreciate that they may require more time than was allocated. The teacher should therefore allocate further time. However, this does not imply longer sessions in front of the computer but more sessions for children or pairs of children. There could be a focused group who will work over a week to complete their task. Although this group will not return to the computer for two or three weeks, the depth of experience over the week will have ensured that these children have had their entitlement to IT.

It is important to give children an understanding of the desired final outcome – i.e. the outcome of the set task. For example, if the outcome is to be a poster teachers must understand the knowledge and the lack of knowledge that children could bring to such a task.

When children think about producing a poster many have a vision of the posters they have seen in shops and on boards around the streets. Whilst some schools may well have the technology to produced high-quality materials such as these, the majority will not. Children need, therefore, to have a concept of what they are able to produce using the technology in their classroom. The use of commercial models for writing fits with this process. Models are used to expand children's knowledge of layout, form, genre. Show children examples of the desired final outcome so that they have a visual concept of what is possible.

Skills-practice tasks should have a time limit (20–30 minutes) set because the purpose is not to produce an outcome for publication.

To print or not?
It is not always necessary to have a printed outcome. If the purpose of the task is to develop a specific skill then there is no need for a printout. Many children have the expectation that they will always print their work. They will, therefore, need to be informed beforehand that this will not be required.

Exploring the full potential for the use of information technology in English

A requirement of the IT programmes of study is that all teachers will consider ways of developing children's use of language:

> Children should be taught to express themselves clearly in both speech and writing, and to develop their reading skills. They should be taught to use grammatically correct sentences and to spell and punctuate in order to communicate effectively in written English.
> (SCAA 1997)

The development of language skills is an entitlement for all children, and information technology is in an unique position to support this development as it is both a subject and a means through which learning takes place.

Specific features of IT are its own set of specialist terms, ever new technologies, and a facility through which children can compose, read, compare, manipulate and transform texts in both printed and electronic form. Information technology offers a medium through which discussion can be stimulated, texts read and explored and writing skills practised and encouraged.

Children's capability in IT, English and literacy

Children need to develop their abilities to use IT tools and information sources effectively to analyse, process and present information (from, for example, computer systems and software packages), to investigate relationships and to model, measure and control external events.

The teaching programmes that teachers plan must ensure that children:

- understand the implications of IT for working life and society (for example, they need to appreciate that texts may be electronically generated, e.g. through word processors and desktop publishing packages using resources such as CD-ROM and the Internet)
- understand how texts work differently (for example, some require reader interaction)
- understand that texts may be non-linear in structure, have multi-authorship, have a spatial dimension, may be conveyed through a combination of still and moving images
- be able to take meaning from this wide variety of texts and understand their distinctive features
- appreciate how through using IT in English they will be enabled to compose texts and alter them with ease, integrating, at times, various media
- understand what the different choices made by writers in medium (text, image, sound, multimedia) and transitional mode (spoken, print, electronic) do to the status and meaning of a text.

It is important that children develop a critical literacy.

Planning for IT in English

In order to ensure rigorous planning of both the English and the information technology programmes of study, medium- and short-term planning will need to be part of an ongoing process of review, further planning and evaluation.

IT teaching and learning activities planned for

These should comprise:

1 Communicating information
2 Handling information
3 Controlling and measuring
4 Modelling.

1 Communicating information

Here information technology is used to organise, present and transmit information in the form of words, numbers, pictures or sounds for particular purposes and audiences (for example the train departure board in a station).

Teachers should encourage children to review their own writing and compare it with that of others, to use appropriate vocabulary which might include technical terms, and to spell and punctuate correctly, making notes from the spell-check facility to identify their most common errors.

2 Handling information

This is concerned with gathering accurate and relevant information, analysing and interpreting it, checking its accuracy and questioning plausibility (for example charts of national data in end of key stage tests!).

Teachers should encourage children to read displayed information accurately in order to identify the relevant, and teach them to use increasingly well skimming and scanning techniques and to be able to distinguish between fact and fiction.

3 Controlling and monitoring

Information technology is used to control events, usually by giving instructions which represent actions to an IT system, to monitor events and measure physical variables (for example the traffic-light system, a lighthouse beam).

Teachers should encourage children to describe the situation or events they wish to control, and to write down the sequence of events whilst using appropriate constructions such as 'if …', 'then …', 'wait until …'.

4 Modelling

Here children use information technology to investigate patterns and relationships through exploring, modifying and creating computer models.

Teachers should encourage children to use language relating to cause and effect, such as '… might increase …', and language that will explore and hypothesise.

English teaching and learning activities planned for

These should comprise:

1 focused opportunities for listening and speaking, by exploring and processing information in pairs or groups with the understanding that, in order to be successful, children must be supportive of and cooperative with each other
2 the reading and transforming of a wide variety of texts, which start with a focus on response to and interpretation of texts and lead to a focus on manipulating the form and changing texts from one genre to another

3 the writing of a wide variety of texts, which has a focus on how texts may be created and structured alongside a focus on the tools of presentation for purpose and audience

4 activities for use in the literacy hour.

How to work the process of review, further planning and evaluation

Review

This is an audit of current provision. Teachers should, with the IT coordinator,

1 look at existing schemes of work in order to identify what IT activities are currently taking place

2 look at the IT National Curriculum programmes of study to see what teachers are required to provide and then note any deficiencies in current provision for the class

3 consider the elements set out in the preceding section, 'Planning for IT in English'

4 re-read the school's policy for IT

5 re-read the school's planning for English and literacy alongside the National Curriculum programmes of study for English and note any deficiencies in current provision

6 identify children's existing competencies and experiences and list aspects of children's learning for IT in English that (1) are not being addressed and (2) need to be revisited

7 consider the suitability and adequacy of resources, identify realistic needs and enquire as to when and how these can be met

8 reflect on their competence and that of colleagues, identify and request training needs and expertise, and be advised as to how training will be provided (for example in school or by the LEA)

9 reflect on the access to computers that ensures equality of opportunity for all children in all classes, identify action that may need to be taken and set timescales.

Further planning

Teachers should now:

1 update planning – both medium and short term – to show where IT is being used and to identify aims and objectives (The coordinator may have altered long-term planning following the experience of school review.)

2 plan for continuity and progression in both IT and English

3 decide on appropriate specialised vocabulary to be learnt

4 identify what useful prompt cue cards could be displayed by the hardware and make them

5 plan strategies for managing children's learning through (1) introducing new applications, (2) reinforcing previous learning, (3) allowing for familiarisation and (4) ensuring equality of access to IT

6 decide on procedures for monitoring children's progress and attainment

7 implement their plans!

Evaluation

Ongoing evaluation is necessary throughout the term. Teachers need to consider how successful they have been in their revised teaching programmes. In evaluating the use of IT in English teachers should ask themselves the following questions:

1 Are children composing texts creatively in a structured way?

2 Can children present texts appropriately for different purposes and audiences?

3 Are children able to read, respond to and interpret a wide range of texts?

4 Can children transform texts into different forms and genres?

5 Are children able to explore, search and process information from a wide range of texts?

Learning from teacher experience and expertise

This section sets out some helpful hints for putting planning into practice.

The early years and Key Stage 1

Speaking and Listening

A tape recorder, often overlooked as a tool in information technology, is an excellent resource at this early stage and, indeed, throughout provision for information technology. It can enable a progression of both listening and speaking skills. Children can:

- record their voices in rhyme and poetry (these could be enhanced with sound effects from musical instruments or children's voices)
- give instructions for another/others to follow
- tell stories
- announce news items
- deliver a miscellany connected to a theme or topic, for example, 'sports day'

- read a newspaper report from a play area, for example from the supermarket, the doctors' surgery, the travel agent, the fast-food restaurant.

From a cassette children can listen, either alone or with others, to:

- a story
- instructions, for example to complete a maze
- the retelling of a story
- interviews with lunchtime helpers, the caretaker, pensioners, office staff, parents.

As teachers move towards the end of Year 1, stories used to promote inferential comprehension, i.e. comprehension beyond the literal, should be explored. Examples of these could be 'Oi! Get Off Our Train' by John Burningham, 'Where the Wild Things Are' by Maurice Sendak , and 'John Brown, Rose and the Midnight Cat' by Jenny Wagner. Such stories can be dramatised with appropriate sound effects and narration for others to share.

Both speaking and listening can be heightened through planned work across the curriculum, for example in music through:

- composition using a program on computer
- composition using a music keyboard and saving into memory
- composition using a tape recorder.

Reading from CD-ROM for information and narrative

The use of CD-ROM can facilitate quality experiences in interaction, cooperation, collaboration and dialogue between primary children, provided that the teacher has, with high expectations, established appropriate ground rules for behaviour, time, turn-taking, rotation of 'hands on' experience and outcomes of task. Children should have had opportunity to practise their mouse skills. Teachers should then ensure that full use is made of the range of facilities on a 'Living Book' CD-ROM:

- having the story read to the children
- interacting with 'hotspots' to discover various hidden activities
- following on-screen spoken instructions, absorbing them, remembering them, and using them later to enable movement around the pages, for example in 'Henry's Party'
- using the microphone and recording facility within a program for the recording of voice as in, for example, 'Rabbits at Home'.

Children need to be led to an understanding that with CD-ROM stories there is a relationship between what they are 'hearing', what is on the screen and the text in the book.

Therefore in order to teach this concept teachers are advised to start the session with a sharing of a copy of the printed book. After this has been experienced teachers should share electronically the remainder of the text as in, for example, 'Harry and the Haunted House'.

Programs such as *My World* will provide an incentive for children to respond to a descriptive passage through the creation of a picture from a written description. Such a task could also be done using 'on screen' text entered by the teacher.

CD-ROM dictionaries provide opportunities for children to read for information through interactive activities.

Warning!

Talking books can present disadvantages. Many deal only with speaking and listening as opposed to reading. Teachers therefore need to know these resources well before the lesson.

Writing

Children should be taught from the earliest years:

- that writing must be for a purpose and for an audience
- to use both computer and desk activity to complement the writing process
- that they can use pen/pencil, paper, screen and keyboard, with planning and writing, alternating from one medium to the other
- the need to save and print work on computers so that they can take it further in thought and edit at their desk.

Teachers should appreciate that story-writing, a time-consuming activity for young children, would not be a good use of computer time. However, these young children could plan their story with setting, characters, events, resolution and title.

Skills learning and differentiated tasks

The skills and processes needed when children learn to word process can be developed through a variety of different tasks allocated to different children at different times. For example, a theme, such as a birthday party, could generate different language activities that should be differentiated across the class group to enable individual children to be challenged according to their ability.

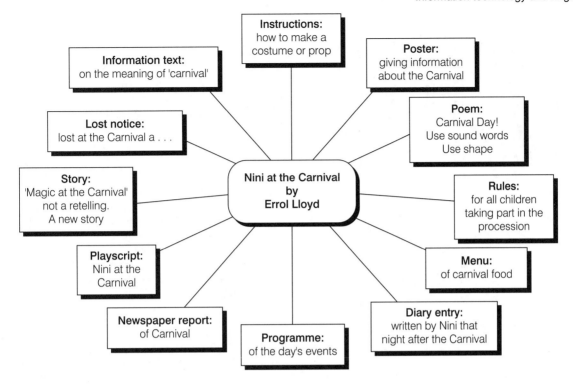

Figure 19.1 Key Stage 1 planning framework for the use of IT with text

Written tasks could range from lists of birthday food and guests (for inexperienced writers), and captions for party photographs, to a recipe for a cake, a letter of invitation, instructions for a party game and a script for a puppet play (for more advanced writers). Such a range of writing activities at the end of Key Stage 1 could stem from literature shared by the whole class. An example from 'Nini at the Carnival' by Errol Lloyd is shown in Figure 19.1.

This figure indicates writing tasks that challenge all abilities of children from the least experienced to the experienced.

Figures 19.2 and 19.3 show samples of such activities.

Key Stage 2

Speaking and Listening
Children can:

- listen to a description and create a picture/scene from it
- incorporate sound to communicate ideas and

information into a multimedia presentation; for example, they can record the reading of a text and then use the 'listen' button
- use tape recorders to add sounds to interact with text and pictures
- create a mini-encyclopaedia on a topic, so producing a combination of sound, information finding and information giving
- use interview situations to ask pre-determined questions, record responses and later transcribe these using a word processor (such activity would fit comfortably with a geographical/environmental issue where there is a real need to communicate information)
- use a video camera with a tripod and monitor to facilitate a combination of sound and picture (teachers should appreciate that a field monitor or an indoor television screen is essential for whole-group appreciation, criticism and framing of shots).

Reading
Children should be taught to:

- skim/scan encyclopaedia text on CD-ROM to find out answers to, for example, an historical enquiry on the Tudors

185

Figure 19.2 'Lost' notice developed through IT based on a text

Figure 19.3 Poster developed through IT based on a text

- read statistical graphs/data in order to interpret them
- use higher-order information-handling skills, i.e. decision-making skills (this could be under an 'umbrella' of modelling where children are asked to make decisions so that the outcome is different from given model outcomes; for example, time, place, date on an invitation are reshaped into a poster for a school fair – a reshaping of the given model)
- extend their skills in classifying, questioning, analysis and explanation
- use a wide range of sources (IT-based reference materials, newspapers, encyclopaedias), including those not specifically designed for children
- find information in computer-based sources through using organisational devices to help them decide which sections of the material to read more closely.

Writing

Teachers should ensure that through their teaching of IT and writing a planned progression of word processing, desktop publishing and multimedia presentation is enabled.

The use of a word processor text-handling package such as the language development programmes *Expose* and *Tray* will help children to generate and communicate ideas. For example, using a cloze procedure programme, children are given a Star Trek scenario where space messages are sent with missing parts to be decoded. Children have to create meaning. They can compose a set of instructions, a response, a label, a list. Through the use of a graphics program children can label diagrams, maps and plans. Such activities directly relate to the programmes of study for English in the National Curriculum. As at Key Stage 1, a range of activities can be promoted through a response to literature.

Figure 19.4 shows differentiated writing activities arising from a study of the text 'Gregory Cool' by Caroline Binch. Figure 19.5 shows a combination of text and specific layout to fulfil a specific purpose.

IT through English is, therefore, consolidated through differing focuses. From the earliest stages models of a wide variety of written genres should be available as models in the classroom (calendars, invitations, business letters, postcards, newspapers, lists, fax, etc.).

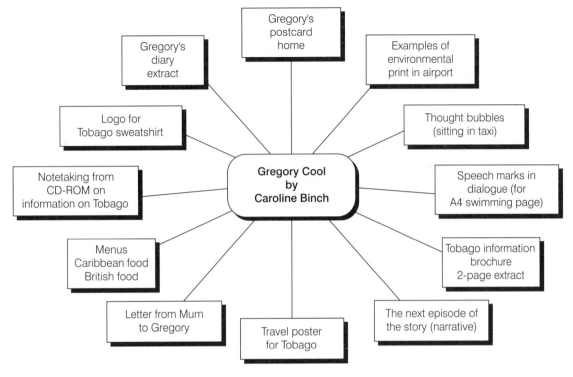

Figure 19.4 Key Stage 2 planning framework for the use of IT with text

BREAKFAST
• Fruit Juice
• Bake and Buljol

LUNCH
• Fried Chicken
• Sweet Bread
• Fruit
• Biscuits

DINNER
• Hot Spicy Meat
• Rice

Figure 19.5 Menus developed through IT based on a text

SUMMARY

This chapter has demonstrated that:

• To allow children to use IT to its full potential the program skills must be taught and practised.

• Children need to be aware of the outcome you desire. Use models and examples to help them develop concepts of the final product.

• IT can be used to write a variety of genres in English, especially using the publication skills of layout and style to suit purpose and audience.

References

SCAA (1997) *Information Technology and the Use of Language*, SCAA

Further reading

NCET (1995) *Approaches to IT Capability, Key Stages 1 and 2*, National Council for Educational Technology
Provides guidance on the development of IT policies, schemes of work and planning a range of classroom experiences.
NCET/DfEE (1997) *English and IT: A Pupil's Entitlement*, SCAA
A leaflet intended to develop and explain pupils' entitlement to IT and English.

20 Working with other people in the classroom

OBJECTIVES

By the end of this chapter you should be able to:

- plan effectively for those whose purpose is to support you or the children in English lessons
- understand the role other adults can play in your professional practice and development
- prepare thoroughly for those whose purpose is to appraise and evaluate your teaching and management of English.

Classrooms with open doors

During the course of a year, a teacher will be visited regularly by a variety of people who have a professional or voluntary relationship with the class. At certain times, colleagues will work with or observe each other. There has been a remarkable 'opening up' of classrooms across the entire educational system. National initiatives such as NOP, LINC and NLS, have created a common basis for professional debate. The introduction of the National Curriculum with its standardised testing (SATs) and a national system of inspection ensured colleagues worked together. Many authorities now group schools together in cluster groups, providing a supportive professional dialogue, and although the pupil–teacher ratio in most primary classes is still unsatisfactorily high, most schools enjoy a strong network of adult support.

Adults in the primary classroom: Who is involved?

There are two main reasons why people may visit a primary classroom.

The supportive role

The support offered in this role may take the form of expertise, time or guidance.

These visitors can be:

1 Unqualified in education and not employed by the school
These include reading volunteers, parent helpers and governors. With the exception of trained reading volunteers, most volunteers cannot perform a 'teaching' role, but they can enhance teacher efficiency by performing practical tasks in English with children, for example finding information, organising school/class library loans, playing word games, etc.

2 Unqualified as teachers but employed by the school as NTAs (non-teaching assistants or classroom helpers)
In some authorities, these members of a school staff are known as support teaching assistants (STAs)or learning support assistants (LSAs) It is important to note here that many classroom helpers and non-teaching assistants are now able to seek training and qualifications. Nursery nurses working in the early years classroom would also belong to this category.

3 Qualified in education and external to the school
These include special needs support teachers, Section 11 teachers, educational psychologists, advisory teachers and educational welfare workers. They provide support for a particular child or children or within a subject area. Student teachers, especially those on their final teaching practice or school experience, could also be included in this category, since they assume increasing responsibility for a class.

4 Qualified as teachers and working within the school
These include curriculum specialists, heads of phase and year, mentors, the deputy head or headteacher. In many schools, teachers work in teams, to plan and implement schemes of work.

The evaluative role

This role relates to quality control, assurance and

accountability. Internal appraisals usually take place annually or every two years. Ofsted inspections take place every four to six years and LEA inspections as necessary. Visits from HMI are rare and are sometimes related to Ofsted inspection outcomes, for example when a school has had serious weaknesses identified. These people are likely to be be experienced and highly qualified professionals. The only exception to this will be the lay inspector in an Ofsted team, who is chosen from a field outside education.

Managing other people in the classroom

If children are going to gain the maximum benefit from having other adults in the classroom, their teachers will need to use these adults' interpersonal skills wisely.

Unfortunately, these may not have been provided for in training and INSET.

Thomas's (1992) research into classroom teams at work suggested that successful school teams depended less on top-down decisions than on what he called the 'fraternity' factor, the informal negotiations among team members.

It is a class teacher's responsibility to ensure that curriculum plans, significant information, resource needs and details of classroom management are communicated clearly to any other adult working in the class. Some schools provide written guidance for all their helpers. A task such as baking, for example, would have not only a recipe but guidance on educational opportunities, group work and safety. All helpers need guidance in the monitoring of learning outcomes and the evaluation of tasks if they are to support the children effectively.

Research into the use of associate staff in several primary schools found that 'Lack of clarity, over what the class teacher wished the associate member staff member to do, sometimes resulted in muddle and mutual irritation' (Mortimore *et al.* 1994).

Communication

Communication between teacher and associate staff is essential but takes time and care. Some teachers use a notebook or support diary. This diary may be attached to a particular subject, such as design and technology, for which a parent comes in every Wednesday to cook with two groups. By using a notebook and inserting a copy of the lesson plan, a teacher can ensure that the parent can be clear about the task and can record any significant learning outcomes for individual children.

Alternatively, the diary may be attached to a particular child or group with whom the helper works regularly, for example another parent who takes a group for extra phonics work once a week, during the literacy hour. In the diary, the teacher can highlight objectives and include follow-up tasks or worksheets.

A photocopiable proforma, such as the example in Figure 20.1, can support this important two-way dialogue. It is important that safety or discipline issues and procedures are made clear.

By sharing the learning objectives and giving organisational guidance, a class teacher can support any adult working with a group of children.

Working with volunteers

There are several ways in which volunteers can enhance the language curriculum for children and teachers (see VRH in the Glossary). One example of a successful partnership with a volunteer involved a retired scientist and a nine-year-old boy who had specific hearing and reading difficulties. The volunteer read a story every visit and discussed the text. A diary, called Philip's Reading Journal, provided a useful record of what they achieved and a channel for teacher–volunteer communication.

Volunteers may also have a particular gift for display, book maintenance, information and communications technology (ICT), sorting and maintaining resources or helping children find information from non-fiction books.

Working with SENCOs and special needs support teachers

In 1978, the Warnock Report (DES 1978) revealed that approximately 20 per cent of schoolchildren will have special needs at some time in their school career. Budget cutbacks limit the provision of one-to-one support in class, so class teachers need to cater for a wide range of ability and

TOPIC:	FOCUS:	DATE:
LESSON FOCUS + OBJECTIVES		TIME ON TASK:
CHILDREN:	OBSERVATIONS:	OUTCOMES:

POINTS TO NOTE: (TEACHER TO HELPER)	IMPLICATIONS FOR FUTURE PLANNING:
COMMENTS: (HELPER TO TEACHER)	

Figure 20.1 Proforma for classroom assistants and volunteer helpers

experience and differentiate the curriculum accordingly.

There may be many reasons for children making slow progress: negative home experiences; difficulties arising from problems with motor control, vision, hearing or behaviour; inadequate challenge for the very able, and so on.

In English, if the child experiences difficulties with speech, listening, reading or writing, an initial 'diagnosis' is needed, supported by activities which will support the child's development in a structured way.

In each school, there is one member of staff known as the special educational needs coordinator (SENCO). This is usually an experienced member of staff who oversees the provision of support for children with specific learning needs. The coordinator will have drawn up a whole-school policy and will be available to offer guidance on the procedures which need to followed.

Special needs support is more likely to be effective if the class teacher works closely with the school SENCO, the child's parents and any other adults involved with the child. Together, using the Individual Education Plan (see below) as a means of communication, these adults can sustain the child's progress and record important benchmarks of progress. Many special needs support teachers introduce specialised materials, language-learning games or intensive teaching approaches, for example Reading Recovery (1985), *PAT* (1996) and Catch Up (1998).

The Special Needs Code of Practice
A child who is struggling may be formally placed on Stage 1 of the Special Needs scale of support, according to the Special Needs Code of Practice (DfEE 1994).

Code of Practice Stage 1: The class teacher
The Code of Practice stipulates that a Stage 1 child should be supported by the class teacher, in consultation with the school SENCO and the child's parents. In English, this support may involve preparing special word banks, providing increased visual support for texts, selecting particular books, devising specific tasks or hearing the child read daily rather than weekly. There may be sufficient auxiliary staff support in the school for regular one-to-one or small group work with a classroom helper. Alternatively there may be voluntary

help available which would suit the needs of this child: for example, a child with speech difficulties may need to practise saying sounds, chants and rhymes away from their peers, to develop confidence.

Code of Practice Stage 2: The SENCO and IEP
If progress is not adequate, a child may then be placed on Stage 2. At this stage, the SENCO will take the lead in coordinating the learning support. The SENCO draws up an Individual Education Plan (IEP). Where this is most successful, the class teacher and SENCO usually sit down together and prioritise achievable targets for the child. In English, these would relate to the National Curriculum levels, for each strand, towards which the child should be working.

The IEP should set out:

- the nature of the child's difficulties
- action needed: the special education provision; the staff involved, including frequency of support; specific programmes, activities, materials, equipment
- help from parents at home
- targets to be achieved in a given time
- any pastoral care or medical requirements
- monitoring and assessment arrangements
- arrangements and a date to review the child's progress.

If, at the Stage 2 Review, the teacher and SENCO agree that more help is needed, the child can be moved into Stage 3.

Code of Practice Stage 3: SEN advisers and the IEP
At Stage 3, the school calls upon external specialist support (SEN advisers, teachers of the hearing impaired, educational psychologists, etc.) to help the child make progress. An IEP again forms the basis of work with the child and a focus for communication between the class teacher, specialist support and the school SENCO.

Code of Practice Stage 4: Statutory assessment
After the Stage 3 review with teachers and parents, a child who has made sufficient progress can revert back to Stages 1 or 2. However, it may be agreed that the child needs to move to Stage 4, which means being referred to the LEA for statutory assessment. A review meeting, with the class teacher, parents, school SENCO and a representa-

tive of the LEA has to take place. Thereafter, reviews are held to ensure that the best provision is made for the child, who may need a change of school, special equipment and funding or a particular programme of specialist support.

Working with bilingual support teachers

The value of working closely with bilingual support teachers has been discussed in Chapter 16.

Together with the class teacher, these colleagues may devise an individual language programme for children to follow. It is important that all adults involved, and the children if they are old enough, are able to monitor the child's progress in English.

Working with LEA advisers and advisory teachers

Occasionally, teachers may find they have the opportunity to work with LEA advisory teachers. Often these professionals will be sharing materials, methodologies, innovations or ideas through practical implementation, in the classroom. Yet it is the class teacher who manages these partnerships, however inexperienced he or she may be. The teacher must accommodate the 'expert' into the learning environment and must ensure that, as a pair, they build on the work the teacher has accomplished with the children.

There may be a programme of authority-wide English INSET, including conferences and seminars. Attending these can be helpful in keeping up to date with developments in language and literacy. There may be opportunities to attend workshops or to hear and meet children's writers and illustrators. By making contact with the local advisory teacher for English, teachers may find that they are able to access valuable expertise which will contribute to the quality of the children's language development and their own professional understanding.

Working with librarians

Sadly, school library services have been greatly reduced but most local authorities still provide support for schools interested in developing their school library or libraries.

A good school library can make a major contribu-

tion to the English curriculum. Most teachers also have a fiction and non-fiction library area within the classroom so that books and 'Booktalk' (Chambers 1993) can form an integral part of daily classroom life.

The National Curriculum has outlined specific requirements for the teaching of information retrieval skills, which centre upon the school library and ICT. For example, pupils should:

Level 3: 'use their knowledge of the alphabet to locate books and find information'
Level 5: 'retrieve and collect information from a range of sources'.

In order to fulfil these objectives, teachers need to teach the children appropriate skills and plan their use of the school library.

Working with outside speakers

When a school wants to highlight reading or writing processes, it may invite a visiting author, storyteller, poet or illustrator to come and work with a few classes or take a whole school session. Teachers can approach a writer's publisher or use arts organisation directories of authors, such as Southern Arts (1997).

Some schools organise an annual Book Week, a whole-school event which may feature the following:

- a bookshop available after school, where parents and children can browse and purchase
- a fancy-dress day when children come to school dressed as a book character
- book-sharing and book-making sessions
- talks for parents about how they might support their child's reading at home.

The school dedicates itself to celebrating reading and books and children find it very exciting to meet the people who work to put books together. Organising such a Book Week is one of many tasks associated with the role of English coordinator.

The curriculum coordinator for English

Coordinators have become increasingly accountable for the teaching and learning within their subject. This accountability has resulted from the following initiatives:

- the introduction of internal staff appraisal
- written job descriptions for coordinators drawn up in negotiation with headteachers
- the central role of school development plans (SDPs)
- in-service training being tied to the achievement of specific targets within the SDP
- the identification of criteria by Ofsted which relate to the teaching and learning of individual subjects and subject coordinators' duties.

Coordinators have to manage not only their subject, but also themselves and their colleagues. They need, therefore, high levels of interpersonal skills. Organisational skills are also essential because of time pressures and a wide range of responsibilities.

The special responsibilities of the primary English coordinator may include:

- drawing up and reviewing policy documents for English
- ensuring key stage plans and schemes of work are in place and being effectively implemented
- monitoring SAT results in English and moderating standards of children's work in English across the school
- advising colleagues about differentiating the English curriculum
- liaising with the SENCO about children with language-learning difficulties
- supervising the ordering of English resources, ensuring balance, suitability and breadth, and managing the English budget
- managing the teaching and assessment of reading
- ensuring adequate provision in and effective use of the library, and linking with schools' library services
- coordinating home–school literacy links
- supporting colleagues in their English teaching by providing good models of practice, organising useful INSET and keeping colleagues up to date with developments in English teaching
- keeping governors and parents informed about the school's approach to teaching language and literacy
- organising special events, e.g. Book Weeks, Theatre-in-Education visits, school performances, sponsored spelling bees, story-writing competitions
- acting as a mentor to less experienced colleagues, providing helpful feedback about ways to improve their classroom practice in English.

It is important that the English coordinator knows about the nature and quality of work going on across the school in English. By making copies of outstanding written work, identifying critical features of successful lessons or sharing achievements, teachers can contribute to the bank of evidence the English coordinator needs to collect to share with colleagues, for example fellow English coordinators within a school cluster group, LEA advisers, parents, or the school governor with responsibility for the National Literacy Strategy.

Auditing the English curriculum

Auditing the curriculum is the process whereby colleagues, led by the English coordinator, examine and evaluate the effectiveness of planning and teaching by asking the following kinds of questions:

- Which English skills and concepts are being taught in each year group?
- How does the children's work reveal progression in standards from year to year?
- Do colleagues enjoy a shared understanding of each level description across the key stages?
- How consistent is teacher assessment and feedback (to children and parents) in each year group?
- Which methods of recording are being used?
- Which resources for English are being used and which may be needed in the future?

The photocopiable sheets in Figures 20.2 and 20.3 may be helpful in the auditing process.

The curriculum coordinator for English has to ensure that colleagues have the resources they need to implement their planning (see Figure 20.4).

Appraisal

In 1986, the Education Reform Act required LEAs and schools to appraise teachers. The best preparation for appraisal is self-appraisal, which may come more easily to recently trained teachers who have been encouraged to see themselves as reflective practitioners (Schon 1983) and reflective teachers (Pollard and Tann 1987).

Increasing emphasis on lifelong learning in education and on continuing professional development has led to recommendations (Craft 1996) that teachers build up, on a continuous basis, a portfolio of evidence of professional development. Such a portfolio could include summaries of appraisal interviews and observations made by mentors and

Programme of Study for English KS1	R	Y1	Y2
1a Range Speaking and Listening a. telling stories, reciting rhymes, reading aloud, discussing ideas b. different purposes and audiences for talk c. listening carefully d. drama – participation and response **2 Key Skills** a. effective communication b. effective listening **3 Standard English and Language Study** a. importance of SE/features b. extend vocabulary through discussion of word meanings, games and associations			

1 Range Reading
a. read range of genres and own writing
   read poems
b. read information texts
   ICT
c. features to stimulate imagination and enthusiasm
d. fantasy
   folk and fairy stories
   range of cultures
 	
2 Key Skills
a. alphabet
   phonological awareness
b. phonic knowledge
   graphic knowledge
   word recognition and sight vocabulary
   grammatical knowledge
   contextual understanding
c. discuss and respond to stories and poems
d. structural devices for organising information
 	
3 Standard English and Language Study
a. characteristics and features of different kinds of text			

1 Range Writing a. understand the value of writing b. writing in response to various stimuli and for different audiences c. write in range of forms, e.g. lists, invitations **2 Key Skills** a. learn to write own name b. plan and review writing c. punctuation – capitals, commas d. spelling – letterstrings e. handwriting **3 Standard English and Language Study** a. written SE b. discussion of words			

Figure 20.2 Proforma for an audit of English teaching, Key Stage 1

Programme of Study for English KS2	Y3	Y4	Y5	Y6

1 Range Speaking and Listening
a. talk for range of purposes/explaining etc.
b. presenting to different audiences
c. reflecting on other speakers' styles
d. drama – performance
         – response
 	
2 Key Skills
a. confidence, clarity, communication of complex
  meanings – expressing self
b. careful listening and questioning, contradicting,
  participating in group discussion
 	
3 Standard English and Language Study
a. use of spoken SE – explanation of language variation
b. extending vocabulary				

1 Range Reading
a. enthusiasm for books – access, response
b. non-fiction – newspapers, encyclopaedias, etc.
  IT – CD-ROM/databases
c. more challenging texts
d. range of fiction and poetry from diverse cultures
 	
2 Key Skills
a. complex phonic/graphic features – fluency,
  accuracy
b. response to plot, characters, language (in
  depth)
c. information and retrieval skills – questioning, note
  taking
d. use of library and classification systems
 	
3 Standard English and Language Study
a. use of appropriate terms to discuss reading				

1 Range Writing a. varied purposes for writing b. writing for extended range of readers and audiences c. use of characteristics of different kinds of writing d. fiction/non-fiction **2 Skills** a. degrees of formality, style, register b. plan, draft, revise, proofread, present c. punctuate correctly d. spell correctly e. legible handwriting for different purposes **3 Standard English and Language Study** a. reflect on written SE vs spoken English b. paragraphs, coherence c. interest in words and vocabulary, e.g. synonyms, prefixes, etc.				

Figure 20.3 Proforma for an audit of English teaching, Key Stage 2

A well-equipped school will be likely to have:	Central store	Library	R	Y1	Y2	Y3	Y4	Y5	Y6
Sets of dictionaries of different levels of ability									
Encyclopaedias, CD-ROM information software									
ICT for English – other software									
Collections of non-fiction books									
Multiple copies of storybooks and novels									
Collections of poetry books									
Examples of a wide variety of text/genres									
Materials to support handwriting or calligraphy									
Materials to support language awareness									
Survival kits for newly arrived EAL children									
Collection of puppets									
Dressing up clothes for drama and role play									
Props and artefacts to encourage descriptive writing									
Materials to support phonics development									
Bookmaking materials									
Materials to support information-retrieval skills									
Materials to support alphabetic knowledge									
Materials to support reading comprehension									
Materials to support speaking and listening									
Listening centres and story tapes									
Materials to support understanding of punctuation									
Materials to support understanding of sentences and syntax, e.g. Breakthrough									
Spelling and phonics guidelines and materials									
Materials to develop and extend vocabulary									
Staff guidelines and materials, e.g. teacher books, *First Steps,* etc.									
Sets of playscripts									
A collection of fiction, for all levels of ability									
Reading Scheme books									
Language support material for SEN									

Figure 20.4 Proforma for an audit of English resources

other colleagues, together with evidence of significant milestones and achievements.

Colleagues as mentors

Schools often designate responsibility to experienced teachers to support colleagues in their initial year of teaching. Mentoring has become widely extended so that most teachers can expect to be evaluated and supported by a range of colleagues.

Appraisal interviews

Appraisal interviews are conducted on a regular basis and generally allow for a period of preparation to allow the appraisee to collect evidence of professional competence.

When conducted constructively, appraisal interviews should enable the teacher to discuss both concerns and achievements. Most importantly, appraisal involves the setting of targets for the immediate or longer-term future.

According to Wragg (1996) appraisal targets should be:

S specific
M measurable
A attainable
R relevant
T time-constrained.

In many ways, these reflect the qualities we look for in lesson objectives (see Chapter 5) or the points for development which make up a whole-school development plan. Teachers need to treat all levels of evaluation, including Ofsted, LEA or HMI inspections, as genuine opportunities for professional development and growth.

Inspection: Ofsted, LEA and HMI

Local authority advisers and inspectors may inspect a school or key stage prior to an Ofsted inspection in order to help a school staff prepare itself thoroughly.

The Ofsted model for inspection, which is also used by many LEAs, has as its main purpose the identification of strengths and weaknesses so that schools may improve:

- the quality of education they provide
- the educational standards achieved by the children

- the management of resources, e.g. time, staff, materials and budget
- the spiritual, moral, social and cultural development of the children.

During an Ofsted inspection, teachers can expect to be visited in a number of lessons across the curriculum. Supply teachers and student teachers are visited in the same way as a class teacher. However, an Ofsted inspector would not include grades given to a student teacher in the school's overall results. Judgements made by the Ofsted team will be made according to specific criteria set out in the official Ofsted inspection handbook. There are three parts in the inspection Framework (1995), concerning:

a) aspects of the school
b) curriculum areas and subjects
c) inspection data.

Ofsted inspectors have to follow the Framework very closely, and teachers can prepare themselves most effectively by consulting the Framework.

Inspectors in the classroom

During an inspection, the quality of teaching will be evaluated as the major factor contributing to children's attainment, progress and response. An Ofsted inspection is probably the most formidable evaluative experience a teacher has to face. However, it is helpful to remember that there is a professional code of conduct for inspectors which is strictly followed, and judgements made have to be secure, first hand, reliable, valid, comprehensive and corporate, i.e. the whole team supports a judgement.

The sections in the Framework which most directly concern class teachers relate to the following areas:

Attainment and progress
The inspection team will ask to see the work of at least three children from each class, covering the full ability range, from below average, through average to above average. The inspector responsible for English will, through talking with children, make judgements about their oral skills, hear readers, discuss the teaching of reading, study samples of work, and look for evidence of challenge, appropriacy of task, progression, standards of presentation, quality of written work and use of language.

Quality of teaching

Teachers are understandably anxious that they will not do themselves justice in a lesson. However, teachers can prepare themselves by carefully planning lessons and by ensuring marking is purposeful and vigorous and records are thorough.

A teacher's quality of teaching will be judged on the extent to which he or she:

- has a secure knowledge and understanding of the subject, e.g. English
- sets high expectations so as to challenge children and deepen their knowledge, skills and understanding
- plans effectively
- employs teaching methods and strategies which match curricular objectives and the needs of all children
- manages children well and achieves high standards of discipline
- uses time and resources (including classroom support) effectively
- makes thorough and constructive assessments of children and uses these to inform planning
- uses homework (including home–school links) to reinforce and/or extend what has been learned in school.

(Ofsted 1995b, p. 18)

Inspectors record their findings on Lesson Observation Forms (LOFs). The headings on observation forms used by inspectors to judge quality are:

- Teaching
- Response (pupils')
- Attainment
- Progress
- Other significant evidence.

Each category is graded and the lesson is given an overall grade. Teachers do not usually see the LOFs but inspectors are permitted to give feedback about lessons they observe.

Curriculum areas and subjects

For the core subjects, English, maths and science, the inspection team have to evaluate:

- pupils' attainment in relation to national expectations or standards, drawing on what the pupils know, understand and can do by the end of the relevant (key) stage
- progress made in relation to pupils' prior attainment
- pupils' attitudes to learning
- any strengths or weaknesses in teaching and other factors which contribute to the standards achieved in the subject.

The inspection of English

Overall, inspectors will be looking for dynamic, stimulating and thorough coverage of the National Curriculum requirements for English. They will look for effective use of the literacy hour and for high standards of achievement in relation to children's prior experiences. They will take account of SAT results and key stage attainment. They will evaluate positively a school where teachers and children display enthusiasm for language and reading, where language diversity is celebrated and where children are taught about language efficiently. They will examine each teacher's planning for English in detail and look for good whole-school subject management from the English coordinator. Inspectors will take into account how efficiently auxiliary staff are used to support English development in the school, and will particularly address the way the school caters for children with special educational needs in language. They will report on the way more able children are extended in English and look at the quality of home–school literacy partnerships.

Speaking and Listening

All inspectors in a team will evaluate the quality of interaction between teacher and children and between children. The quality of teachers' and children's questioning, attentiveness and response will contribute to an overall judgement about speaking and listening in the school.

Judgements made will be based not only on classroom-based interaction but on observations made in and around the school throughout the inspection period.

Reading

The inspection team will share the close monitoring of standards in reading across the school. Each year group will be asked to indicate three readers, one from each ability band, average, below and above average. Inspectors will analyse children's responses and comprehension skills, strategies used when encountering unfamiliar words and the breadth of their reading experience and knowledge of authors and genres. They will examine the ways teachers support struggling readers and challenge the more able. They will monitor reading records and parental involvement in literacy. They will look at reading test results and evaluate the quality and management of book provision throughout the school.

Writing

Inspectors will look back through class anthologies, yearbooks and previous work in order to establish whether there is continuity and progression in writing. Each year group will be asked to submit all the work of a below-average, average and above-average child. The team will spend some time going through all the work of all these children, looking for evidence of progression and attainment.

The standards of writing, in relation to content, range, skills, handwriting and presentation, will be judged not only within English lessons but across the curriculum. In the Ofsted Framework, there is special mention made of the cross-curricular links with English.

The Ofsted report

The inspection process culminates in the Ofsted team writing a report which is a public document, available to parents and the world at large. Ofsted reports can be accessed through the Internet at the following address: http://www.ofsted.gov.uk

The report includes a summary of the inspection, called the main findings. There is also a list of key issues for action, which have to be responded to and acted upon by staff and governors within the time period following the inspection.

The section on English will not identify individual teachers by name but there may be oblique references to significant practice (weak or strong) in a certain key stage or year group.

Positive outcomes largely depend upon teachers' willingness to collect evidence to support them in the 'telling' of their own stories during the inspection. Ofsted inspectors need tangible evidence in the form of documentation, observation forms or learning outcomes, such as examples of children's work. By collecting this evidence well in advance and by labelling it clearly, teachers can approach the inspection process with confidence.

SUMMARY

Key points identified in this chapter include:

- the importance of planning carefully so that other adults are clear about their role in the classroom

- the need to allow time to communicate with other adults in the classroom, e.g. the SENCO or bilingual support teacher

- the value of good home–school parental partnerships

- the benefits of working cooperatively with colleagues

- the value of perceiving appraisal as a growth process

- the importance of careful preparation for Ofsted inspections.

References

Chambers, A. (1993) *Tell Me: Children, Reading and Talk*, Thimble Press

Craft, A. (1996) *Continuing Professional Development: A Practical Guide for Teachers and Schools*, Open University Press

DES (1978) *Special Educational Needs* (The Warnock Report), HMSO.

DfEE (1994) *Special Needs Code of Practice*, HMSO

Mortimore, P. (1994) *Managing Associate Staff: Innovation in Primary and Secondary Schools*, Paul Chapman

Ofsted (1995) *The New Inspection Framework*, HMSO

Pollard, A. and Tann, S. (1987) *Reflective Teaching in the Primary School*, Cassell

Schon, D. (1983) *The Reflective Practitioner: How Professionals Think in Action*, Temple Smith

Thomas, G. (1992) *Effective Classroom Teamwork*, Routledge

Wragg, E. C. , Wikeley, F. J., Wragg, C. M., and Haynes, G. S. (1996) *Teacher Appraisal Observed*, Routledge

Further reading

Clipson-Boyles, S. B. (1996) *Language and Literacy*, David Fulton
A clearly structured and highly practical set of guidelines, which were originally designed to support learning support assistants or teachers' aides. However, they also provide very useful guidance to young teachers who are keen to raise literacy standards and make the most of their human and textual resources.

Laar, W. (1996) *The TES Guide to Surviving School Inspection*, TES/Butterworth Heinemann
A practical book which guides teachers through the Ofsted Framework, with advice about effective preparation for Ofsted inspections.

Mills, J. and Mills, R. (eds) (1997) *Primary School People: Getting to Know Your Colleagues*, Routledge
Written primarily for student teachers and NQTs, this very readable book offers perceptive insights into the different perspectives of support staff and other adults connected with primary schools. It provides practical advice about working in partnerships and teams and gives opportunities for reflection.

Peel, R. (1994) *The Primary Language Leader's Handbook*, David Fulton
This is a comprehensive overview of the role of a language coordinator in a school. It deals with the external agencies with which a coordinator would be involved and gives a detailed description of the role of language specialists. In a general sense, it also provides helpful perspectives on the teaching of primary English.

Reason, R. (1994) *Helping Children with Reading and Spelling: A Special Needs Manual*, Routledge
This book offers practical approaches to working with children with language difficulties. There are many examples of materials which it would be helpful to adapt or adopt. The style and layout are clear, and important issues relating to special language needs are discussed.

Webb, R. and Vulliamy, G. (1996) *Roles and Responsibilities in the Primary School*, Open University Press
A comprehensive and practical overview of the responsibilities of the curriculum coordinator and other staff.

Wolfendale, S. and Topping, K. (1996) *Family Involvement in Literacy*, Cassell
This book provides an overview of recent family literacy initiatives in the UK and elsewhere. It examines community projects and reading partnerships.

21 Language variety: accent, dialect and standard English

OBJECTIVES

By the end of this chapter you should:

- understand the key issues related to language variety, accent, dialect and standard English

- understand the requirements of the sections on Standard English and Language Study in the English programmes of study and the relevant objectives in the National Literacy Strategy: Framework for Teaching

- be able to choose activities which build children's awareness of language difference and promote appropriate use of standard English.

Attitudes to language

> When it comes to a contest between attitudes on the one hand and information which challenges those attitudes on the other, attitudes often prove the stronger.
>
> Language in the National Curriculum (LINC) project materials

Language is never neutral. It is often surrounded by controversy and conflict. It frequently arouses strong feelings and reveals ingrained attitudes, particularly in relation to accent and dialect. A recent newspaper report demonstrated this only too well. A soccer star had asked for a transfer from Queens Park Rangers in West London, to save his wife from the daily teasing and ridicule about her West Country accent. The wife was apparently dubbed a 'thick yokel' and 'farmer' by her work colleagues, and to add insult to injury she was told not to answer the phone in case her accent 'put customers off.' Her Bristol accent would probably have included an elongated *r*, and maybe a dropping of the *h*. Her new colleagues in Farnham, Sur-

rey may have spoken with the classic BBC accent, or possibly, the so called Queen's accent, whereby 'off' becomes *orf*, 'house' is *hice* and 'tower' is *tar*.

Most of us would surely wish to challenge such narrow, prejudiced reactions to language and foster a tolerance of the diverse uses of language in our classroom But before we do we need to be really sensitive to the complexity and delicacy of the issues involved. It is also important that new teachers are prepared for the considerable pressure and contradictory opinions they are likely to encounter.

The language debate

A three-year project known as Language in the National Curriculum, or LINC, was set up in 1989 following recommendations from the Kingman Report (DES 1988). The LINC project recognised the importance of standard English, nationally and internationally. It also recognised that different accents and dialects have different social status, as we saw in the attitudes to the accent of the Bristol woman above. But LINC took on board the general linguistic view that standard English was not inherently superior to other dialects and that no accent was better than another. Instead the project suggested that schools have a responsibility to give children pride and confidence in their own accent and dialect by encouraging them to talk about and reflect upon how language varies and how it is appropriate in different contexts. This LINC model of language is the one used by contributors to this book and is implicit in much of the Framework for Teaching (DfEE 1998a). (See Module 3: Sentence Level Work, in the *National Literacy Strategy: Literacy Training Pack* (DfEE 1998b), and particularly the accompanying tape. The presenters discuss the importance of children learning to use language appropriate to purpose and context.)

Students or newly qualified teachers will, however, come across very strong opposing views. In 1987 the Centre for Policy Studies published John Marenbon's *English Our English: The New Orthodoxy Examined*. In many ways this still represents the current right-wing thinking on language in education. Marenbon and many others have described the LINC model of language as a 'new orthodoxy' which devalues standard English. They have argued that grammar should be prescribed and that standard English is superior to dialect. Moreover they have attributed a perceived fall in standards in education to this so called 'new orthodoxy'. (It was probably these views that led the DES in 1992 to disown the LINC project and reject the materials produced. They restricted them to use in INSET for the professional development of teachers.)

All of this should give us a sense of the political and controversial nature of language. Students and new teachers would be well advised to read more widely on attitudes to language, and particularly those related to accent and dialect and standard English (see Bain (1992), Trudgill (1975) and Davidson (1994)).

Developing our own knowledge about language

In order to support children's knowledge about language we should aim to be secure in our own knowledge! Language is central to the processes of teaching and learning, and all of us need knowledge about language in order to appreciate children's achievements with language. Knowledge about language helps us to diagnose children's difficulties and intervene at different stages to promote their abilities as talkers, readers and writers. Knowledge about language also helps us to deal with some of the narrow, prejudiced views we have discussed above.

The importance of language variety

Schools today are extremely rich and varied linguistic environments in which children use and demonstrate knowledge of a wide variety of language around them, as is illustrated by these examples of children talking to adults (taken from *TALK* 1990):

'My mum doesn't like being posh but she has to because everyone else is, where she works.'

'You just switch languages; Welsh here, English at home. You don' think about it. I can choose – that's all.'

'At Chinese school we talk English secretly just as in English schools we talk Chinese secretly.'

(In role-play)

Hostage We don't have no money in this shop.
Robber Well you'll have to get some, won't you?
Hostage We say we have no money.
Robber They ain't got no money. Let's get out of here!

Ann (on TV) Hello. Today we have a serious crime at Desmond's butcher's shop. We have a few pictures of them when they were young.

Child 1 I'm going to write on my drawing in Urdu.
Child 2 Oh I can write that in Bengali.

The eloquent voices of these children remind us that people all over the world have a tremendous variety of experiences and languages to share with those around them. They also reinforce just how much language varies from one context to another according to the purpose, place and time, and how we all work along a kind of continuum of language, adapting it according to the context and audience.

What do we mean by accent, dialect and standard English?

Accent

All of us have an accent. Accent is the distinctive pronunciation that we use to produce the sounds of our language. It is normally associated with a specific town or geographical area. So some of us might have a Liverpool, Birmingham, Black Country or Yorkshire accent. It is extremely important to remember that just because someone speaks with a strong accent this does not indicate that they are using dialect. Accent is purely to do with pronunciation. It is also very important to note that the National Curriculum does not require children to lose their local accents when they learn about standard English.

Dialect

The term dialect refers to the actual words that speakers or writers use (vocabulary) and the way they put words in order in a sentence (syntax). Dialect characterises the language of a particular area or region of the country. For example, in Yorkshire we would hear many people using the words 'ginnel' or 'snicket' to mean an alleyway. In Peterborough they often use the word 'dodds' for sweets, and in the Fenland area 'dockey' means a mid-morning snack.

Received Pronunciation (RP)

This is an accent which relates more to social and educational background. It is often associated with public schools and may be called the Queen's English or BBC English.

Standard English

Standard English is the official dialect of English and used by the Government, the law courts and the education system. Since it is the variety of English which is usually used in writing, it is what we teach in schools and to those learning English as a foreign language. It is also the variety which is normally spoken by educated people and used in news broadcasts and other formal situations.

It is useful for us to have a sense of the historical development of standard English. It developed in the fifteenth century when William Caxton chose the East Midland dialect for his printing, and then became used by the influential merchants of the time and the universities of Oxford and Cambridge. In the eighteenth century a decision was made to standardise this one particular dialect and make it 'official'. Gradually standard English became the written form used by all writers of English, no matter which dialect area they come from. Because it is the written form it is used not only in Britain but by all writers of English throughout the world.

Standard English: other important ideas

- Standard English is not *fixed*. It constantly changes over time, like any other language. The media, travel and international relations all contribute to change, which will continue because language is always changing.
- Standard English has many *variations*. There is no one form of standard English; the standard form in England is not the same as standard United States English. For example, Americans would use *color* for colour, *sidewalk* for pavement, *cookie* for biscuit, *fall* for autumn. In Standard Scottish English we would hear *aye* for yes, *burn* for stream, *loch* for lake, and so on.
- All children must have access to standard English because the subjects they learn at school are taught through standard English. If children are to master these subjects they must therefore learn to read and write in standard English.
- Language and identity are inseparable, so when we criticise someone's language they often feel we are criticising them as a person. Rather than criticism or negative comment about children's home speech, we should instead talk of languages as being appropriate or inappropriate.

Most English specialists agree that there is no one correct English, nor do they regard dialect errors as errors as such. Similarly most classroom teachers are unlikely to think of language, accent and dialect in terms of being good or bad or right and wrong because they, in particular, recognise the link between a child's language and self-esteem. In reality we all make choices according to what is most appropriate to the context, purpose and audience.

Differences between standard English and non-standard dialect

Dialects, as we have already discussed, are essentially local to particular parts of a particular country. In these different areas, special words and phrases are often used to talk about local and domestic life. But there are other key differences to note: standard English, as we have seen, is used in writing and can be more formal. It includes specialised vocabulary not part of any non-standard dialect. Standard English also has sentence features which have no equivalent in non-standard dialects, for example 'The teachers discussed Jim and Mick respectively'.

Here are some examples of dialect forms:

- multiple negation, e.g. 'We didn't buy no sweets'
- past-tense verb forms, e.g. 'He come home on Saturday'
- relative pronouns, e.g. 'This is the girl what said it'
- demonstrative pronouns, e.g. 'Them ones over there'
- personal pronouns, e.g. 'Us don't like that'
- forms of the verb to be, e.g. 'I ain't going today', 'We isn't happy'.

The National Curriculum

In the National Curriculum we find reference to many of these key ideas of variety, appropriateness and entitlement. The General Requirements stress that all pupils are entitled to a full range of language opportunities. They emphasise 'the richness of dialects and other languages' and that spoken standard English is not the same as received pronunciation but can be expressed in a variety of accents.

The National Curriculum also places considerable emphasis upon standard English. In order to develop effective speaking and listening, pupils should be taught to use the vocabulary and grammar of standard English and to speak, write and read standard English fluently and accurately.

The National Curriculum also distinguishes standard English from other forms of English by its vocabulary, and by rules and conventions of grammar such as how pronouns, adverbs and adjectives should be used. In each programme of study there is a section entitled Standard English and Language Study; these are gathered together in Figures 21.1 and 21.2.

Speaking and Listening	Reading	Writing
a. Pupils should be introduced with appropriate sensitivity to the importance of standard English. Pupils should be given opportunities to consider their own speech and how they communicate with others, particularly in more formal situations or with unfamiliar adults. Pupils should be encouraged to develop confidence in their ability to adapt what they say to their listeners and to the circumstances, beginning to recognise how language differs, eg *the vocabulary of standard English and that of dialects, how their choice of language varies in different situations.* They should be introduced to some of the features that distinguish standard English, including subject–verb agreement and the use of the verb 'to be' in past and present tenses. Pupils may speak in different accents, but they should be taught to speak with clear diction and appropriate intonation. b. Pupils' vocabulary should be extended through activities that encourage their interest in words, including exploration and discussion: • the meanings of words and their use and interpretation in different contexts; • words with similar and opposite meanings; • word games; • words associated with specific occasions eg *greetings, celebrations* • characteristic language in storytelling eg *'Once upon a time'*	Pupils should be given opportunities to consider the characteristics and features of different kinds of texts eg *beginnings and endings of stories.* They should be taught to use their knowledge about language gained from reading to develop their understanding of standard English.	a. Pupils should be introduced to the vocabulary, grammar and structures of written standard English including subject–verb agreement and the use of the verb 'to be' in past and present tenses. They should be taught to apply their existing linguistic knowledge, drawn from oral language and their experience of reading, to develop their understanding of the sentence and how word choice and order are crucial to clarity of meaning. Pupils should be given opportunities to discuss the organisation of more complex texts, and the way sentences link together. b. Pupils' interest in words and their meanings should be developed, and their vocabulary should be extended through consideration and discussion of words with similar meanings, opposites and words with more than one meaning.

Figure 21.1 Standard English and Language Study Key Stage 1 programmes of study

Speaking and Listening	Reading	Writing
a. Pupils' appreciation and use of standard English should be developed by involvement with others in activities that, through their content and purpose, demand the range of grammatical constructions and vocabulary characteristic of spoken standard English. They should be taught to speak with clear diction and appropriate intonation. Pupils should be taught how formal contexts require particular choices of vocabulary and greater precision in language structures. They should also be given opportunities to develop their understanding of the similarities and differences between the written and spoken forms of standard English, and to investigate how language varies according to context and purpose and between standard and dialect forms. b. Pupils should be taught to use an increasingly varied vocabulary. The range of pupils' vocabulary should be extended and enriched through activities that focus on words and their meanings, including: • discussion of more imaginative and adventuruos choices of words; • consideration of groups of words eg *word families, the range of words relevant to a topic;* • language used in drama, role-play and word games.	Pupils should be introduced to the organisation, structural and presentational features of different types of text, and to some of the appropriate terms to enable them to discuss the texts they read eg *author, setting, plot, format.* They should be encouraged to use their knowledge gained from reading to develop their understanding of the structure, vocabulary and grammar of standard English.	a. Pupils should be given opportunities to reflect on their use of language, beginninng to differentiate between spoken and written forms. They should be given opportunities to consider how written standard English varies in degrees of formality. b. Pupils should be given opportunities to develop their understanding of the grammar of complex sentences, including clauses and phrases. They should be taught how to use paragraphs, linking sentences together coherently. They should be taught to use the standard written forms of nouns, pronouns, verbs, adjectives, adverbs, prepositions, conjunctions and verb tenses. c. Pupils should be taught to distinguish between words of similar meaning, to explain the meanings of words and to experiment with choices of vocabulary. Their interest in words should be extended by the discussion of language use and choices.

Figure 21.2 Standard English and Language Study Key Stage 2 programmes of study

End of key stage: level descriptions

In the level descriptions for Speaking and Listening we can identify the relevant strand for language variety, including standard English, as follows:

Speaking and Listening

Level 1: '[Pupils] listen to others and usually respond appropriately.'

Level 2: 'They usually listen carefully and respond with increasing appropriateness to what others say. They are beginning to be aware that in some situations a more formal vocabulary and tone of voice are used.'

Level 3: 'They begin to adapt what they say to the needs of the listener, varying the use of vocabulary

... They are beginning to be aware of standard English and when it is used.'

Level 4: 'They use appropriately some of the features of standard English vocabulary and grammar.'

Level 5: 'They begin to use standard English in formal situations.'

Level 6: 'They are usually fluent in their use of standard English in formal situations.'

Notice that there is a welcome emphasis here on many of the ideas explored in this chapter, such as the importance of variety and appropriateness; how language changes according to context; and the need to use standard English in more formal situations.

The National Literacy Strategy: Framework for Teaching

The Framework for Teaching has considerable potential to develop children's knowledge about language, including an awareness of the importance of language variety. It requires teachers to use a range of literature and teach skills at word, sentence and text level within the literacy hour. The areas discussed in this chapter mostly appear in the sentence-level work columns under grammatical awareness and sentence construction and punctuation. Earlier work tends to focus upon parts of speech: pronouns, adjectives, verbs and adverbs, for example. In Year 3, Term 2, however, children should understand the need for grammatical agreement in speech and writing, for example 'I am'; 'we are'.

Direct references to standard English appear more in Year 5 and Year 6. In Term 1 of Year 5 children should understand the basic conventions of standard English and consider when and why standard English is used. At this stage they should be able make nouns and verbs agree, and understand the need for consistency of tense and subject. They should also avoid double negatives and non-standard dialect words. (One would need to be careful here, as many celebrated authors and poets make excellent use of non-dialect forms (see later examples).)

Now let us look at how we can develop meaningful activities which will develop children's ability to use standard English as required in the programmes of study and the Framework for Teaching.

Accent, dialect and standard English in the classroom

Some guiding principles

It is important to value the language of the child and their home and community, and to appreciate that 'No child should be expected to cast off the language and culture of the home' (DES 1975). When children come to school they already know a lot about language, and this should be our starting point

We should also remember that we can teach standard English most effectively through discovery learning. Language can and should be fun; children seem to have a natural feeling for language and this can be exploited. Often it is a case of looking for signs of children's implicit knowledge and competence in using language and then encouraging them to reflect and analyse upon its particular features.

Most of all, children should be encouraged to feel positive about their own accents and dialects and see standard English as an alternative and not a rival. What we can do is discuss the similarities and differences of standard and non-standard English in real, meaningful activities, and because children learn through language and learn about language simultaneously a cross-curricular approach is essential (see Chapter 15). In cross-curricular contexts we can often draw attention to the inappropriacy of dialect in a natural way.

Finally, remember that drama, media studies and IT all have a very important role to play in developing children's awareness of the varieties of language, accent and dialect.

Some practical suggestions

Most activities in the classroom provide an opportunity for language work, but here are some possible starting points. They are listed under seven major headings and deliberately start with the child and the immediate environment.

Many of these ideas could be incorporated into discussions around texts during the shared reading and writing slot of the literacy hour, whilst others could be used during the group sessions.

Children and their experiences

- A language survey: Which language do children speak when and to whom?
- Studying children's own dialects and then drawing out comparisons between non-standard and standard, highlighting differences in vocabulary and grammar, e.g. 'I aren't'/'I am not'.
- Language logs/diaries: Who do they talk to, why and in what context? A log can be kept over an hour, a day or several days. Later, children could produce a language profile of themselves which provides a context for discussion on linguistic diversity.
- Sharing varieties of circumstances in which they use language: at a party, at a football match, in a library, in a hospital, in a church, temple or mosque. How and why do they adapt? For what purpose?
- Reflecting upon differences between speech and writing, for instance using transcripts of a spoken and written version of the same event.
- Analysing extracts of children's talk: How

might/does the language differ if the children write a report on the same activity?

The language environment at home/in the community

- Involving parents: using letters and questionnaires to find out about their language histories. Discussion of differences between generations.
- Discussing children's local dialect: making a list/web of local dialect words and perhaps involving parents and grandparents in their collection.
- Discussing language use at home: comparisons between language used at home and school.
- Exploring the speech environment of a local restaurant, workshop, building site, hospital (use of role play interviews or questionnaires). Discussing how vocabulary changes.

Class/school activities

- Practising interviewing: considering how to structure questions and answers; choice of vocabulary; sentence construction. Interviews can be taped, transcribed and used in discussion to help children evaluate their use of language and discuss grammatical features of standard English.
- Class discussions: sharing experiences and advising each other about the appropriateness of language. For example: How would you talk to the Queen/a policeman/a baby/friend/grandmother/brother/sister? What words would you choose? What types of sentence, etc.?
- Using schools' broadcasts which feature different dialects, e.g. the BBC schools' programme *Geordie Racer*, and later providing opportunities for explicit discussion and comparisons of accent and dialect in the literacy hour.
- Accent stereotypes: playing a variety of accents to children, ask them to write down their impression of the person. Discussing implications.
- Listening to and reading examples of different dialects. Identifying dialect words and checking their meanings. Discovering rules relating to tenses and singular and plural.
- Writing down the verbal instructions for an activity.
- Taping teachers as they revert to their original accents; discussing with children.
- Book-making, incorporating use of dual-language texts.

Play

Role-play areas can encourage children to consider the different types of language they have to use appropriate to the context; for example, communication between:

- a buyer and a seller in a shop
- a customer and a waiter in a restaurant
- police/witnesses and a criminal in a police station
- the teacher/headteacher/children in a school.

Note that we can provide a model for using language by taking on some of these parts ourselves!

Literature

Literature is obviously an extensive and rich resource for thinking and talking about language. During the literacy hour we can use the range of literature required by the Framework for Teaching to analyse and enjoy the variety and richness of language.

Story books

- Discussing the appropriateness of language in a range of stories: use of any dialect features; how characters speak formally and informally.
- Using Leon Garfield's *Fair's Fair*, which uses non-standard English: 'I bring back your dog'; 'Shove off I got no food'; 'Ain't that enough'; 'Them what lives in this house';'It were late when me and the dog came'. Comparing and discussing use of verb to be/tenses/subject verb agreement, etc.

Poetry

Many poems use dialect. We can explore their richness and maybe discuss the difference with standard English. Some use standard English and non-standard dialects together. (See 'When We Was Fab' by George Harrison (1988). Harrison moves freely between a poetic standard English – 'Caressers fleeced you in the morning light' – and dialect – 'When we was fab'.)

Other suggestions:

- Using dual-language poems.
- Using poems by Grace Nicholls and Jane Berry.

Rhymes

- Using rhymes, such as cockney rhyming slang on the body, e.g. head/crust of bread, mouth/north and south.

Media

- Listening to the weather forecast, the news, the radio; discussing the role of standard English and issues of formality and appropriateness.

Emphasising the importance of standard English in public life.

- Using popular soaps from TV, e.g. *EastEnders*, *Brookside*, to explore issues of accent, dialect, and standard English and appropriateness.
- Using examples of dialect in popular newspapers to draw comparisons with standard and non-standard forms.
- Discussing the choice of vocabulary and language of DJs and children's TV presenters.

IT

- Playing with language; discussing range and forms.
- Composing a range of texts on the computer:
  - drafting and discussing features of standard English required in a text for publication
  - emphasising the importance of standard English for this purpose.

Assessment and record keeping

When we assess and record children's abilities in using a variety of language it is important to consider many of the principles explored in this chapter. For example, children will need to be observed using language in a range of contexts across the curriculum. This is because spoken language is particularly influenced by the social and learning context – whether children are working in pairs, threes, fours or large groups, or whether they are sharing stories, making a book, solving a problem, taking on a part in drama, or reporting an event on a formal occasion.

It is important to remember that the quality of the talk may not always relate to ability but can be greatly affected by factors such as:

- the nature of the activity
- the responses of the listener
- previous experience
- the atmosphere in the class.

Elements of progress

When looking for progression, students and newly qualified teachers might like to draw on some of these elements:

- increased confidence when talking in a wider range of situations, i.e. informal to formal (use of standard English)
- expressing ideas using appropriate language
- using different forms of language for learning
- increased ability to stand back and reflect upon

language varieties and their own use of these varieties

- Using a range of vocabulary, including the more specialised
- Using a range of sentence structures, including those of standard English.

Gathering evidence of achievement

Observations in all areas of experience and learning can be recorded as verbatim comments in note-books. More structured observations can be recorded on simple sheets or proformas, whereas detailed observations of one child over a period of time, and across a range of contexts, can be recorded in note form and added to the child's profile.

Samples of talk

Audio or video tapes of children demonstrating knowledge of language varieties can be recorded for further analysis. Samples of talk, for example a conversation around a story or a picture, can be assessed and kept as evidence of a child's use of appropriate language.

Notes from conversations with parents, other adults in school and with children themselves can also help build an all-round, reliable picture of the child's language repertoire.

Record keeping

In this example a teacher has made summary notes on a young bilingual child. The notes record the different learning and social contexts together with the child's achievements and behaviours.

Speaking and listening

Baljinder speaks English and Sylheti fluently. She will tell stories into a tape and share them with small groups. She is not yet confident to tell stories to the whole class. She will however report on maths and science activities to the whole class. She seems very interested in these subjects and asks very interesting questions. She coped particularly well with the book we made on Bangladesh and used her language knowledge combined with her general knowledge of books. She can be shy and is easily dominated in group situations. This term I have tried to pair her with girls who will give her more support. This seems to have given her more confidence.

Source: Birmingham Curriculum and Advisory Service

SUMMARY

This chapter has attempted to celebrate the diversity and richness of language in terms of accent, dialect and standard English. It has briefly explored the highly contentious nature of language and suggested how we should develop our own knowledge about language in key areas. It has also offered approaches which can help children to reflect upon language and continue to make their own choices, as they explore language in a range of contexts across the curriculum.

You should now:

- have more understanding of the key issues related to language variety, accent, dialect and standard English and be more aware of some of the tensions and conflicts

- understand the basic requirements of the sections on Standard English and Language Study in the English programmes of study and be aware of the relevant objectives in the National Literacy Strategy Framework for Teaching

- have more confidence and ability to choose child-centred, enjoyable activities which can develop children's awareness of language variety, including the importance of standard English.

References

Bain, Fitzgerald (1992) *Looking into Language*, Hodder and Stoughton

Davidson, K. (1994) 'Double Standards', *English Today* 10, 2 (April)

DES (1975) *A Language for Life* (The Bullock Report), HMSO.

DES (1988) *Report of the Committee of Inquiry into the Teaching of English* (The Kingman Report), HMSO

DfEE (1998a) *The National Literacy Strategy: Framework for Teaching*, DfEE

DfEE (1998b) *The National Literacy Strategy: Literacy Training Pack*, DfEE

Marenbon, J. (1987) *English Our English: The New Orthodoxy Examined*, Centre for Policy Studies

TALK (Journal of the National Oracy Project) (1990) No. 3 (Summer)

Trudgill, P. (1975) *Accent, Dialect and School*, Edward Arnold

Further reading

Barrs, M., Ellis, S., Hester, H. and Thomas, A. (1988) *The Primary Language Record*, Centre for Language in Primary Education
This booklet celebrates the range and richness of children's language and offers practical guidance for assessing and recording their achievements

Carter, R. (ed.) (1990) *Knowledge about Language and the Curriculum: The LINC Reader*, Hodder and Stoughton
This book offers useful theoretical background to knowledge about language together with interesting examples of children developing their own knowledge of language variety in real contexts across the curriculum

Crystal, D. (1987) *The Cambridge Encyclopedia of Language*, Cambridge University Press
A large book on language which can be dipped into. It contains helpful background information on accent, dialect and standard English useful for developing teachers' knowledge about language.

Edwards, V. (1983) *Language in Multicultural Classrooms*, Batsford
A book full of classroom examples set within a rationale for celebrating linguistic diversity.

Wray, D. and Medwell, J. (1997) *QTS English for Primary Teachers: An Audit and Self-Study Guide*, Letts Educational
An invaluable and comprehensive audit and self-study guide. The book enables the reader to audit their knowledge of language and then provides guidance, advice and support materials to develop knowledge in many areas of language, including dialect, accent and standard English. See pages 20 and 42 in particular.

Glossary

accent
the distinctive way in which speech is pronounced, usually related to region or class

alliteration
a phrase or sentence in which each word starts with the same letter sound (phoneme), e.g. several sparkling silvery stars

alphabetic method
the traditional way of teaching reading through teaching letter names

analogy
making links between something already known to something new. In reading and spelling, using knowledge of one word to read and spell other new words with the same letter string, e.g. light, might, night, etc.

ascenders
letters with tall strokes, e.g. *b*, *h*

BICS
Basic Interpersonal Communication Skills, the level of English required to interact with others and cope socially

big book
a large book which can be seen by the whole class and used to demonstrate text

book talk
children, teachers, other adults sharing conversations about any aspect of a book, e.g. the author, the genre, the structure, characters, plots, setting, meaning, use of language, etc.

Bookstart
an initiative devised in Birmingham which has enabled books to be given to babies and toddlers

Breakthrough to Literacy
a literacy programme which encourages children to use their own experience and language as starting points for reading and writing. It includes words, letters and punctuation – all of different sizes – which can be slotted into sentence stands, displayed as wall charts or added to individual children's folders.

CALP
Cognitive Academic Language Proficiency, the level of English required to succeed at school, e.g. at GCSE level

Catch Up Programme
a ten-minute-a-week reading intervention programme for Year 3 children who are struggling with reading. The teacher's pack combines a training video with reading support materials (Oxford Brookes University, 1998).

CILT
Centre for Information on Language Teaching

cloze procedure
a way of testing comprehension by deleting words or letters from a continuous text and asking the reader to fill in the blanks

CLPE
Centre for Language in Primary Education

consonant cluster
two or more letters which are pronounced running together, e.g. *bl*, *sp*

consonants
the letters that arc not vowels

criterion-referenced tests
tests assessed against specific criteria

DES
Department of Education and Science, renamed the Department for Education (DfE) in 1992

descenders
letters with long downward strokes, e.g. *p*, *g*

DfE
Department for Education (1992–95)

DfEE
Department for Education and Employment,

formed in 1995 by the merger of the DfE and the Employment Department

dialect
the vocabulary, construction and pronunciation of language which is local to a particular area or community

digraph
two letters which combine to make one sound, e.g. *ph, sh, ee*

EAL
English as an additional language

EFL
English as a foreign language

ESL
English as a second language

ESOL
English for speakers of other languages

First Steps
a series of teachers' guides, which are based on a developmental approach to English teaching. Originally developed in Western Australia and thoroughly researched there and elsewhere, *First Steps* was introduced by Heinemann Education in 1997, alongside a nationwide INSET programme.

formal testing
assessment through published, standardised tests

genre
a text type with a distinctive form and content, e.g. narrative, instruction, explanation

grammar
the structure of a language – its vocabulary and word order

guided reading
an approach to teaching reading with small groups of children. The teacher sets the purpose for the reading and then works intensively with the group to support the reading.

guided writing
the process whereby the teacher works with a group to model aspects of the writing task as a prelude to children attempting this task unaided

heritage language
the language of a child's parents

HMI
Her Majesty's Inspector

homophones
words spelled the same way but which have different meanings according to context

hot seating
a method whereby an individual or group takes on the role of others in order to answer questions

ICT
information and communications technology

IEP
Individual Education Plan, for children with special educational needs

improvisation
the playing out of an unscripted situation, either planned or spontaneous

informal testing
testing devised by an individual or school which has not been standardised

interlanguage
the mixture of English syntax and vocabulary with structures and words from the child's mother tongue or other languages

intonation
how the voice is modulated to indicate meaning; for example, questions usually rise at the end

IT
information technology

IT capability
the effective use of IT tools and information sources to analyse, process and present information and to model, measure and control external events

Jolly Phonics
a popular, multi-sensory phonics programme, designed to support children's early encounters with sound–symbol correspondence

letter formation
how a child forms letters of the alphabet

LINC
Language in the National Curriculum, a three-year project set up in 1989

Living Book
an interactive story on CD-ROM

lower-case letters
letters of the alphabet not written in capitals

media studies
learning about and through the media

miscue analysis
a system of recording and analysing what a child says when reading aloud when the reading differs from the text

motor skill
an action that the body 'learns', which then becomes automatic

NATE
National Association for the Teaching of English

NLS
National Literacy Strategy

non-linear text
text not written in long and narrow lines as it would be in a narrative

NOP
National Oracy Project, 1988–91

NQT
newly qualified teacher

norm-referenced test
a test which compares children with a standard or norm – often expressed in terms of a reading age

Ofsted
Office for Standards in Education, responsible for school inspections

onset
the initial consonant or consonant cluster before a vowel, e.g. *str*ing, *c*at, *pl*ug

oracy
speaking and listening skills

PAT
Phonological Awareness Training programme (Buckinghamshire County Council, 1993), devised to develop an awareness of onsets and rimes in children who were experiencing difficulties with reading.

PE
physical education

PEEP
Peers Early Education Partnership (1997), one of many community initiatives concerned with family literacy. Based in Oxford, it combines funds raised by business with charitable trusts in order to introduce babies to books (*see* Bookstart).

phoneme
the smallest unit of sound within a word. The sound can be represented by one, two, three or four letters, e.g. *h* in 'hat', *sh* in 'shoe', *igh* in 'night', *ough* in 'through'.

phonics
the study of the relationship between the sounds and the written symbols of a language

phonological awareness
awareness of similar and different sounds in words. Anyone who recognises that two words rhyme and therefore have a sound in common possesses a degree of phonological awareness.

prefix
a morpheme (the smallest unit of meaning) which is added to the beginning of a word to change its meaning, e.g. *dis*appear, *un*happy

pronunciation
how phonemes and words are spoken

QCA
Qualifications and Curriculum Authority (England)

RE
religious education

Reading Recovery
In 1987, Marie Clay developed a reading intervention programme to bring the six least confident six-year-olds in any class up to the level of their peers. Reading Recovery teachers have to undergo intensive training. They then work intensively, for a 12-week period one-to-one, with each child.

received pronunciation (RP)
a specific accent in English, associated with middle-class speech and traditionally used by BBC announcers

register
the result of an interaction between three elements: the field, mode and tenor. The field is what the author is writing about (content). The mode is how the author is using and expressing language (e.g. use of cohesion, choice of vocabulary, etc). The tenor is the author's attitude to the subject and to the reader (the mood of a text; use of active/passive voice; level of formality, etc.).

response partners
peers with whom children can test the effectiveness of writing drafts

rime
the vowel and final consonant(s) of a word or syllable, e.g. c*at*, b*ull*, b*ike*, sw*iftly*

role play
taking on the role and character of another person, real or imagined

role-play area
part of a classroom converted into a themed play area with furniture, props and dressing-up clothes

running record
a simplified version of miscue analysis

SAT
Standard Assessment Task

SCAA
School Curriculum and Assessment Authority (England)

scan
to look over a text very quickly in order to locate a key word or phrase

SEN
special educational needs

SENCO
Special Educational Needs Coordinator, a teacher (there is one in every school) responsible for the coordination of special needs agencies and the supervision of IEPs

sight words
words instantly identified by a child on sight and without visual or contextual clues

silent letters
letters not sounded in a word, e.g. com*b*, *g*nome

skim
to read quickly to get an initial overview of the general meaning of a particular text

spelling string
a string of letters which spells part of a word. It may combine two or more phonemes, e.g. *-ing*, *-tion*, *-tch*, *-ity*, *cr-*, *-ough*, and can come at the beginning, middle or end of a word.

standard English
the grammatically correct form of English used in formal interactions and taught to speakers of other languages

story ingredients
essential components of a successful story

Storysacks
an initiative which seeks to support parents more practically when sharing books with their children. A Storysack is a fabric bag with a book, soft-toy props and characters together with pre-reading and reading activities, a non-fiction book, a cassette of the story and anything else which is relevant to the picture book. The National Storysacks Project in Swindon is funded by the Basic Skills Agency.

suffix
a morpheme (the smallest unit of meaning) which is added to the end of a word. Inflectional suffixes change the tense or status of a word from present to past (e.g. jump*ed*) or from singular to plural (e.g. boy*s*). Derivational suffixes change the class of a word from adjective to noun (e.g. kind*ness*), verb to noun, etc.

supported writing/scribing
a process whereby the teacher undertakes the secretarial role and the children concentrate upon the compositional aspects of writing

syntax
the structure of sentences, and the grammatical rules which govern the structure

tableau
a three-dimensional image of a scene in still form

THRASS
Teaching Handwriting, Reading and Spelling Skills, a programme developed at Manchester Metropolitan University. It is marketed as a special needs programme but it sets out to introduce the 44 phonemes in English systematically to children of all abilities.

trigraph
three letters which combine to make one sound or phoneme, e.g. *-igh*

UKRA
United Kingdom Reading Association

unaided writing
the process whereby children write to the best of their ability without the support of the teacher

upper-case letters
capital letters

USSR
uninterrupted, sustained silent reading, a half-

hour session of concentrated reading which enables children to read silently as individuals.

vowels
the letters *a, e, i, o, u* and sometimes *y*

VRH
Volunteer Reading Help Organisation, a nation-wide network of reading volunteers

writing process
the stages by which a piece of writing is undertaken

writing product
the end result of a writing task

Index